THIS BOOK IS SPONSORED

By

....

....

As a Gift to

....

....

On this Day

....

'For I was an hungred, and ye gave me meat:
I was thirsty, and ye gave me drink:
I was a stranger, and ye took me in:
Naked, and ye clothed me:
I was sick, and ye visited me:
I was in **prison**, and ye came unto me'
(Matthew 25:35-36)

TEARS IN PRISON

THE PRISONERS OF HOPE

PRAYER M. MADUEKE

TEARS IN PRISON: THE PRISONERS OF HOPE

Copyright © 2012

PRAYER M. MADUEKE

ISBN: 1463765363

Prayer Publications

All rights reserved. No part of this work may be reproduced or transmitted in any form or by any means without written permission from the publisher

Unless otherwise indicated, all Scripture quotations are taken from the King James Version of the Bible, and used by permission. All emphasis within quotations is the author's additions.

First Edition, 2012

For further information of permission

1 Babatunde close, off Olaitan Street, Surulere, Lagos, Nigeria
+234 803 353 0599
Email: pastor@prayermadueke.com,
Website: www.prayermadueke.com

TABLE OF CONTENTS

COMPREHENSIVE PRAYER LIST

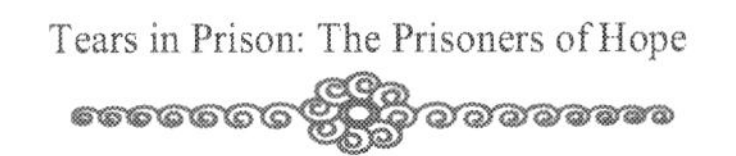

DEDICATION

This book is dedicated to all prisoners of hope all over the world. Sooner or later, prison doors will be opened for your sakes.

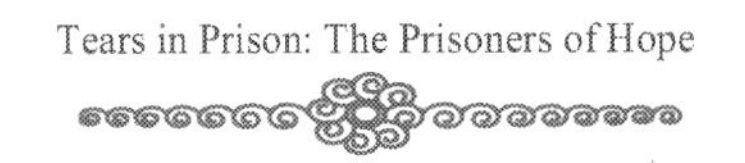

ACKNOWLEDGMENT

First, I acknowledge God Almighty for the gift of the Holy Spirit that inspired me to write this book in honor of the most abandoned class of people on earth – prisoners.

Am deeply grateful to our Lord Jesus Christ and the Holy Spirit who provided all the wisdom, strength and enabling to complete this book.

Special thanks to my lovely wife, Mrs. Roseline Chinwe Madueke, for her immense contribution in encouraging me during this project, and to my lovely children.

I thank God also for inspiring and strengthening the editor of this book, Mr. Tochi Maduba Ejiofor, and Mr. Andrew Nwobodo, who provided resourceful information needed for this project. May God bless you two. May God bless you two.

Lastly, I must acknowledge the body of Christ who are engaged in prison ministries and evangelism, and individuals who are committed, over the years, to seeing that basic necessities like Bibles, clothes, soaps and medication are provided to prisoners all over the world. May God bless all of you richly Amen.

INTRODUCTION

Data on Prison Population and Conditions Worldwide

The number of people serving jail terms has been on the increase in recent years. This appears to confirm the view held by the law enforcement community that the best deterrent for crime is putting people behind bars. This view is being increasing challenged but with little success.

The data on prison population and conditions from all over the world is shocking to say the least.

Here is what Wikipedia says about incarceration in the United States:

> *"According to the U.S. Bureau of Justice Statistics (BJS) 2,292,133 adults were incarcerated in U.S. federal and state prisons, and county jails at year-end 2009 — about 1% of adults in the U.S. resident population. Additionally, 4,933,667 adults at year-end 2009 were on probation or on parole. In total, 7,225,800 adults were under correctional supervision (probation, parole, jail, or prison) in 2009 — about 3.1% of adults in the U.S. resident population. In addition, there were 86,927 juveniles in juvenile detention in 2007."*

An article on Commondreams.org has this to say-

> Tough sentencing laws, record numbers of drug offenders and high crime rates have contributed to the United States having the largest prison population and the highest rate of incarceration in the world, according to criminal justice experts.

Maricopa County female inmates march for chain gang duty in Phoenix, Arizona in this file photo. Tough sentencing laws, record numbers of drug offenders

A U.S. Justice Department report released and high crime rates have contributed to the United States having the largest prison population and the highest rate of incarceration in the world, according to criminal justice experts. REUTERS/Shannon, Stapletonon, November, 30 showed that a record 7 million people - or one in every 32 American adults -- were behind bars, on probation or on parole at the end of last year. Of the total, 2.2 million were in prison or jail.

According to the International Centre for Prison Studies London, more people are incarcerated in the United States than in any other country in the world. China ranks second with 1.5 million prisoners, followed by Russia with 870,000.

The U.S. incarceration rate of 737 per 100,000 people in the highest followed by 611 in Russia and 547 for St. Kitts and Nevis. In contrast, the incarceration rates in many Western industrial nations range around 100 per 100,000 people.

"The United States has 5 percent of the world's population and 25 percent of the world's incarcerated population. We rank first in the world in locking up our fellow citizens," said Ethan Nadelmann of the Drug Policy Alliance, which supports alternatives in the war on drugs.

Another article on cnn.com echoed the same grim statistics:

> A record number of Americans served time in corrections systems across the country in 2007, according to a report released Monday by the Pew Center on the States.
>
> The U.S. correctional population -- those in jail, prison, on probation or on parole -- totaled 7.3 million, or one in every 31 adults.
>
> The Pew Center on the States compiled the information from Justice Department and Census Bureau statistics.
>
> America's prison population has skyrocketed over the past quarter century. In 1982, 1 in 77 adults were in the correctional system in one form or another, totaling 2.2 million people.

Do prisons stop people from committing crime? An article from the economist.com has this to say:

> Some people argue that the system works: that crime has fallen in the past two decades because the bad guys are either in prison or scared of being sent there. Caged thugs cannot break into your home. Bernie Madoff's 150-year sentence for running a Ponzi fraud should deter imitators. In addition, indeed the crime rate continues to drop, despite the recession, as Michael Rushford of the Criminal Justice Legal Foundation, an advocacy group, points out. This, he says, is because habitual criminals face serious consequences. Some research supports him: after raking through

decades of historical data, John Donohue of Yale Law School estimates that a 10% increase in imprisonment brings a 2% reduction in crime.

Others disagree. Using a more recent data, Bert Useem of Purdue University and Anne Piehl of Rutgers University estimate that a 10% increase in the number of people behind bars would reduce crime by only 0.5%. In the states that currently lock up the most people, imprisoning more would actually increase crime, they believe. Some inmates emerge from prison as more accomplished criminals. Moreover, raising the incarceration rate means locking up people who are, on average, less dangerous than the ones already behind bars. A recent study found that, over the past 13 years, the proportion of new prisoners in Florida who had committed violent crimes fell by 28%, whereas those inside for "other" crimes shot up by 189%. These "other" crimes were non-violent ones involving neither drugs nor theft, such as driving with a suspended license.

How about the cost of maintaining such large prison population? Economist.com has this to say:

> Crime is a young man's game. Muggers over 30 are rare. Ex-cons who go straight for a few years generally stay that way: a study of 88,000 criminals by Mr. Blumstein found that if someone was arrested for aggravated assault at the age of 18 but then managed to stay out of trouble until the age of 22, the risk of his offending was no greater than that for the general population. Yet America's prisons are crammed with old folk. Nearly 200,000 prisoners are over 50. Most would pose little threat if released. And since people age faster in prison than outside, their medical costs are vast. Human Rights Watch, a lobby-group, talks of "nursing homes with razor wire".
>
> Jail is expensive. Spending per prisoner ranges from $18,000 a year in Mississippi to about $50,000 in California, where the cost per pupil is but a seventh of that. "We are well past the point of diminishing returns," says a report by the Pew Center on the States. In Washington State, for example, each dollar invested in new prison places in 1980 averted more than nine dollars of criminal harm (using a somewhat arbitrary scale to assign a value to not being beaten up). By 2001, as the emphasis shifted from violent criminals to drug-dealers and thieves, the cost-benefit ratio reversed. Each new dollar spent on prisons averted only 37 cents' worth of harm.

A summary of prison population by country

SOURCE: International Centre for Prison Studies

Country	Prison population	Population per 100,000	Jail occupancy level %	Un-sentenced prisoners %	Women prisoners %
US	2,193,798	737	107.6	21.2	8.9
CHINA	1,548,498	118	N/A	N/A	4.6
RUSSIA	874,161	615	79.5	16.9	6.8
BRAZIL	371,482	193	150.9	33.1	5.4
INDIA	332,112	30	139	70.1	3.7
MEXICO	214,450	196	133.9	43.2	5
UKRAINE	162,602	350	101.3	19.5	6.1
SOUTH AFRICA	158,501	334	138.6	27.5	2.1
POLAND	89,546	235	124.4	16.8	3
ENGLAND/WALES	80,002	148	112.7	16.4	5.5
JAPAN	79,052	62	105.9	14.7	5.9
KENYA	47,036	130	284.3	45.6	42
TURKEY	65,458	91	77.4	47.7	3.3
NIGERIA	40,444	30	101.5	64.3	1.9
AUSTRALIA	25,790	125	105.9	21.6	7.1
SCOTLAND	6,872	134	107.5	21	4.4
N IRELAND	1,375	79	91.5	37.4	2.2

The above screenshot from bbc.co.uk captures it all:

Treatment of Prisoners

Here is what an article from cepprobation.org says about the treatment of prisoners in various countries:

Conditions of detention

Prison conditions vary tremendously between nations and generally reflect the social and economic situation of each country. In many countries, foreign national prisoners suffer violations of their human rights through poor treatment and conditions. In developing countries, local prisoners rely on

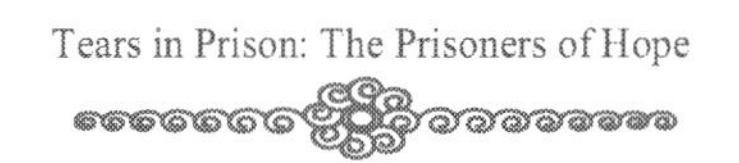

their family to supplement their diet by bringing in food for them to the prisons. Foreign prisoners are at a disadvantage as they are dependent on money sent to them by their families back home. Many of foreign prisoners' families however cannot afford to send money.

In some prisons, the prisoners spend twenty-three hours a day locked up, often sharing a cell with many others, sometimes sleeping on mattresses or the floor. Foreign nationals face these conditions with the additional difficulties of being isolated from most other inmates through cultural differences and language barriers. They are further isolated through distance from family and friends and by the mental anguish of not knowing what is happening and will happen to them.

Lack of sanitation, poor hygiene and severe overcrowding in some countries mean that foreign prisoners have little hope of staying healthy. In some jails, prisoners have to pay for their cell, mattress and bedding and sometimes end up having to sleep on the floor of the cell due to overcrowding.

How about Torture?

The same article has this to say:

For some prisoners, their status as foreign prisoners protects them from the treatment handed out to local prisoners. Nonetheless, the effect of being held in situations where violence and ill treatment is endemic can be deeply traumatizing for prisoners.

To see someone's legs tied, suspended upside down while their feet are beaten has a disturbing effect. Even the sound I shall never forget, not just the screaming but also the swash of the hose coming down on their body.

In some places, foreign prisoners may themselves be subject to torture and ill treatment, particularly when they are first arrested and are being questioned by the police. Their lack of understanding of the local language makes them especially vulnerable in these situations.

A Sad Situation

The conditions of people serving prison terms have been a cause for concern among human rights advocates. Nevertheless, there appears to be little that can be done on a global scale to improve things. This is the realm of governments.

However, much can be done for prisoners on a spiritual level. This is where this book comes in. The aim is to help those in prison to ask for God's intervention in their situation.

A much-touted benefit of imprisonment is reform of prisoners. It is doubtful if this objective is being achieved in today's prisons. A book of this nature can help prisoners change their behavior because the Word of God id power and can change even the hardest criminals.

Personally, I am not advocating the scrapping of the prison system, no. There will always be people who need to be restrained to safeguard the larger society. However, governments should cater more adequately to the spiritual

needs of prisoners. If a man is changed in the mind, it manifests in the physical behavior.

This book contains prayer points targeting various needs of those in prison and the needs of their families and relatives.

Chapter

PRISONERS OF HOPE

Prison has no decency or respect for no one, regardless of rank or status in society. Once convicted and imprisoned, you become an ordinary person and a prisoner regardless of how much respect you command in the society. On Friday July 27, 2007, a former Nigerian governor was convicted and sentence to twelve (12) years imprisonment for money

laundering and false declaration of assets.[1] He was convicted on six counts out of thirty-three (33) count charges leveled against him by Nigerian anti-graft agency, the Economic and Financial Crimes Commission.

Though he had been an Executive governor of one of Nigerian states and an officer in Nigerian Air Force for nineteen years, he was impeached, arrested, removed from governor's lodge, office, and arraigned in court. He lost his immunity and glamorous position as a privileged citizen of Nigeria that lived in splendor of government benefits, and was confined to an ordinary cubicle of prison. He was not even allowed to entertain visitors or family members.

In his own words, this former governor later lamented, *'Since my arrest in London in September 15, 2005, I have been through a dehumanizing journey. I was brought back into the country by the British government. In London, I was kept with mad people for fifteen days. I have been bleeding ever since then due to the manner of my arrest and deteriorating state of health. The President sent a battalion of solders and Air Force helicopters flying over my house. I was not impeached but physically removed. As a result, I have had surgical operations five times since then. I did this for two reasons; I am 55 years old, and have lost a wife and children. I have neither paid any legal fees nor earned a kobo. I have gone through the valley of the shadow of death severally. I am still carrying metals fixed on my body, which are due for removal. However, the Economic and Financial Crimes Commission (EFCC) whisked me out of Dubai without my doctors' consent.*

Prison is not a pleasant place to be. It is a place of absolute confinement or captivity, physical and spiritual. It is a place

[1] The Punch Newspaper (Nigeria), Friday, July 27, 2007 pg. 4

[3] ~~**Chief Olusegun Obasanjo**, Nigerian elder statesman and former Head of State~~

where convicts are kept in bounds under control of guards and wardens. Most prisoners who are not as influential as the governor is die without being noticed. Hundreds of people die every day in prisons across the world without being giving opportunities to witness Jesus Christ.

Prison can also be defined as an institution where persons convicted of serious crimes are confined. It is home to prisoners of wars and politics. Therefore, prisoners are people deprived of liberty and kept under involuntary restraints, confinement or custody, including those on or awaiting trials, or those who committed minor crimes.

We have four major categories of prisoners. They include:

1. *The first group is Suspects, who are arrested and remanded in prison. This group of prisoners is classified as Awaiting trials.*
2. *The second group is Prisoners, who are arrested, convicted and sentenced by a court of law to serve jail terms for a given number of months or years.*
3. *The third group is Prisoners, who are convicted and sentenced to life imprisonment, otherwise known as life jail.*
4. *The last group is Prisoners referred to Condemned Criminals (CC), but yet to be executed or killed.*

People go to prisons for different reasons. While some survive and regain freedom, others die or come out worse than they were before jail. Many others come out of prison only to go back into prison after a short while. When you go to prison and afterwards fail to fulfill the purpose of going to prison, you are likely to return to prison eventually. God always establish a purpose for allowing most people to go to prison, likewise the devil. So the question of the hour is, whose terms or purpose are you serving?

'To everything there is a season, and a time to every purpose under the heaven: A time to be born, and a time to die; a time to plant, and a time to pluck up that which is planted; A time to kill, and a time to heal; a time to break down, and a time to build up; A time to weep, and a time to laugh; a time to mourn, and a time to dance' (Ecclesiastes 3:1-4).

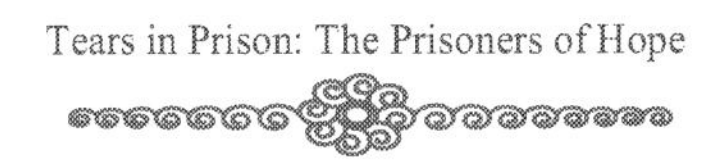

GOD'S AND SATAN'S PURPOSES FOR PRISONERS

1. DEVIL'S PURPOSE FOR PRISONERS

Times apportioned to every prisoner to spend in prison have purpose. The day you come into prison marks the time you were spiritually born in prison. It is your birthday in that prison. People always cry as they enter prison yards just as newborn babies cry as they enter into the world. From the day you were confined, you will agree it is possible devil has chosen the best place to kill you. He has also set a day aside to plant evil into your life.

> *'A time to be born, and a time to die; a time to plant, and a time to pluck up that which is planted'* (Ecclesiastes 3:2).

The death we are talking about here can be complete or partial. Devil can kill a prisoner completely or partially. When he plans to kill a prisoner completely and fails, he ruins that person partially through planting of evil seeds into such prisoners. There are many satanic agents in prisons across the world today. They are planted in different prisons to deliver evil counsels to fellow prisoners, or force them into evil covenants or atrocities inside prisons.

They kill fellow inmates by planting evil seeds into their lives. This explains why you see good people go to prison but come out alive with suicidal characters. There are demonic agents that are more poisonous than deadliest vipers in many prisons. There are equally many spiritual and evil intercourses going on in many prisons today.

Many prisoners come out of prison impregnated with all manner of abominations, adulterous intentions, and possessed by demons against Christianity. Many have gone into prisons as Christians but come out well equipped to fight Christ. Others come out with corrupted or infested minds filled with evil devices, enmity, discouragement, unforgiving, envy, fault finding, fear, grudge, hatred, rebellion, heresies, homosexual affections, fake repentance, cruelty, intimidation, evil inventions, jealousy, lack of fear of God, satanic knowledge, laziness, love of money, pleasure, lusts, malice, murdering spirit, oppressive spirit, merrymaking Spirit, pleasure in sin, pollution, pride, quarrelling, riot, ruthless, sedition, self-will, slander, stealing, anger, violence, ingratitude, witchcraft, ungodliness and so many other evil vices. Devil takes people to prison to waste their lives and commit them to suffer eternally in hell.

> '*The thief cometh not, but for to steal, and to kill, and to destroy: I am come that they might have life, and that they might have it more abundantly*' (John 10:10).

Many people get to prison and allow the devil to plant all manner of evil into their lives. Devil converts so many people's prison terms to seasons of planting and nurturing evil, only to use them upon release from prisons as instruments to fight God and His people on earth. These are people we call jail breakers. They break free from prisons without godly plans. A prisoner who overcomes devil's purpose will not waste any other time returning to prison. This is because all that he lost while in prison will be fully restored by God after he or she must have fulfilled God's purpose in prison.

> *'And Pharaoh said unto Joseph, Forasmuch as God hath shewed thee all this, there is none so discreet and wise as thou art: Thou shalt be over my house, and according unto thy word shall all my people be ruled: only in the throne will I be greater than thou. And Pharaoh said unto Joseph, See, I have set thee over all the land of Egypt. And Pharaoh took off his ring from his hand, and put it upon Joseph's hand, and arrayed him in vestures of fine linen, and put a gold chain about his neck; And he made him to ride in the second chariot which he had; and they cried before him, Bow the knee: and he made him ruler over all the land of Egypt. And Pharaoh said unto Joseph, I am Pharaoh, and without thee shall no man lift up his hand or foot in all the land of Egypt'* (Genesis 41:39-44).

It is possible to be wrongly accused, arrested, remanded, sentenced and even condemned to death. But if you trust entirely in God, you will recover all you lost and lifted higher above all your enemies. Joseph was wrongly accused. He was hated by his brethren without a just cause.

> *'And when his brethren saw that their father loved him more than all his brethren, they hated him, and could not speak peaceably unto him. And Joseph dreamed a dream, and he told it his brethren: and they hated him yet the more. And he said unto them, Hear, I pray you, this dream which I have dreamed: For, behold, we were binding sheaves in the field, and, lo, my sheaf arose, and also stood upright; and, behold, your sheaves stood round about, and made obeisance to my sheaf. And his brethren said to him, Shalt thou indeed reign over us? Or shalt thou indeed have*

> *dominion over us? And they hated him yet the more for his dreams, and for his words'* (Genesis 37:4-8).

Devil may mark you for destruction, or even cause your own family members to either hate or accuse you wrongly and speak all manner of evil against you. However, if you can determine to make good use of your prison terms in godly way, you will be exalted above all those that hated you. You may have been thrown into prison by people who hated or envied you, but if you can entrust your prison terms to God, He will promote you in the end. Your own brothers and colleagues may reject your kingship, and even conspire against you to stripe your kingship, and cast you into prison. Trust God for He will not forsake you.

> *'And when they saw him afar off, even before he came near unto them, they conspired against him to slay him. And they said one to another, Behold, this dreamer cometh. Come now therefore, and let us slay him, and cast him into some pit, and we will say, Some evil beast hath devoured him: and we shall see what will become of his dreams. And Reuben heard it, and he delivered him out of their hands; and said, Let us not kill him. And Reuben said unto them, Shed no blood, but cast him into this pit that is in the wilderness, and lay no hand upon him; that he might rid him out of their hands, to deliver him to his father again'* (Genesis 37:18-23).

It is easy for people to plan against you, or sell you out to make money, or testify against you to be imprisoned. Look up to God, for He will surely remember you and bring you out of your prison to make you better than all your enemies.

This was why David cried unto God, *'Bring my soul out of prison, that I may praise Thy name....'* (Psalms 142:7).

> *'Then there passed by Midianites merchantmen; and they drew and lifted up Joseph out of the pit, and sold Joseph to the Ishmeelites for twenty pieces of silver: and they brought Joseph into Egypt'* (Genesis 37:28).

However, when you refuse to fulfill Satan's purpose with your prison terms, and determine in your heart to serve your God with your terms, you will receive all the strength that you need, which can thrust you to an exalted position of being listened to and obeyed, making you a fruitful bough like Joseph.

> *'And when all the land of Egypt was famished, the people cried to Pharaoh for bread: and Pharaoh said unto all the Egyptians, Go unto Joseph; what he saith to you, do'* (Genesis 41:55).

> *'Joseph is a fruitful bough, even a fruitful bough by a well; whose branches run over the wall'* (Genesis 49:22).

It is also possible to be thrown into prison because of being favorite son, daughter, or a visionary, but I encourage you to be faithful to God even in hard times.

> *'And Joseph was brought down to Egypt; and Potiphar, an officer of Pharaoh, captain of the guard, an Egyptian, bought him of the hands of the Ishmeelites, which had brought him down thither. And the Lord was with Joseph, and he was a prosperous man; and he was in the house of his master the Egyptian. And his master saw that the Lord was with*

him, and that the Lord made all that he did to prosper in his hand. And Joseph found grace in his sight, and he served him: and he made him overseer over his house, and all that he had he put into his hand. And it came to pass from the time that he had made him overseer in his house, and over all that he had, that the Lord blessed the Egyptian's house for Joseph's sake; and the blessing of the Lord was upon all that he had in the house, and in the field. And he left all that he had in Joseph's hand; and he knew not ought he had, save the bread which he did eat. And Joseph was a goodly person, and well favored' (Genesis 39:1-6, 20-23).

In this prison, decide to overcome every temptation. You could be a governor or president in the making but reduced to a slave and thrown into prison. But do not fight God. Remain faithful, work hard to please God and seek for His glory. Do not allow adverse conditions in prisons to make you enemy of God.

'Flee fornication. Every sin that a man doeth is without the body; but he that committeth fornication sinneth against his own body' (1 Corinthians 6:18).

'Dearly beloved, I beseech you as strangers and pilgrims, abstain from fleshly lusts, which war against the soul; Having your conversation honest among the Gentiles: that, whereas they speak against you as evildoers, they may by your good works, which they shall behold, glorify God in the day of visitation' (1 Peter 2:11-12).

Joseph was thrown into prison unjustly. He had all opportunities to speak against God and take sides with devil. But he remained faithful to God and humanity in his prison until the day God occasioned his release. Even when all the people Joseph helped in and outside prison forgot and forsook him, he remained steadfast and did not thwart God's salvation plan.

> *'Yet within three days shall Pharaoh lift up thine head, and restore thee unto thy place: and thou shalt deliver Pharaoh's cup into his hand, after the former manner when thou wast his butler. But think on me when it shall be well with thee, and shew kindness, I pray thee, unto me, and make mention of me unto Pharaoh, and bring me out of this house: For indeed I was stolen away out of the land of the Hebrews: and here also have I done nothing that they should put me into the dungeon…. Yet did not the chief butler remember Joseph, but forgat him'* (Genesis 40:13-15, 23).

It is possible also, that, because of your imprisonment, all your friends and people you helped may have forsaken you. Remain steadfast and be sure God will not forget you in prison. You may need to spend more time engaging yourself in the service of God right there in prison, and see if God will not deliver you.

> *'And it came to pass at the end of two full years, that Pharaoh dreamed: and, behold, he stood by the river…. Then Pharaoh sent and called Joseph, and they brought him hastily out of the dungeon: and he shaved himself, and changed his raiment, and came in unto Pharaoh… And when all the land of Egypt was famished, the people cried to Pharaoh for bread: and Pharaoh said unto all the Egyptians, Go unto Joseph; what he saith to you, do. And the famine was over all the face of the*

> *earth: and Joseph opened all the storehouses, and sold unto the Egyptians; and the famine waxed sore in the land of Egypt. And all countries came into Egypt to Joseph for to buy corn; because that the famine was so sore in all lands'* (Genesis 41:1, 14, 55-57).

You may be suffering in the prison now while other people are out there enjoying the fruits of your labor. Do not be troubled, but always be assured that God will not forsake you there forever, when you remain faithful to Him in prison. You could also have been there in prison because you refused to do or engage income wrong or evil things at the detriment of your soul. Jesus said, *'Rejoice, and be exceedingly glad: for great is your reward in heaven: for so persecuted they the prophets which were before you'* (Matthew 5:12).

Many people in prisons today are so bitter with God, accusing God for failing to vindicate them in court, thus leading them to backslide in their faith in God, while seeking solace in other faiths, which they believe can provide them relief. You can get angry with God, the judges, or the government and in fact, every one for not giving you what you think is a fair judgment. But will that profit you? Joseph was falsely accused by Potiphar's wife. Did he get bitter with God in prison? No, he did not. Where did he end up? He ended up becoming a boss of his former boss, Potiphar, and boss to his former boss's wife.

> *'And it came to pass, when she saw that he had left his garment in her hand, and was fled forth, That she called unto the men of her house, and spake unto them, saying, See, he hath brought in an Hebrew unto us to mock us; he came in unto me to lie with me, and I cried*

> *with a loud voice: And it came to pass, when he heard that I lifted up my voice and cried, that he left his garment with me, and fled, and got him out. And she laid up his garment by her, until his lord came home. And she spake unto him according to these words, saying, The Hebrew servant, which thou hast brought unto us, came in unto me to mock me: And it came to pass, as I lifted up my voice and cried, that he left his garment with me, and fled out. And it came to pass, when his master heard the words of his wife, which she spake unto him, saying, After this manner did thy servant to me; that his wrath was kindled'* (Genesis 39:13-19).

When Potiphar ordered for Joseph's imprisonment without fair hearing (*of Joseph's side of the story*), Joseph remained faithful while in prison. He blamed neither God nor man. He did not ask God, *why me*? He did not complain or murmur; he was not bitter, and did not write petition in his defense. He did not harbor revenge in his heart and did not plan to fight back. His humility made God to come down when the time was right and identified with him in prison.

> *'And Joseph's master took him, and put him into the prison, a place where the king's prisoners were bound: and he was there in the prison. But the Lord was with Joseph, and shewed him mercy, and gave him favor in the sight of the keeper of the prison. And the keeper of the prison committed to Joseph's hand all the prisoners that were in the prison; and whatsoever they did there, he was the doer of it. The keeper of the prison looked not to anything that was under his hand; because the Lord was with him, and that which he did, the Lord made it to prosper'* (Genesis 39:20-23).

When you find yourself in prison, having labored your entire life to avoid prison, calm your spirit and determine to remain faithful. Spend time serving God while in prison, and remain in hope for divine intervention. God will not forsake you when you put all your trust in Him.

> *'But Zedekiah the son of Chenaanah went near, and smote Micaiah on the cheek, and said, Which way went the Spirit of the Lord from me to speak unto thee? And Micaiah said, Behold, thou shalt see in that day, when thou shalt go into an inner chamber to hide thyself. And the king of Israel said, Take Micaiah, and carry him back unto Amon the governor of the city, and to Joash the king's son; And say, Thus saith the king, Put this fellow in the prison, and feed him with bread of affliction and with water of affliction, until I come in peace'* (1 Kings 22:24-27).

> *'Then Asa was wroth with the seer, and put him in a prison house; for he was in a rage with him because of this thing. And Asa oppressed some of the people the same time'* (2 Chronicles 16:10).

People who spend their time well in prison serving the Lord will come out to reign over all their enemies including who had labored to put them in prison, including the proverbial Potiphar's wife.

> *'For out of prison he cometh to reign; whereas also he that is born in his kingdom becometh poor'* (Ecclesiastes 4:14).

2. GOD'S PURPOSE FOR PRISONERS

There are many people today awaiting their trials that God will deliver out of devil's grip with power. God can intervene before you are convicted and sentenced wrongly. God can also choose to intervene while you are awaiting trial or in court. Other times, He may deliberately allow you to go to prison for a short while, or allow you to pass through severe suffering before He intervenes in your case. The most important thing is that you must remain faithful and trusting in God, regardless of where He chooses to show up to deliver you.

> *'Now there cried a certain woman of the wives of the sons of the prophets unto Elisha, saying, Thy servant my husband is dead; and thou knowest that thy servant did fear the Lord: and the creditor is come to take unto him my two sons to be bondmen. And Elisha said unto her, What shall I do for thee? tell me, what hast thou in the house? And she said, Thine handmaid hath not anything in the house, save a pot of oil. Then he said, Go, borrow thee vessels abroad of all thy neighbors, even empty vessels; borrow not a few. And when thou art come in, thou shalt shut the door upon thee and upon thy sons, and shalt pour out into all those vessels, and thou shalt set aside that which is full. So, she went from him, and shut the door upon her and upon her sons, who brought the vessels to her; and she poured out. And it came to pass, when the vessels were full, that she said unto her son, Bring me yet a vessel. And he said unto her, There is not a vessel more. And the oil stayed. Then she came and told the man of God. And he said, Go, sell the oil, and pay thy*

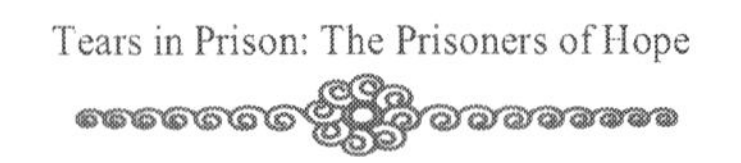

> *debt, and live thou and thy children of the rest'* (2Kings 4:1-7).

God allowed Jesus to drink from the cup of suffering, humiliation and death for a purpose, even when Jesus cried out unto Him. Whether God decides to meet you at the beginning of your trouble, in the middle or at the end, you must trust in Him and remain completely faithful. Where and when He meets you should not be your worry. The most important thing you need to understand and believe is that God loves you and knows the best place and time to show up. And wherever He decides to meet a person is always the best place. God has a purpose for everything including allowing you to go through problems sometimes.

> *'And lo a voice from heaven, saying, This is my beloved Son, in whom I am well pleased'* (Matthew 3:17).

Jesus was rejected, hated and despised by His people. It got to a point when Jesus became sorrowful and filled with grief. He bore the grief and sorrow of all humanity, born and unborn, upon the cross, but God did not appear immediately out of emotions. Jesus was afflicted and wounded not for His own sins (*He does not have one*), but for transgressions of others. Jesus was bruised for our iniquities, and chastised severely for offences He never committed.

> *'Surely, he hath borne our grief, and carried our sorrows: yet we did esteem him stricken, smitten of God, and afflicted. But he was wounded for our transgressions, he was bruised for our iniquities: the chastisement of our peace was upon him; and with his stripes, we are healed. All we like sheep have gone astray; we have turned everyone to his own way; and*

the Lord hath laid on him the iniquity of us all. He was oppressed, and he was afflicted, yet he opened not his mouth: he is brought as a lamb to the slaughter, and as a sheep before her shearers is dumb, so he openeth not his mouth. He was taken from prison and from judgment: and who shall declare his generation? for he was cut off out of the land of the living: for the transgression of my people was he stricken And he made his grave with the wicked, and with the rich in his death; because he had done no violence, neither was any deceit in his mouth. Yet it pleased the Lord to bruise him; he hath put him to grief: when thou shalt make his soul an offering for sin, he shall see his seed, he shall prolong his days, and the pleasure of the Lord shall prosper in his hand' (Isaiah 53:4-10).

Unfortunately, the people Jesus suffered for abandoned Him. All His trusted friends turned their backs on Him and ran away. He took upon Him the sins of all humanity. The iniquities of all, born and unborn, was laid upon him. He was oppressed and unjustly afflicted. He was taken from one prison to another. Multiple judgments were delivered on him. He was condemned to death for crimes He did not commit.

Devil deceived people Jesus came to deliver and they sentenced Jesus to death, hanging Him on a cross. Jesus did not fight back for He knew He has to die to reconcile us with His Father.

'And Jesus stood before the governor: and the governor asked him, saying, Art thou the King of the Jews? And Jesus said unto him, Thou sayest. And when he was accused of the chief priests and elders, he answered

nothing. Then said Pilate unto him, Hearest thou not how many things they witness against thee? And he answered him to never a word; insomuch that the governor marvelled greatly' (Matthew 27:11-14).

Recall that Jesus also became a prisoner. However, when an opportunity came for His release, His enemies subverted it and preferred a notable and deadly criminal called Barnabas. He was condemned and sentenced to die a shameful death.

'The governor answered and said unto them, Whether of the twain will ye that I release unto you? They said, Barabbas. Pilate saith unto them, What shall I do then with Jesus, which is called Christ? They all say unto him, Let him be crucified. And the governor said, Why, what evil hath he done? But they cried out the more, saying, Let him be crucified. When Pilate saw that he could prevail nothing, but that rather a tumult was made, he took water, and washed his hands before the multitude, saying, I am innocent of the blood of this just person: see ye to it. Then answered all the people, and said, His blood be on us, and on our children. Then released he Barabbas unto them: and when he had scourged Jesus, he delivered him to be crucified' (Matthew 27:21-26).

When Jesus was sentence to death, the soldiers of the governor took Him into the common hall, stripped Him and put a scarlet robe on Him. They designed a crown with thorns and put upon His head, and a reading in His right hand. He was mocked, spited upon and smitten on the head. His clothes were taken away from Him. He was crucified

and was given vinegar mingled with gall to drink when He was thirsty (*See* Matthew 27:27-38).

When Jesus was made a prisoner, we saw how he accepted His persecution without bitterness. God did not intervene at the beginning of His suffering, or at the middle or at the end, which cumulated to His death. God waited for the right time. He intervened on the third day after His death and burial. So, it is for most prisoners. God is waiting for the right time to intervene. You have to learn how to trust God without any piece of bitterness found anywhere in your heart.

> *'Jesus, when he had cried again with a loud voice, yielded up the ghost. And, behold, the veil of the temple was rent in twain from the top to the bottom; and the earth did quake, and the rocks rent; And the graves were opened; and many bodies of the saints which slept arose, And came out of the graves after his resurrection, and went into the holy city, and appeared unto many'* (Matthew 27:50-53).

Do not blame or accuse God or any man or woman for being responsible for your imprisonment, even though they are. God has a purpose for allowing you get to this level in your life. He will never fail to deliver you at the right and appointed time. Jesus was faithful until the end, and God honored Him above all the angels in heaven and all creatures.

> *'Wherefore God also hath highly exalted him, and given him a name which is above every name: That at the name of Jesus every knee should bow, of things in heaven, and things in earth, and things under the earth; And that every tongue should confess that Jesus*

> *Christ is Lord, to the glory of God the Father'* (Philippians 2:9-11).

There is always promotion waiting for every prisoner who accepts his or her affliction in good faith and serve God until the end. Peter was condemned to die for devil had marked him for death, but God delivered him miraculously. Joseph was never bitter with God and he never accused his brothers for betraying him while in prison. God allowed these people to enter into prisons with death sentences hanging over their heads. The same God broke every protocol and set them free. Who says God cannot do the same on your behalf?

> *'Now about that time Herod the king stretched forth his hands to vex certain of the church. And he killed James the brother of John with the sword. And because he saw it pleased the Jews, he proceeded further to take Peter. (Then were the days of unleavened bread.) And when he had apprehended him, he put him in prison, and delivered him to four quaternions of soldiers to keep him; intending after Easter to bring him forth to the people'* (Acts 12:1-4).

When Peter was in prison waiting for his death under the watch of four fierce soldiers, prayers were organized for him by the church. I have written effective prayers that can set you free in this book. I encourage you to prepare yourself for prayers. Every evil sentence hanging your life must be broken.

> *'Peter therefore was kept in prison: but prayer was made without ceasing of the church unto God for him. And when Herod would have brought him forth, the same night Peter was sleeping between two soldiers, bound with two chains: and the keepers before the door*

kept the prison. And, behold, the angel of the Lord came upon him, and a light shined in the prison: and he smote Peter on the side, and raised him up, saying, Arise up quickly. And his chains fell off from his hands' (Acts 12:5-7).

Prayers in this book can break every spiritual chain binding you now and allow light to shine upon you there in prison. When every spiritual chain is broken, it becomes easy for physical ones to lose freely. Your prison's garment of shame will be torn and every prison gate miraculously opens for your sake. All condemned prisoners in the Bible that trusted God were all set free in different ways.

'Therefore because the king's commandment was urgent, and the furnace exceeding hot, the flame of the fire slew those men that took up Shadrach, Meshach, and Abed-nego. And these three men, Shadrach, Meshach, and Abed-nego, fell down bound into the midst of the burning fiery furnace. Then Nebuchadnezzar the king was astonied, and rose up in haste, and spake, and said unto his counselors, Did not we cast three men bound into the midst of the fire? They answered and said unto the king, True, O king. He answered and said, Lo, I see four men loose, walking in the midst of the fire, and they have no hurt; and the form of the fourth is like the Son of God' (Daniel 3:22-25).

Shadrach, Meshach and Abednego were condemned to die in fiery furnace heated seven times more. The mightiest men in the army were commanded to cast them into burning furnace. However, God miraculously delivered them and the ravenous and exceedingly hot burning flames slew all their enemies instead. Many good people have entered prisons in the past, but prison fires burned their entire virtues. That was not the case with these three young Hebrew children. Jesus came and identified with them in that isolated prison of burning tongues of fire. They walked, rejoiced and sang in the midst of the fire with a fourth person, who was our Lord Jesus Christ.

> *'Then Nebuchadnezzar the king was astonied, and rose up in haste, and spake, and said unto his counselors, Did not we cast three men bound into the midst of the fire? They answered and said unto the king, True, O king. He answered and said, Lo, I see four men loose, walking in the midst of the fire, and they have no hurt; and the form of the fourth is like the Son of God'* (Daniel 3:24-25).

So, when you enter into any prison and refuse to invite Jesus into your life, the prison fires will consume every good virtue in your life. Without Jesus, no man or woman can enter into any prison and come out unhurt. Your decision to invite Christ into your life right in this prison can change the course of your life, overturn every decree against you and reposition you for good by the time you finish your prison terms. If you surrender your life to Christ and serve Him in this prison, you will recover all that you have lost, including all the years that were productive and you will be promoted highly among all your equals. By the time you come out of this prison with Christ, your invested prayers will be waiting to usher you into divine store of blessings. The time of imprisonment is always a potential time of preparations for greater things.

> *'Then Nebuchadnezzar came near to the mouth of the burning fiery furnace, and spake, and said, Shadrach, Meshach, and Abed-nego, ye servants of the most high God, come forth, and come hither. Then Shadrach, Meshach, and Abed-nego, came forth of the midst of the fire. And the princes, governors, and captains, and the king's counselors, being gathered together, saw these men, upon whose bodies the fire had no power, nor was an hair of their head singed, neither were their coats changed, nor the smell of fire had passed on them. Then Nebuchadnezzar spake, and said, Blessed be the God of Shadrach, Meshach, and Abed-nego, who hath sent his angel, and delivered his servants that trusted in him, and have changed the king's word, and yielded their bodies, that they might not serve nor worship any god, except their own God. Therefore I make a decree, That every people, nation, and language, which speak anything amiss against the God of Shadrach, Meshach, and Abed-nego, shall be cut in pieces, and their houses shall be made a dunghill: because there is no other God that can deliver after this sort. Then the king promoted Shadrach, Meshach, and Abed-nego, in the province of Babylon'* (Daniel 3:26-30).

Joseph came out of prison a better person for he knew and trusted his God. He was not ordinarily promoted, he was promoted above all his masters and all that hated him served under his government and bowed down to him. Everything depends on how you wanted things to be for whatever you desire can be achieved in this place of confinement.

'And the ill-favored and lean fleshed kine did eat up the seven well-favored and fat kine. So Pharaoh awoke… And when all the land of Egypt was famished, the people cried to Pharaoh for bread: and Pharaoh said unto all the Egyptians, Go unto Joseph; what he saith to you, do' (Genesis 41:4, 55).

If you can obey God by accepting His only begotten Son, Jesus, into your life, and repent, confessing and determining to forsake all your sins while in this prison, you will not regret your decision. Daniel was once condemned and cast into a lion's den to die, but God spared his life and promoted him.

'Then the king commanded, and they brought Daniel, and cast him into the den of lions. Now the king spake and said unto Daniel, Thy God whom thou servest continually, he will deliver thee. And a stone was brought and laid upon the mouth of the den; and the king sealed it with his own signet, and with the signet of his lords; that the purpose might not be changed concerning Daniel… Then said Daniel unto the king, O king, live forever. My God hath sent his angel, and hath shut the lions' mouths, that they have not hurt me: forasmuch as before him innocency was found in me; and also before thee, O king, have I done no hurt' (Daniel 6:16-17, 21-22).

You may have been condemned today, but am sure nobody wants to die in prison. You have to get up and start praying. Repent and surrender your life to Christ and witness Him. He will set you free. When God delivers a person, He will not leave that person at his or her former state. He takes him or her to a higher ground, mostly beyond human expectation. So, you have to initiate the process of your deliverance through your prayers in prison.

> *'Then was the king exceeding glad for him, and commanded that they should take Daniel up out of the den. So, Daniel was taken up out of the den, and no manner of hurt was found upon him, because he believed in his God. And the king commanded, and they brought those men which had accused Daniel, and they cast them into the den of lions, them, their children, and their wives; and the lions had the mastery of them, and brake all their bones in pieces or ever they came at the bottom of the den. Then king Darius wrote unto all people, nations, and languages, that dwell in all the earth; Peace be multiplied unto you. I make a decree, That in every dominion of my kingdom men tremble and fear before the God of Daniel: for he is the living God, and steadfast forever, and his kingdom that which shall not be destroyed, and his dominion shall be even unto the end. He delivereth and rescueth, and he worketh signs and wonders in heaven and in earth, who hath delivered Daniel from the power of the lions. So this Daniel prospered in the reign of Darius, and in the reign of Cyrus the Persian'* (Daniel 6:23-28).

It is true that those who sent you to prison wanted your life and destiny destroyed, but how you respond would go a long way to determine the actual turn out of events. God is the one who determines your end, not your enemies. You may have entered in prison as the worst person on earth, but you can actually leave prison as one of the greatest persons on earth by accepting Jesus as your Lord and personal Savior while in prison. Many people who are influencing great nations of the world today with the gospel of Jesus actually met Jesus while they were in prison.

It does not matter whether you belong to any other religion besides Christianity. But if you can repent now and accept Christ, He can cause you to be delivered from prison and promoted to greater heights. And as you come out of prison a real Christian, all your enemies will be put far behind you. A single miracle from Jesus can make all the deference.

> *'And the king commanded, and they brought those men which had accused Daniel, and they cast them into the den of lions, them, their children, and their wives; and the lions had the mastery of them, and brake all their bones in pieces or ever they came at the bottom of the den'* (Daniel 6:24).

It is very possible that the purpose of God for allowing you to enter prison is to change your life and destiny for good. So, you do not have to complain or blame anyone for being very responsible for your coming to this prison. God has great plan and purpose, and if you would cooperate with Him, the works of God will be made manifest in you.

> *'And as Jesus passed by, he saw a man which was blind from his birth. And his disciples asked him, saying, Master, who did sin, this man, or his parents, that he was born blind? Jesus answered, Neither hath this man sinned, nor his parents: but that the works of God should be made manifest in him'* (John 9:1-3).

There was a man in the scriptures called Jeremiah. He was greatly destined and he knew it. He started his ministry and God really prospered him. He was a great prayer warrior who prayed for a whole nation and the entire world until he was nicknamed a weeping prophet. His lamentation for Israel was great. He prayed fervently against idolatry (*See* Jeremiah 10:8-15). He also prayed against the affliction of the children of Israel. He was wrongly persecuted and imprisoned many times (*See* Jeremiah 20:7-13).

Jeremiah prayed for kings of Israel and prophesied about their captivity. He was a man who knows how to pray, fast and wait upon God. He took many remarkable decisions in the Bible. He obeyed God and preached to sinners of his day and pleaded with them to return to God (*See* Jeremiah 3:1, 12-14, 23). He assured all sinners of God's promises if only they would return to God (*See* Jeremiah 4:1, 14, 30). Even when righteous men decreased in Israel, he still prayed to God for the nation of Israel (*See* Jeremiah 5:1-6). He confronted sinners in Israel and exposed their sins by announcing to them what their ends will be if they refuse to repent (*See* Jeremiah 17:9-11, 13-14).

Jeremiah was a great man of God who believed the Word of God. He entered into troubles many times, but he prayed and God gave him mighty deliverances and great promises (*See* Jeremiah 15:15-21). Afterwards, Jeremiah was arrested, remanded in prison and later condemned to death. When he found himself condemned as a criminal, his countenance failed him and he almost forgot all the promises of deliverance God gave to him. He almost forgot that God promised to make him a fenced brazen wall. He almost forgot that God promised to be with him, to save and deliver him out of the hand of the wicked.

> *'And I will make thee unto this people a fenced brazen wall: and they shall fight against thee, but they shall not prevail against thee: for I am with thee to save thee*

> *and to deliver thee, saith the Lord. And I will deliver thee out of the hand of the wicked, and I will redeem thee out of the hand of the terrible'* (Jeremiah 15:20-21).

When Jeremiah spent so many days in prison under awful conditions of prison, he began to lose hope of survival. He began to forget to pray, fast, and trust God's Word and promises. Though he knew the Word of God, he focused on the negative realities in his prison.

> *'Moreover the word of the Lord came unto Jeremiah the second time, while he was yet shut up in the court of the prison, saying, Thus saith the Lord the maker thereof, the Lord that formed it, to establish it; the Lord is his name'* (Jeremiah 33:1-2).

At some point, Jeremiah lost hope of deliverance and surrendered his wits to death. He became spiritually and physically weak and his hope could not carry him through. While his deliverance was more desirous of him, Jeremiah preoccupied his thoughts with his execution and death. The prison brought him discouragement and suffering, and he foresaw death instead of life. Then in Jeremiah chapter 32, he dropped his writing materials and surrendered to death. But God later reminded him that there are many chapters unwritten by him. Jeremiah wrote chapters 33to 52 afterwards, including five chapters of the book of Lamentation before death. To Jeremiah, prison meant his death, but to God, there was much more to do.

When God condemned Hezekiah to death and confirmed it through prophet Isaiah, Hezekiah rejected it and through prayers, he reversed God's verdict. He gave God the reason why he was not ready to die and God listened to him.

> *'Call unto me, and I will answer thee, and shew thee great and mighty things, which thou knowest not'* (Jeremiah 33:3).

He reminded God what he has done, and begged God to allow him more time on earth and God reversed the death verdict.

> *'In those days was Hezekiah sick unto death. And Isaiah the prophet the son of Amoz came unto him, and said unto him, Thus saith the Lord, Set thine house in order: for thou shalt die, and not live. Then Hezekiah turned his face toward the wall, and prayed unto the Lord, And said, Remember now, O Lord, I beseech thee, how I have walked before thee in truth and with a perfect heart, and have done that which is good in thy sight. And Hezekiah wept sore. Then came the word of the Lord to Isaiah, saying, Go, and say to Hezekiah, Thus saith the Lord, the God of David thy father, I have heard thy prayer, I have seen thy tears: behold, I will add unto thy days fifteen years'* (Isaiah 38:1-5).

You still have many empty chapters to write in your life, so do not accept death yet. God is not done with you. In fact, your life is just beginning.

The lawyer to the convicted former governor I mentioned at the earlier told the court that his client did not intend to contest the six counts charges proffered against him. The lawyer pleaded with the court to tamper justice with mercy and show utmost leniency in given out any sentence to the accused. He advocated that his client could still be useful in gainful service to the country. It was based on this plea that

the former governor was sentenced to only two years imprisonment.[2]

Therefore, God would deliver prisoners, who repent and remain faithful in His service. Through the prayers in this book, we will be talking to our heavenly judge who gives better judgment than earthly judges do.

> *'And he spake a parable unto them to this end, that men ought always to pray, and not to faint; Saying, There was in a city a judge, which feared not God, neither regarded man: And there was a widow in that city; and she came unto him, saying, Avenge me of mine adversary. And he would not for a while: but afterward he said within himself, Though I fear not God, nor regard man; Yet because this widow troubleth me, I will avenge her, lest by her continual coming she weary me. And the Lord said, Hear what the unjust judge saith. And shall not God avenge his own elect, which cry day and night unto him, though he bear long with them? I tell you that he will avenge them speedily. Nevertheless when the Son of man cometh, shall he find faith on the earth?'* (Luke 18:1-8).

One practical example is writing a list of what you want God to do for you in and outside prison, and then spend some time and cry to God. God will not delay to answer your prayers. Moreover, as you pray, remain faithful so that when the Son of man comes with answers, He will find you practicing a consistent Christian life.

> *'Come unto me, all ye that labor and are heavy laden, and I will give you rest. Take my yoke upon you, and learn of me; for I am meek and lowly in heart: and ye shall find rest unto your souls. For my yoke is easy, and my burden is light'* (Matthew 11:28-30).

You are in prison for a reason. Your prayers should be to serve your godly purpose well and never to overstay or under stay in this prison. Then allow things to happen the way Christ has planned them from the beginning. Regardless of what your offence was, what you do with Christ in this prison will determine a lot in years ahead. No prisoner of any category has ever encountered Christ and remained the same. Accept Christ into your heart now and see how sweet Christ is. It has happened severally in the past, and if you believe, it will happen in your life.

As God did in the lives of people like Joseph, He can and will do it in your life. Joseph was taken away from his beloved father and his country. He became a salve boy and later a prisoner. Yet, his trust and belief in God were never shaken. Rather he remained faithful to God. He worked hard to promote God with his gift of interpreting dreams. He worked diligently, seeking nothing but the glory of God. He was an encouragement to other prisoners and introduced God to them. I pray you will not die but you shall live to leave the prison fulfilling God's purpose.

> *'For David, after he had served his own generation by the will of God, fell on sleep, and was laid unto his fathers, and saw corruption'* (Acts 13:36).

Do not complain or compare yourself with other people outside prison. You are here to be made better than others are.

'Then Pharaoh sent and called Joseph, and they brought him hastily out of the dungeon: and he shaved himself, and changed his raiment, and came in unto Pharaoh... And Pharaoh said unto his servants, Can we find such a one as this is, a man in whom the Spirit of God is? And Pharaoh said unto Joseph, Forasmuch as God hath shewed thee all this, there is none so discreet and wise as thou art: Thou shalt be over my house, and according unto thy word shall all my people be ruled: only in the throne will I be greater than thou. And Pharaoh said unto Joseph, See, I have set thee over all the land of Egypt. And Pharaoh took off his ring from his hand, and put it upon Joseph's hand, and arrayed him in vestures of fine linen, and put a gold chain about his neck; And he made him to ride in the second chariot which he had; and they cried before him, Bow the knee: and he made him ruler over all the land of Egypt. And Pharaoh said unto Joseph, I am Pharaoh, and without thee shall no man lift up his hand or foot in all the land of Egypt' (Genesis 41:14, 38-44).

'And one of the malefactors which were hanged railed on him, saying, If thou be Christ, save thyself and us. But the other answering rebuked him, saying, Dost not thou fear God, seeing thou art in the same condemnation?' (Luke 23:39-40).

What you need is a simple decision to open the door of your heart for Christ to come in, and your level will change forever.

Chapter

WHO ARE PRISONERS OF HOPE?

The reason believers are special people is that believers are God's covenanted partners on earth. The new life in Christ makes them heavenly partners and ambassadors of Christ on earth. By the reason of a believer's faith in Christ, he or she is automatically translated into God's kingdom as a worthy son or daughter on earth.

> *'But as many as received him, to them gave he power to become the sons of God, even to them that believe on his name'* (John 1:12).

Devil does not underestimate true believers spiritual capabilities because he knows how powerful and equipped they are. It is only non-breakthrough believers who think or believe that devil is too strong, thus fearing devil and all his agents. A true believer cannot be afraid of devil. Devil is the one who is afraid of true believers.

> *'And I say also unto thee, That thou art Peter, and upon this rock I will build my church; and the gates of hell shall not prevail against it'* (Matthew 16:18).

No power can defeat a prayerful Christian because he or she is rightly equipped with the name of Jesus; a name that is above every other name on the universe, that at the mention of the name of Jesus every knee bows. The gate of hell trembles at the voice of a true child of God and cannot withstand him or her. You can only prevail over devil if you are a true child of God, whom Christ redeemed, guides and protects through the power of the Holy Spirit. When you become born again, you receive spiritual transformation and you become a new creature.

> *'Therefore if any man be in Christ, he is a new creature: old things are passed away; behold, all things are become new'* (2 Corinthians 5:17).

By the virtue of being born again, you can no longer be that unworthy, wretched and poor man of the flesh. All believers are brothers to the Lord Jesus Christ and will be defended by Christ at the mention of His name, even in prison. A wise demon cannot enter your territory when it knows that you are a true Christian carrying fire of God inside of you in the name of Jesus.

'He suffered no man to do them wrong: yea, he reproved kings for their sakes; Saying, Touch not mine anointed, and do my prophets no harm' (Psalms 105:14-15).

'And from Jesus Christ, who is the faithful witness, and the first begotten of the dead, and the prince of the kings of the earth. Unto him that loved us, and washed us from our sins in his own blood, And hath made us kings and priests unto God and his Father; to him be glory and dominion forever and ever. Amen' (Revelation 1:5-6).

As kings and priests, we have been made to reign over devil and all his agents. This also means we, and not devil or our enemies, have final authority or the final say. However, while it is possible for true believers to enter into troubles or prison, by remaining faithful and prayerful, they shall always come out better and greater people. Therefore, I encourage you to maintain your position in Christ. All believers, especially those who repent and receive Jesus while in prison are referred to as *Prisoners of Hope*.

'The Spirit of the Lord God is upon me; because the Lord hath anointed me to preach good tidings unto the meek; he hath sent me to bind up the brokenhearted, to proclaim liberty to the captives, and the opening of the prison to them that are bound' (Isaiah 61:1).

'Turn you to the strong hold, ye prisoners of hope: even to day do I declare that I will render double unto thee' (Zechariah 9:12).

Prisoners of hope are great destinies that should not waste in prison. Before a prisoner of hope enters into prison, the Lord has already made a way of escape for him or her. Those who hear the gospel and obey it, even in prison, will be delivered, promoted and made better.

Where you have been broken and maltreated, Jesus will bind up your broken heart and liberate you. It is always a fulfilling and joyful thing to serve Jesus inside prison. He will never forget all your labor of love. So many great people today who are doing well started their ministries while they were serving prison sentences. God will never fail to reward all who serve Him diligently, restoring them back to their destinies to recover every loss.

You are a prisoner of hope. A miraculous way to escape death is waiting in Christ Jesus. This prison will not terminate your life because prison is not an end-of-the-road for true believers. However, prisoners of hope many enter into diverse trials and difficulties and even imprisoned, but they will not be consumed.

> *'Many are the afflictions of the righteous: but the Lord delivereth him out of them all'* (Psalms 34:19).

One good thing about prisoners of hope is that even at death, they still remain winners. They cannot lose any battle because, to them, death is already defeated. God has overcome the world for all prisoners of hope.

> *'When they heard these things, they were cut to the heart, and they gnashed on him with their teeth. But he, being full of the Holy Ghost, looked up steadfastly into heaven, and saw the glory of God, and Jesus standing on the right hand of God, And said, Behold, I see the heavens opened, and the Son of man standing on the right hand of God. Then they cried out with a*

> *loud voice, and stopped their ears, and ran upon him with one accord, And cast him out of the city, and stoned him: and the witnesses laid down their clothes at a young man's feet, whose name was Saul. And they stoned Stephen, calling upon God, and saying, Lord Jesus, receive my spirit. And he kneeled down, and cried with a loud voice, Lord, lay not this sin to their charge. And when he had said this, he fell asleep'* (Acts 7:54-60).

Prisoners of hope who lost their lives in battlefields are not dead. Once their eyes close in physical death, they open them in heaven where the enemy does not have power to reach. Though prisoners of hope can be taken out of the physical world, heaven will always open to receive them. You may physically stone them to death, but death cannot overpower them for they will live eternally in heaven forever and ever.

BIBLICAL EXAMPLES OF PRISONERS OF HOPE

1. *ABEL*

Abel took an unshakeable decision to worship God the right way despite all pressures from his elder brother, Cain. He gave God the right offering in righteousness. And even though he died in the battlefield, he was recognized by God and heaven avenged his death.

> *'And she again bare his brother Abel. And Abel was a keeper of sheep, but Cain was a tiller of the ground. And in process of time it came to pass, that Cain brought of the fruit of the ground an offering unto the Lord. And Abel, he also brought of the firstlings of his flock and of the fat thereof. And the Lord had respect unto Abel and to his offering'* (Genesis 4:2-4).

A prisoner of hope does not compromise true worship. He or she is always determined to do the right thing regardless of dire consequences. Therefore, as a prisoner of hope, take a decision now to obey God and His Word regardless of all visible and invincible sufferings. Abel's sacrifice was accepted and respected by God because he offered it in faith and righteousness. I pray that you do not give up halfway, but fight until your freedom is restored so you can come out alive to enjoy your life in Christ.

The only mistake Abel did was following his brother to an evil field where he has no grace to resist his brother on time. He was manipulated and bewitched, but he stood his ground and remained faithful and thankful to God for blessing him. He resisted with his blood, but he did not start early.

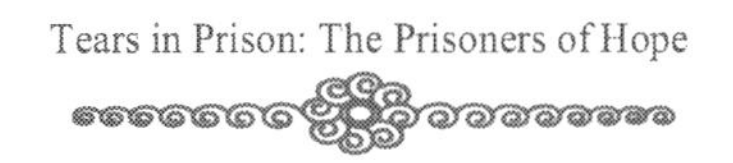

'Submit yourselves therefore to God. Resist the devil, and he will flee from you' (James 4:7).

If you start now to resist your enemy, the Lord will appear in the battlefield and set you set free.

2. *ENOCH*

In Enoch's generation, worshiping and serving God, or doing what was right was so unpopular. People of his generation walked with devil. They walked out on God in their groups. It was very common for people in that generation to serve devil. They were rooted in evil worship and witchcraft. Nevertheless, Enoch was different. He chose to walk with the LORD God.

'Finally, my brethren, be strong in the Lord, and in the power of his might' (Ephesians 6:10).

The only place we are exhorted in the Scriptures to be strong is in the Lord. But in our generation today, a lot of people are either strong in occultism, or wickedness, violence and robbery. Paul advised the church of Christ in Ephesus to be strong only in the Lord and in the power of His mighty.

'And Jared lived an hundred sixty and two years, and he begat Enoch: And Jared lived after he begat Enoch eight hundred years, and begat sons and daughters: And all the days of Jared were nine hundred sixty and two years: and he died. And Enoch lived sixty and five years, and begat Methuselah: And Enoch walked with God after he begat Methuselah three hundred years, and begat sons and daughters: And all the days of Enoch were three hundred sixty and five years: And

> *Enoch walked with God: and he was not; for God took him'* (Genesis 5:18-24).

In the days of Enoch, people were very much interested in gathering wealth and begotten sons and daughters without reference to God. They multiplied to themselves many wives, lived long lives and expired without serving God. But Enoch lived for God. He took unpopular decision and separated from his generation and remained alone with God. Prisoners of hope walk with God regardless of degree of worldly influences around them.

Believers who are prisoners of hope are called to separate and distance themselves from those whose affections and desires are ungodly, so that they can walk with God. Prisoners of hope are believers who shun carnal programs, demonic gatherings, evil motivated festivities and worldly conversion in and outside prison yard.

> *'But fornication, and all uncleanness, or covetousness, let it not be once named among you, as becometh saints; Neither filthiness, nor foolish talking, nor jesting, which are not convenient: but rather giving of thanks'* (Ephesians 5:3-4).

As true ambassador of Christ, a true prisoner of hope does not compete with the world or strive outside God's will. He or she knows for sure how to get to destinations with God. They separate themselves from worldly fashions, demon motivated relationships and worldly cares. They follow God gradually and do not struggle to get rich quick and fast. It is a blessing for prisoners of hope to be rich and even far beyond the children of this world. They avoid companies of day dreaming worldly people, who labor to be rich at all, cost or by all evil means necessary.

'The thought of foolishness is sin: and the scorner is an abomination to men' (Proverbs 24:9)

'He that loveth silver shall not be satisfied with silver; nor he that loveth abundance with increase: this is also vanity. When goods increase, they are increased that eat them: and what good is there to the owners thereof, saving the beholding of them with their eyes? The sleep of a laboring man is sweet, whether he eat little or much: but the abundance of the rich will not suffer him to sleep. There is a sore evil which I have seen under the sun, namely, riches kept for the owners thereof to their hurt. But those riches perish by evil travail: and he begetteth a son, and there is nothing in his hand. As he came forth of his mother's womb, naked shall he return to go as he came, and shall take nothing of his labor, which he may carry away in his hand' (Ecclesiastes 5:10-15).

A true believer purposes in his or her heart to align with godliness, and does not allow worldly people to influence them. True believers regard worldly pleasures as sin, and do not pursue anything outside God's will. They reject worldly enjoyments. They neither attend evil parties nor take part in demonic inspired entertainments.

3. *NOAH*

Prisoners of hope are not helpless people but they are people that believe in Christ and are better prepared for the future. Age does not matter to them for they remain faithful to God even unto death. Noah is one of the practical evidences of prisoners of hope. When Noah was over five hundred years, he heard God's voice. He believed it and went ahead to construct an ark.

> *'Make thee an ark of gopher wood; rooms shalt thou make in the ark, and shalt pitch it within and without with pitch. And this is the fashion which thou shalt make it of: The length of the ark shall be three hundred cubits, the breadth of it fifty cubits, and the height of it thirty cubits. A window shalt thou make to the ark, and in a cubit shalt thou finish it above; and the door of the ark shalt thou set in the side thereof; with lower, second, and third stories shalt thou make it. And, behold, I, even I, do bring a flood of waters upon the earth, to destroy all flesh, wherein is the breath of life, from under heaven; and everything that is in the earth shall die. But with thee will I establish my covenant; and thou shalt come into the ark, thou, and thy sons, and thy wife, and thy sons' wives with thee. And of every living thing of all flesh, two of every sort shalt thou bring into the ark, to keep them alive with thee; they shall be male and female. Of fowls after their kind, and of cattle after their kind, of every creeping thing of the earth after his kind, two of every sort shall come unto thee, to keep them alive. And take thou unto thee of all food that is eaten, and thou shalt gather it to thee; and it shall be for food for thee, and for them.*

> *Thus did Noah; according to all that God commanded him, so did he'* (Genesis 6:14-22).

When God commanded Noah to construct an ark of deliverance and salvation, all the people mocked God. Only Noah and his family believed that God is able to do what He said He would do. Noah's obedience can be attributed to his personality as a prisoner of hope. Prisoners of hope do not hesitate to enter into covenants with God. Today, true believers are still building the ark of God and only those in covenant with God will escape impending doom. We need to accept Lord Jesus and answer the call of salvation.

> *'Come unto me, all ye that labor and are heavy laden, and I will give you rest'* (Matthew 11:28).

Noah was the only righteous and just man in his generation (*See* Genesis 7:1-24, 8:1-22). He believed God. Moreover, when he obeyed Him, he found grace and his life and that of his family were spared from destruction. The people in Noah's days were soaked in sin. But Noah was busy with God building the ark of salvation. The difference was clear; Noah became dead to sin, dead to the world, deaf to things of the world and was perfectly separated from worldly activities that did not glorify God.

> *'For ye are dead, and your life is hid with Christ in God'* (Colossians 3:3).

> *'God forbid. How shall we, that are dead to sin, live any longer therein?.... For he that is dead is freed from sin. Now if we be dead with Christ, we believe that we shall also live with him: Knowing that Christ being raised from the dead dieth no more; death hath no more dominion over him. For in that he died, he died unto*

sin once: but in that he liveth, he liveth unto God. Likewise, reckon ye also yourselves to be dead indeed unto sin, but alive unto God through Jesus Christ our Lord… Being then made free from sin, ye became the servants of righteousness' (Romans 6:2,7-11,18).

Prison is a place of isolation where people who are broken in spirit have opportunity to make friends with God. It is a place where such people prepare themselves for greatness. I encourage you to take this imprisonment as an opportunity to kill all evil affections. Ask God to make you unconscious to sin forever. To be dead to sin means to be free from sin, and separated from all appearances of evil. Set your affections on things that are above and things that are in heaven, and let all your ambitions be perfectly regulated and controlled by the Word of God.

'All things are lawful for me, but all things are not expedient: all things are lawful for me, but all things edify not' (1 Corinthians 10:23).

You have to let go of whatever you left behind in the world and ask God for new things. Focus your mind on pleasing God and living for Him all the days of your life. Before you finish your divine purpose in prison on time, you will receive miracles. If you prepare yourself very well in prison, you will have a perfect place to fit into when you come out of prison. At all times, set your affection on Christ and get rid of inordinate affections for things, places or persons. Noah's ambition on earth that singled him out and made him a prisoner of hope was to be holy and to serve God. Ambition to love others, serve them, and obey God at all cost will always see you through at all times.

As you are in prison now, pray that your understanding will be delivered from powers of darkness. Destroy every deceit devil has buried inside you. Ask God to deliver your conscience from defilement and uproot every root of sin in your life. That was what Noah did and God delivered him in his generation as a prisoner of hope.

4. *ABRAHAM*:

Prisoners of hope lose a lot of things to gain much more in their lifetimes. As a prisoner of hope, you must be willing to suffer losses or to leave your comfort zone to where God prefers to start a new life with you.

> *'Now the Lord had said unto Abram, Get thee out of thy country, and from thy kindred, and from thy father's house, unto a land that I will shew thee: And I will make of thee a great nation, and I will bless thee, and make thy name great; and thou shalt be a blessing: And I will bless them that bless thee, and curse him that curseth thee: and in thee shall all families of the earth be blessed. So Abram departed, as the Lord had spoken unto him; and Lot went with him: and Abram was seventy and five years old when he departed out of Haran'* (Genesis 12:1-4).

Abraham was called by God to abandon all his investments in his country. He was asked to give up all that he had labored for seventy-five years on earth. This is massive. It is possible that the reason you may be in prison now is that God wants to calm your spirit so that you can hear His voice. Most people are ready to fight for their rights at all costs to reclaim their positions in their countries, kindred and fathers' houses, which are often outside the will of God.

Do you know that God may have allowed you to come to this prison to compel you to listen to Him.

You will spend more years in this prison when you refuse to learn your lessons early. If you can identify what brought you to prison and repent of it instead of persisting in sin, God will arrange for your release. Abraham heard the voice of God clearly and abandoned everything he worked for and left. You can always give up something in order to get to where God wants you to be. The reason why you are in this prison may be for you to have time with God, so you can change and begin to live a new life. When God is showing you a way and you insist in your own way, you may stay longer in a particular spot.

God told Abraham to leave his country, and he left in obedience. Your friends and relatives may have abandoned you in prison. It happened to Joseph too. Abraham abandoned his personal lands and properties. Had he not left may be they would have killed him or manipulate him to commit offence that would have took him to jail, who knows? If you can abandon your evil ways in this prison, God will make you great.

Leaving the prison without leaving your sins behind is useless because they will surely bring you back to prison or put you in a more severe condition. Prisoners of hope who really repented are always made great. In the days of Abraham, he never struggled over anything that will take him away from God.

> *'And Abram went up out of Egypt, he, and his wife, and all that he had, and Lot with him, into the south. And Abram was very rich in cattle, in silver, and in gold. And he went on his journeys from the south even*

to Bethel, unto the place where his tent had been at the beginning, between Bethel and Hai; Unto the place of the altar, which he had made there at the first: and there Abram called on the name of the Lord.... And Abram said unto Lot, Let there be no strife, I pray thee, between me and thee, and between my herdmen and thy herdmen; for we be brethren. Is not the whole land before thee? separate thyself, I pray thee, from me: if thou wilt take the left hand, then I will go to the right; or if thou depart to the right hand, then I will go to the left. And Lot lifted up his eyes, and beheld all the plain of Jordan, that it was well watered everywhere, before the Lord destroyed Sodom and Gomorrah, even as the garden of the Lord, like the land of Egypt, as thou comest unto Zoar. Then Lot chose him all the plain of Jordan; and Lot journeyed east: and they separated themselves the one from the other. Abram dwelled in the land of Canaan, and Lot dwelled in the cities of the plain, and pitched his tent toward Sodom' (Genesis 13:1-4, 8-12).

To maintain peace and keep his relationship with God, Abraham allowed Lot to choose first where he wanted to stay. He lost something to get something better (*See* Genesis 13:8-11, 13-18). Have you ever asked God these questions – Why am I on earth? Why am I in this prison? What is my assignment and reason of being here? Once you can get answers to these questions, your deliverance is easy.

Abraham never bore grudges against people that offended him. He forgave them and threw all offenses behind him. Your being in prison can also be as result of your unforgiving, malicious and revengeful spirit. Abraham never bore grudges against Lot. Learn from him.

> *'And there came one that had escaped, and told Abram the Hebrew; for he dwelt in the plain of Mamre the Amorite, brother of Eschol, and brother of Aner: and these were confederate with Abram. And when Abram heard that his brother was taken captive, he armed his trained servants, born in his own house, three hundred and eighteen, and pursued them unto Dan. And he divided himself against them, he and his servants, by night, and smote them, and pursued them unto Hobah, which is on the left hand of Damascus. And he brought back all the goods, and also brought again his brother Lot, and his goods, and the women also, and the people'* (Genesis 14:13-16).

He helped him in times of need, rescued him and his possessions without a charge (*See* Genesis 13:5-7, 11-13, 14:17-24). These were characters that made Abraham an excellent prisoner of hope. Being a prisoner of hope can as well mean that though a child of God may enter into trouble, but hope for deliverance will abound more. Regardless of the amount of sin, you have committed in the past, if you would repent and accept Jesus to save and forgive you, then there is hope. You may have spent many years in prison before now, but if you can repent now and start living your life according to God's will, after confessing your sins and asking God for forgiveness, you will become better than the richest person outside prison who does not know God.

Abraham started with nothing and God blessed him mightily and made a great nation out of him. It does not matter when you started with God. Abraham was seventy-five years old when he started with God. Yet he became greater than all the nations and families of the earth. When you come out of this prison, a single opportunity can make you greater than your entire village. Do you know of a man in Nigeria called Obasanjo?[3] He was once a prisoner, but he accepted Jesus while he was in prison. Soon later, he was elected the president of Nigeria and he made history by changing the shape of Nigeria economy. In Nigeria today, Obasanjo is richer and more popular that all citizens of some African countries.

It is absolutely a matter of decision. When Abraham became a prisoner of hope through his decision to obey God, he was empowered by God to win all his battles. He confronted and conquered his wife's barrenness after the Lord gave him a promise (*See* Genesis 11:29-30, 15:1, 4-7, 18-21).He entertained angles of God, interceded for Sodom and Gomorrah, and sent his second wife and her child away in obedience to God. He was going to offer his only son, Isaac, before God intervened (*See* Genesis 18:1-8,25-33, 21:9-21, 22:1-19). Abraham became the father of Isaac, grandfather of Jacob, the founder of great nation called Israel. Jesus came into this world through the linage of Abraham and David.

> *'The next day John seeth Jesus coming unto him, and saith, Behold the Lamb of God, which taketh away the sin of the world'* (John 1:29).

No nation on earth can successfully defeat the nation of Israel without God fighting for them. So, rejecting Jesus and Christianity is the same as rejecting God entirely. In Christ is where your safety is.

> *'Who is the image of the invisible God, the firstborn of every creature: For by him were all things created, that are in heaven, and that are in earth, visible and*

---

[3] **Chief Olusegun Obasanjo**, Nigerian elder statesman and former Head of State

> *invisible, whether they be thrones, or dominions, or principalities, or powers: all things were created by him, and for him: And he is before all things, and by him all things consist'* (Colossians 1:15-17).

When you receive Jesus into your life, repent of all your sins and determine to forsake them. God will come to you and bless your life. With Jesus in your life, you can now pray and fight your battles and be sure of winning all your battles.

> *'For in him dwelleth all the fulness of the Godhead bodily. And ye are complete in him, which is the head of all principality and power'* (Colossians 2:9-10).

Unless you backslide and go back into sin, there is no power that can defeat a prisoner of hope in any battle. By the reason of Christ dwelling in you, there is no power that can keep you forever in prison. Your release is sure regardless of how long it takes (Genesis 14:13-24). Abraham fought many kings and defeated them all because he was faithful to God. Simon, the great grandson of Abraham, fought a whole nation and defeated them (Genesis 34:25-31). Demons and all spiritual forces from every evil department cannot stop any prisoner of hope from winning all battles. Not even an angel of God can prevail over a determined and prayerful prisoner of hope.

> *'And Jacob went on his way, and the angels of God met him. And when Jacob saw them, he said, This is God's host: and he called the name of that place Mahanaim… And Jacob said, O God of my father Abraham, and God of my father Isaac, the Lord which saidst unto me, Return unto thy country, and to thy kindred, and I will deal well with thee: I am not worthy of the least of all the mercies, and of all the*

truth, which thou hast shewed unto thy servant; for with my staff I passed over this Jordan; and now I am become two bands. Deliver me, I pray thee, from the hand of my brother, from the hand of Esau: for I fear him, lest he will come and smite me, and the mother with the children. And thou saidst, I will surely do thee good, and make thy seed as the sand of the sea, which cannot be numbered for multitude.... And Jacob was left alone; and there wrestled a man with him until the breaking of the day. And when he saw that he prevailed not against him, he touched the hollow of his thigh; and the hollow of Jacob's thigh was out of joint, as he wrestled with him. And he said, Let me go, for the day breaketh. And he said, I will not let thee go, except thou bless me. And he said unto him, What is thy name? And he said, Jacob. And he said, Thy name shall be called no more Jacob, but Israel: for as a prince hast thou power with God and with men, and hast prevailed. And Jacob asked him, and said, Tell me, I pray thee, thy name. And he said, Wherefore is it that thou dost ask after my name? And he blessed him there. And Jacob called the name of the place Peniel: for I have seen God face to face, and my life is preserved. And as he passed over Penuel the sun rose upon him, and he halted upon his thigh. Therefore the children of Israel eat not of the sinew which shrank, which is upon the hollow of the thigh, unto this day: because he touched the hollow of Jacob's thigh in the sinew that shrank' (Genesis 32:1-2, 9-12, 24-32).

The Egyptian kings defeated other nations and took them as slaves forever, but they failed to keep the children of Israel imprisoned forever because they are prisoners of hope. Do you want to be a prisoner of Hope? Then repent now, confess all your sins and forsake them. Ask Jesus to come into your heart and bless you. He will.

> *'He that covereth his sins shall not prosper: but whoso confesseth and forsaketh them shall have mercy'* (Proverbs 28:13).

Pharaoh, the Egyptian king, has never lost any battle until he met with prisoners of hope in the battlefield. Pharaoh used many wicked tactics, invoked all his evil powers, and set taskmasters to afflict his enemies with heavy burdens. He used them as slaves to build his treasure cities, Pithom and Raamses. He made them to serve with rigor more than what prison wardens do to you. They were insulted without regard far above all insults and shame you are getting now. In fact, it was recorded that the Egyptians made their lives bitter with hard bondage.

It might interest you to know that those wardens and jailers you have in that prison today are very much kind to you and cannot be compared to jailers and wardens of those days and what they did to the people of God. They forced the children of Israel to serve with their blood in mortar and bricks. It got to a stage when Pharaoh ordered every Hebrew male to be murdered. But because they were prisoners of hope, God was with them. (*See* Exodus 1:8-22).

If you join prisoners of hope today, your life will never remain the same. God will come and identified with you in that prison. God delivered His people out of Egyptian prison and destroyed all their captors and jailers in the Red Sea. Beloved, let these scriptures speak your spirit out of the prison (*See* Exodus 9:13-33, 10:1-28, 12:29-36, 14:23-31 and 15:1-21).

You also know that even when they came out of that hard labor, the Amalekites fought them at Rephidim. Moses, the leader of these prisoners of hope, held up his hands and Israel prevailed. The army captain at that time called Joshua entered into the battlefield with his forces at the going down of the sun and prevailed over them, destroying all of them with sword.

> *'Remember what Amalek did unto thee by the way, when ye were come forth out of Egypt; How he met thee by the way, and smote the hindmost of thee, even all that were feeble behind thee, when thou wast faint and weary; and he feared not God. Therefore it shall be, when the Lord thy God hath given thee rest from all thine enemies round about, in the land which the Lord thy God giveth thee for an inheritance to possess it, that thou shalt blot out the remembrance of Amalek from under heaven; thou shalt not forget it'* (Deuteronomy 25:17-19).

And also immediately after that battle, the Canaanites blocked their way to the Promised Land, and fought Israel with all their strength. But again the Canaanites were utterly destroyed and their cities taken. Those were very fierce battles. The major lesson that stood out of all was that no one could forever keep prisoners of hope out of victory or in bondage for too long.

> *'And when king Arad the Canaanite, which dwelt in the south, heard tell that Israel came by the way of the spies; then he fought against Israel, and took some of them prisoners. And Israel vowed a vow unto the Lord, and said, If thou wilt indeed deliver this people into my hand, then I will utterly destroy their cities.*

> *And the Lord hearkened to the voice of Israel, and delivered up the Canaanites; and they utterly destroyed them and their cities: and he called the name of the place Hormah'* (Numbers 21:1-3).

However, battles for their lives lingered for a very long time, but by their reason of being prisoners of hope they always prevailed. The Amorites faced them in battle and were easily defeated and smitten with the edge of the sword and their land was taken from Arnon unto Jabbok (*See* Numbers 21:21-32). All the nations of the earth at that time hated Israel and were determined to stop them from entering that land God promised Abraham, but they all failed. Bashan blocked their way with the host of his trained soldiers but he was defeated, smitten and none of them was let alive, after which the prisoners of hope possessed their land till this day.

> *'And they turned and went up by the way of Bashan: and Og the king of Bashan went out against them, he, and all his people, to the battle at Edrei. And the Lord said unto Moses, Fear him not: for I have delivered him into thy hand, and all his people, and his land; and thou shalt do to him as thou didst unto Sihon king of the Amorites, which dwelt at Heshbon. So they smote him, and his sons, and all his people, until there was none left him alive: and they possessed his land'* (Numbers 21:33-35).

The greatest decision one can make in a lifetime is to decamp and join the camp of prisoners of hope. There is no entry fee attached to it. Just believe in the Lord Jesus Christ and you will be enlisted by heaven as one of the prisoners of hope on earth.

'The Horims also dwelt in Seir beforetime; but the children of Esau succeeded them, when they had destroyed them from before them, and dwelt in their stead; as Israel did unto the land of his possession, which the Lord gave unto them. Now rise up, said I, and get you over the brook Zered. And we went over the brook Zered. And the space in which we came from Kadesh-barnea, until we were come over the brook Zered, was thirty and eight years; until all the generation of the men of war were wasted out from among the host, as the Lord sware unto them. For indeed the hand of the Lord was against them, to destroy them from among the host, until they were consumed. So it came to pass, when all the men of war were consumed and dead from among the people, That the Lord spake unto me, saying, Thou art to pass over through Ar, the coast of Moab, this day: And when thou comest nigh over against the children of Ammon, distress them not, nor meddle with them: for I will not give thee of the land of the children of Ammon any possession; because I have given it unto the children of Lot for a possession. (That also was accounted a land of giants: giants dwelt therein in old time; and the Ammonites call them Zamzummims; A people great, and many, and tall, as the Anakims; but the Lord destroyed them before them; and they succeeded them, and dwelt in their stead: As he did to the children of Esau, which dwelt in Seir, when he destroyed the Horims from before them; and they succeeded them, and dwelt in their stead even unto this day: And the Avims which dwelt in Hazerim, even unto Azzah, the Caphtorims, which came forth out of Caphtor,

> *destroyed them, and dwelt in their stead)'* (Deuteronomy 2:12-23).

They were hated everywhere they went even by their own relatives, but as usual they always prevailed over their enemies. Among many kings and nations that fought them were the king of Sihon, Heshbon, Jericho, Ai, all the kings in the other side of Jordan, the king of Hazor, Eglon, Moab, Jabin and the king of Midianites. Nevertheless, in all, they all failed. It took them time but at the end they had good testimonies and well settled life in the land of promises.

> *'And the Lord gave unto Israel all the land which he sware to give unto their fathers; and they possessed it, and dwelt therein. And the Lord gave them rest round about, according to all that he sware unto their fathers: and there stood not a man of all their enemies before them; the Lord delivered all their enemies into their hand. There failed not ought of any good thing which the Lord had spoken unto the house of Israel; all came to pass'* (Joshua 21:43-45).

These were true believers with focus and determination. The Lord gave them all the land which He promised to give unto their father. Every enemy was dealt with as God gave them rest round about. The end of the story was that all their enemies were on the floor and none could stand up to challenge them. Every promise, dreams and all their expectations were fulfilled as they settled without any enemy in the promise land.

Chapter 3

POWERS THAT TAKE PEOPLE TO PRISON

There are spiritual powers that drag people to prison by all means, to either waste their precious lives or time inside prison. Praying, fasting and making plans to be released from prison are all good, but it would be better and more effective to deal with powers that take people to jail. These powers are extremely wicked and have no human feelings. Most people do not even get to know about these real powers behind their imprisonment and hence keep blaming wrong persons. This is due to the fact that these powers operate underground.

In other words, most physical actions and behaviors that earn most people prison sentences are often not the real causes of their imprisonments. There are invisible powers responsible for most of those evil behaviors, and when those wicked and satanic powers are not dealt with properly, the problems cannot be said to be solved or over. That is why you see many come out of prison only to be re-arrested and imprisoned many more times later.

Again, while most convicts are not taken back to prison all over again, their evil behaviors that earned them prison terms linger on in their lives. Many of these victims are beginning to find out that they have no power over these dangerous and demonic invisible powers.

> *'For we know that the law is spiritual: but I am carnal, sold under sin. For that which I do I allow not: for what I would, that do I not; but what I hate, that do I'* (Romans 7:14-15).

While in prison, do not make any commitment that you are not determined to fulfill. Many prisoners vow and make numerous promises that they will never go back to their evil ways. But once released, they dive back into more deadly evil lifestyles and old vomits. These wicked powers are deadly and are determined to waste lives of their victims. These powers capture their victims and influence them with demonic spirits to carry out evil assignments compulsorily.

> *'That made the world as a wilderness, and destroyed the cities thereof; that opened not the house of his prisoners?'* (Isaiah 14:17).

> *'Know ye not, that to whom ye yield yourselves servants to obey, his servants ye are to whom ye obey;*

whether of sin unto death, or of obedience unto righteousness? But God be thanked, that ye were the servants of sin, but ye have obeyed from the heart that form of doctrine which was delivered you. Being then made free from sin, ye became the servants of righteousness. I speak after the manner of men because of the infirmity of your flesh: for as ye have yielded your members servants to uncleanness and to iniquity unto iniquity; even so now yield your members servants to righteousness unto holiness. For when ye were the servants of sin, ye were free from righteousness. What fruit had ye then in those things whereof ye are now ashamed? For the end of those things is death' (Romans 6:16-21).

Prophet Isaiah was talking about spiritual prisons where victims are first locked up before they are physically imprisoned. The reality is there are millions of spiritual prisoners all over the world that have not been physically imprisoned yet. Most of these people, mostly ignorant of their spiritual imprisonments, wallow in things they never dreamt of doing. But on things they are expected to do, they are always found wanting. They can only nurture wills to do good things but lack the power to execute them. This justifies confirms that the spiritual that controls the physical.

A victim of these evil powers can only nurture willingness to do right but usually acts in the opposite.

'I find then a law, that, when I would do good, evil is present with me. For I delight in the law of God after the inward man: But I see another law in my members, warring against the law of my mind, and bringing me into captivity to the law of sin which is in my

> *members. O wretched man that I am! who shall deliver me from the body of this death?'* (Romans 7:21-24).

This is the major battle of life that every prisoner ought to fight first before any other. There is a spiritual war going on inside the human mind that takes its victims captive and makes them wretched and useless. Oftentimes, these wicked powers darken the understanding of their victims before dealing with them finally.

> *'Having the understanding darkened, being alienated from the life of God through the ignorance that is in them, because of the blindness of their heart'* (Ephesians 4:18).

When your understanding is darkened, you will be made to see masquerading benefits of wrong actions and choices, including urgency for quick action. The only thing you will be prevented from initially is to comprehend the consequences of such actions and choices. This is how many peoples' understanding is being darkened daily. However, regardless of your high intelligence and profile, your understanding can be driven far away from truth of the outcome of your foolish actions so you do not get any chance to think right before acting.

Usually, at the course of action, you will be manipulated to forget about God and His Word. Satan manipulates most Christians to believe they will return to God after their evil and wicked actions or choices and be forgiven immediately. The eyes of such peoples' hearts are successfully blinded to truth.

> *'But the natural man receiveth not the things of the Spirit of God: for they are foolishness unto him:*

> *neither can he know them, because they are spiritually discerned'* (1 Corinthians 2:14).

> *'The heart is deceitful above all things, and desperately wicked: who can know it?'* (Jeremiah 17:9).

Wicked deeds and choices always take place before darkened hearts are allowed to reason rightly. That explains why regrets always follow suit. Like I said earlier, praying and fasting, or using connections and influence to get yourself out of physical prison are not wrong, but they are far from winning the battle. The battle is a spiritual battle. The problem lies inside your mind and all over the conscience which is already defiled. When you refuse to address this fundamental front, you might as well be fighting spiritual battles in your entire lifetime.

> *'Unto the pure all things are pure: but unto them that are defiled and unbelieving is nothing pure; but even their mind and conscience is defiled'* (Titus 1:15).

Your freedom might be taken away from you today, as the case may be, but the truth remains that every root of sin in your life must be uprooted before true freedom can be gained. The chain of evil cycles in your life must be broken completely. These include all forms of filthiness and carnal lusts manifesting in your thoughts and actions. In addition, if concrete and decisive steps are not taken to root out those evil seeds out of your life, you remain a prisoner even if you are released today. Evil characters can be inherited, acquired or fired into victims in form of evil arrows. If you think you have any enemy, evil characters are more dangerous than all your enemies put together.

Oftentimes, when these evil powers notice that certain victims of theirs have stopped cooperating, they do whatever is in their powers to lure such victims to seek for different routes of escape, which they normally provide secretly. In any attempt to escape, such victims are forced into deadly mistakes that can lead to death. These invisible principalities can influence you to join secret cults and societies, or force you into robberies that will get you back into prison.

> *'Then there was a famine in the days of David three years, year after year; and David inquired of the Lord. And the Lord answered, It is for Saul, and for his bloody house, because he slew the Gibeonites. And the king called the Gibeonites, and said unto them; (now the Gibeonites were not of the children of Israel, but of the remnant of the Amorites; and the children of Israel had sworn unto them: and Saul sought to slay them in his zeal to the children of Israel and Judah)'* (2 Samuel 21:1-2).

Saul the first king of Israel wanted to please the children of Israel and that led him to shed blood. Many people justify their decisions to sell out to devil with realities of their families' sufferings and poverty. Others go into robberies and end up killing and shedding innocent blood. The blood of all innocent people they killed will never cease to cry to God for vengeance, especially when any of such victims is a covenanted child of God.

> *'And Joshua made peace with them, and made a league with them, to let them live: and the princes of the congregation sware unto them… And Joshua called for them, and he spake unto them, saying, Wherefore have*

ye beguiled us, saying, We are very far from you; when ye dwell among us? Now therefore ye are cursed, and there shall none of you be freed from being bondmen, and hewers of wood and drawers of water for the house of my God… And Joshua made them that day hewers of wood and drawers of water for the congregation, and for the altar of the Lord, even unto this day, in the place which he should choose' (Joshua 9:15, 22-23, 27).

Many young women commit abortion to avoid being ridiculed or shamed. They sell their bodies, tell lies and engage in all sorts of evil maneuvers. In some cases, the blood your ancestors shed could be the blood that has been crying for your head before you made that costly mistake that brought you into this prison. You may be innocent though, but if you fail to deal with your past and your ancestral foundation, you may continue to suffer future losses and spiritual freedom. Just like David and the children of Israel really suffered for a very long time because of what Saul did when he was alive. Who could have imagined that consequences of Saul's sin would affect a whole nation that God loved so much?

You may even argue that you are innocent of the crime that brought you to prison. However, have you taken time to look at some pattern of events that have surrounded your life over the years? Your educational certificates are worthless for now because you are in prison. Your wife and children are out there, but they cannot enjoy your company and you cannot enjoy theirs. What about your houses? They are just there while you live and suffer inside the prison. You have ideas, talent, gift, energy, inheritance and positions, but they are not with you in prison. Some of these evil patterns are not ordinary as they seem. There is largely a spiritual connotation to them that you have not bothered to know about. David was a righteous king but he suffered for three good years under famine. You may be righteous and yet, you are suffering in prison now for what another person has done in the past. May these never be your portion in the name of Jesus.

> *'Our fathers have sinned, and are not; and we have borne their iniquities'* (Lamentations 5:7).

> *'Thou shalt betroth a wife, and another man shall lie with her: thou shalt build a house, and thou shalt not dwell therein: thou shalt plant a vineyard, and shalt not gather the grapes thereof. Thine ox shall be slain before thine eyes, and thou shalt not eat thereof: thine ass shall be violently taken away from before thy face, and shall not be restored to thee: thy sheep shall be given unto thine enemies, and thou shalt have none to rescue them. Thy sons and thy daughters shall be given unto another people, and thine eyes shall look, and fail with longing for them all the daylong: and there shall be no might in thine hand… Thou shalt beget sons and daughters, but thou shalt not enjoy them; for they shall go into captivity'* (Deuteronomy 28:30-32,41)

Many prisoners today are married but other men out there are physically enjoying their wives. The bed, houses and cars they bought when they were free citizens are all left for their enemies to use. Businesses they established have fallen into the hands of their enemies. In addition, all the money they made through armed robbery is being enjoyed by their colleagues. How could it be that you are all alone in prison now, forsaken by your so-called gangs, friends and relatives? How could you have planted and labored while strangers are now enjoying the fruits of your labors? You need Jesus to restore and lift you up in righteousness. You cannot afford to go back to your former evil ways.

Many prisoners have daughters who have been married in their absences. Let me tell you the truth, if you refuse to do something now to fight against those powers that took you to prison, you may die in prison. You can even be released today and the same evil powers of darkness sent you back to prison the next day. None of those people who have taken over your properties, inheritance and even your wife is your real enemy. Your real enemy is those principalities that took you to prison. If you do not fight them, you can be released and they force you to commit a greater crime afterwards.

Oftentimes, people you consider your enemies are nothing but instruments those principalities and powers use to incarcerate you. If you come out of prison today and get such people you think are your enemies killed, you have not done anything good for yourself because those same wicked powers and principalities can yet enter into other persons and use them against you. How many more people can you kill? Attacking people is like chasing the shadow. You have to confront the evil powers and principalities if gainful freedom is to be won.

My advice is that you rise up and deal with those powers spiritually. It will be more suitable to fight your battle while you are still in prison now. If your father entered into any cult, or killed people to make money and used the blood money to pay your mother's dowry, then you should know today that you were sold to devil before you were born. So many foolish ancestral parents entered into evil covenants with death, idols, secret cults, and all manner of evil spirits to either make money or get protection. But time has proven that they have all succeeded in pulling all generations of their children and children's children into an unending war with Satan.

Though they have lived and died, the consequences of their deeds linger on in your life. Houses they built and all properties they acquired are all covenanted to Satan. That is why devil has foothold in your marriage, children and all your achievements. You grew up without knowing the terms of the covenant between your father and devil. And breaking such covenants ignorantly starts spiritual battle you have no idea of its source. This is because you were put in bondage before you were born.

> *'Now there cried a certain woman of the wives of the sons of the prophets unto Elisha, saying, Thy servant my husband is dead; and thou knowest that thy servant did fear the Lord: and the creditor is come to take unto him my two sons to be bondmen'* (2 Kings 4:1).

> *'Wherefore hear the word of the Lord, ye scornful men, that rule this people which is in Jerusalem. Because ye have said, We have made a covenant with death, and with hell are we at agreement; when the overflowing scourge shall pass through, it shall not come unto us: for we have made lies our refuge, and under falsehood have we hid ourselves: Therefore thus saith the Lord God, Behold, I lay in Zion for a foundation, a stone, a tried stone, a precious corner stone, a sure foundation: he that believeth shall not make haste. Judgment also*

> *will I lay to the line, and righteousness to the plummet: and the hail shall sweep away the refuge of lies, and the waters shall overflow the hiding place. And your covenant with death shall be disannulled, and your agreement with hell shall not stand; when the overflowing scourge shall pass through, then ye shall be trodden down by it'* (Isaiah 28:14-18).

If your ancestors entered into any covenant with death, hell or a family god, you are in big trouble. That means you have a battle to fight before your freedom can be perfected and won. The problem with many prisoners today is that they do not know the meaning of covenant. Does it bother you at all? Well, let me remind you what evil covenant is all about so it can awaken your heart to start praying.

First, a covenant is a mutual understanding between two or more parties, where each party binds itself to fulfill specific and stipulated obligations. Covenant is a legal contract, which when broken attracts a consequence. There are physical and spiritual covenants, as well as there are good and evil covenants. A marriage union is a good covenant, which legally binds a man and a woman together till death. Spiritual covenants are always difficult and tough covenants, which demands strict compliance. God entered into covenants with so many notable people in the Bible including Abraham, Isaac and Jacob.

Likewise, devil deceived a lot of people to enter into evil covenants with them. A covenant with devil is dangerous and deadly. While God can have mercy when you break a covenant with Him, there is no mercy with devil. Breaking evil covenants result in bloodshed and death. Many dangerous men and women today are in powerful covenant with demons. Most of these wicked people are extremely wealthy and always appear very beautiful and handsome, but they are in covenants with terrible serpents, death and hell. Many have equally initiated lots of ignorant and unsuspecting people into satanic covenants.

It could start as a simple agreement to marry and when later you decide against it, you open an evil war front for yourself. In such circumstances, most people would think they could decide to do what seems right to them, but as soon as the other party reports them to their evil group or take their names to evil altar, their spiritual problems will start. Covenant is a very dangerous thing when evil spirits are involved. You can even end up in prison because of an ordinary promise, especially when you handle it carelessly.

> *'Brethren, I speak after the manner of men; Though it be but a man's covenant, yet if it be confirmed, no man disannulleth, or addeth thereto'* (Galatians 3:15).

The question is this, how can a covenant be confirmed? Covenants can be confirmed by a wave of hand after ordinary discussion. With that, the convent is sealed without your signature or physical witness. It can also be confirmed by a kiss, shaking of hands, signing of signature. The deadliest is when it is confirmed by sexual intercourse. If you do not break such covenants, you will die and go straight to hell fire. You can inherit an evil covenant, and you can acquire it yourself through your actions and choices. As soon as a covenant is confirmed, it becomes very dangerous and forceful.

Another important thing to know about covenants is that representatives (witnesses) of covenants, whether evil or good, are legal representatives. Covenants bind people that stated them, children, born and unborn of every generation, and their families. It is an irrevocable commitment and you have to know how to break it before freedom can be secured. Otherwise, you will live a futile life on earth.

> *'And afterward when David heard it, he said, I and my kingdom are guiltless before the Lord for ever from the blood of Abner the son of Ner: Let it rest on the head of Joab, and on all his father's house; and let there not fail from the house of Joab one that hath an issue, or that is a leper, or that leaneth on a staff, or that falleth on the sword, or that lacketh bread'* (2 Samuel 3:28-29).

A young virgin enters into blood covenant with the person that breaks her virginity. Abortion is a blood covenant that cries bitterly against women who commit abortion. All these things can cry until you make a mistake that can get you into trouble or prison.

> *'As the bird by wandering, as the swallow by flying, so the curse causeless shall not come'* (Proverbs 26:2).

There is no smoke without fire. You have to discover the root of your problem, and then deal with it and your deliverance will take place. This is the fundamental thing you need to do, rather than regretting and blaming others for your incarceration.

Evil powers can permit you to reach the top of your career before they deal with you. They can allow you to go to the best schools, get the best certificates, and secure the best jobs or invest here and there. But they will never permit you to enjoy any of those benefits. These evil powers at the prime of your success may create a demonic roadblock that can lead you into a heart breaking and unpardonable mistake. At other times, they can force you to settle for life of non-achievement, making you to live your life under struggle.

Evil powers can induce frustration at the edge of a miracle, and force people to make foolish mistakes that can cause them to be arrested, tried in court and imprisoned. Powers that take people to prison can place a mark of rejection and hatred upon you. In the past, people have been rejected and hated almost by everyone they come across until they become frustrated and took drastic decisions that led them to disaster and confinement. They can block your marriage or cause you to marry a wrong person that will cause you to be imprisoned.

Evil powers can drag their victims into serious troubles, backwardness, mysterious problems and loss of hope for the rest of their lives. These powers are wicked and do not know mercy.

> '*And thy life shall hang in doubt before thee; and thou shalt fear day and night, and shalt have none assurance of thy life: In the morning thou shalt say, Would God it were even! And at even thou shalt say, Would God it were morning! For the fear of thine heart wherewith thou shalt fear, and for the sight of thine eyes which thou shalt see*' (Deuteronomy 28:66-67).

These powers can program a prodigal spirit into your life that can cause your wealth to disappear suddenly. They can program discouragement to you so you can get tired of life and be forced to consider evil options like robbery, murder, stealing, smoking and drinking all manner of drinks until you get addicted to wicked characters that will lead you to prison. They can attack you and rob you of good reasoning or make you to become uncontrollable, pulling you away from your divine helpers. That is when you begin to meet wrong people, who would eventually destroy you.

> *'And he said, A certain man had two sons: And the younger of them said to his father, Father, give me the portion of goods that falleth to me. And he divided unto them his living. And not many days after the younger son gathered all together, and took his journey into a far country, and there wasted his substance with riotous living. And when he had spent all, there arose a mighty famine in that land; and he began to be in want. And he went and joined himself to a citizen of that country; and he sent him into his fields to feed swine. And he would fain have filled his belly with the husks that the swine did eat: and no man gave unto him'* (Luke15:11-16).

At some point, if you do not come to your senses early, they will drag you into sleepless and restless lifestyle when you will begin to have terrifying dreams. Victims can become unreasonable and harsh in dealing with other people. This explains why many people settle for unfaithfulness, foolishness, fruitlessness and all manner of vices. At some point, they are possessed with demons of lesbianism, homosexuality, bankruptcy, and memory failures and are easily manipulated to get tired of life and commit a crime that will take them to prison.

Once the crime is committed, they return to their senses to face the consequences of their actions, often in prison. That is why many people always have regrets for their mistakes instead of repenting from them and praying against further occurrences. Instead of praying for true salvation and deliverance from evil powers that brought them to prison, they will begin to contemplate thoughts of revenge. Some will even start to wish they are dead, or to commit suicide instead of confronting their problems. I pray the Holy Spirit of God will lead you to do what is right for your deliverance to manifest now, in Jesus name.

> '*And she said unto him, How canst thou say, I love thee, when thine heart is not with me? thou hast mocked me these three times, and hast not told me wherein thy great strength lieth. And it came to pass, when she pressed him daily with her words, and urged him, so that his soul was vexed unto death; That he told her all his heart, and said unto her. There hath not come a razor upon mine head; for I have been a Nazarite unto God from my mother's womb: if I be shaven, then my strength will go from me, and I shall become weak, and be like any other man. And when Delilah saw that he had told her all his heart, she sent and called for the lords of the Philistines, saying, Come up this once, for he hath shewed me all his heart. Then the lords of the Philistines came up unto her, and brought money in their hand. And she made him sleep upon her knees; and she called for a man, and she caused him to shave off the seven locks of his head; and she began to afflict him, and his strength went from him*' (Judges 16:15-19).

Samson was manipulated, deceived, tortured and put in prison. While in prison, he began to suffer in the hands of wicked tormentors. He was under serious affliction and his strength went away. Instead of repenting and praying for restoration of strength, he prayed for death and revenge.

> *'And she said, The Philistines be upon thee, Samson. And he awoke out of his sleep, and said, I will go out as at other times before, and shake myself. And he wist not that the Lord was departed from him. But the Philistines took him, and put out his eyes, and brought him down to Gaza, and bound him with fetters of brass; and he did grind in the prison house'* (Judges 16:20-21).

Unfortunately, his prayers did not spare his life. He fought carnally and instead of complete deliverance, he received a partial deliverance for he died with his enemies.

> *'And Samson called unto the Lord, and said, O Lord God, remember me, I pray thee, and strengthen me, I pray thee, only this once, O God, that I may be at once avenged of the Philistines for my two eyes. And Samson took hold of the two middle pillars upon which the house stood, and on which it was borne up, of the one with his right hand, and of the other with his left. And Samson said, Let me die with the Philistines. And he bowed himself with all his might; and the house fell upon the lords, and upon all the people that were therein. So the dead which he slew at his death were more than they which he slew in his life'* (Judges 16:28-30).

When you see yourself in a prison like Samson, or involved in any kind of land dispute, the right prayer to pray is not to die. Another reason why many people end up in prison is the activities of evil men and women in the world. There are envious people around who are enemies of progresses, merchants of souls, growers and harvesters of evil. These people can do whatever it takes to manipulate you out of your destiny and take over your position. You may not be seeing how great your destiny is, but they see it and can work against it from their evil altars. They can kill, steal and destroy. They monitor peoples' destinies and can kill people spiritually. They can do anything possible to get rid of greatly destined people to take over their positions and possessions. They can fire arrows of death to kill you physically.

> *'And when the child was grown, it fell on a day, that he went out to his father to the reapers. And he said unto his father, My head, my head. And he said to a lad, Carry him to his mother. And when he had taken him, and brought him to his mother, he sat on her knees till noon, and then died'* (2Kings 4:18-20).

If they cannot kill you physically, they will manipulate you to commit an offence that can send you to prison. While in prison, they enjoy your possessions and position and if you do not know how to pray yourself out of prison, you will rot and waste away in prison.

> *'And when he came to him, behold, he stood by his burnt offering, and the princes of Moab with him. And Balak said unto him, What hath the Lord spoken?'* (Numbers 23:17).

When they discover God's plan for your life from their evil altars and mirrors, they labor to waste it. When they seize your international passport spiritually and you do not know how to withdraw them, you will die as a local champion, unproductive element and a waste product. Some of these evil powers specialize in allowing people to appear physically beautiful and handsome, yet they steal their original destinies to prosper in their businesses.

'And it came to pass, as we went to prayer, a certain damsel possessed with a spirit of divination met us, which brought her masters much gain by soothsaying: The same followed Paul and us, and cried, saying, These men are the servants of the most high God, which shew unto us the way of salvation. And this did she many days. But Paul, being grieved, turned and said to the spirit, I command thee in the name of Jesus Christ to come out of her. And he came out the same hour. And when her masters saw that the hope of their gains was gone, they caught Paul and Silas, and drew them into the marketplace unto the rulers' (Acts 16:16-19).

Your deliverance will hinder their operations, which is why they do not want you to be delivered. These principalities do not want you to pray aggressive prayers. They may allow you to recite your rosary, do the sign of the cross or practice religion but will not allow you to pray serious prayers that can set you free. They understand that your deliverance would mean the end of their gains over your life on earth through their evil businesses. In order to stop you, they fire evil arrows of drug addictiveness, evil delays, and excessive anger, and can make you to have uncontrollable sexual desires that will expose you to mistakes that would lead you to prison. They can plant evil seeds of bad behaviors and addictions that waste destines. You have to wake up now and start praying.

'And in them is fulfilled the prophecy of Esaias`, which saith, By hearing ye shall hear, and shall not understand; and seeing ye shall see, and shall not perceive: For this people's heart is waxed gross, and their ears are dull of hearing, and their eyes they have

> *closed; lest at any time they should see with their eyes, and hear with their ears, and should understand with their heart, and should be converted, and I should heal them. But blessed are your eyes, for they see: and your ears, for they hear. For verily I say unto you, That many prophets and righteous men have desired to see those things which ye see, and have not seen them; and to hear those things which ye hear, and have not heard them. Hear ye therefore the parable of the sower. When any one heareth the word of the kingdom, and understandeth it not, then cometh the wicked one, and catcheth away that which was sown in his heart. This is he which received seed by the way side. But he that received the seed into stony places, the same is he that heareth the word, and anon with joy receiveth it; Yet hath he not root in himself, but dureth for a while: for when tribulation or persecution ariseth because of the word, by and by he is offended. He also that received seed among the thorns is he that heareth the word; and the care of this world, and the deceitfulness of riches, choke the word, and he becometh unfruitful. But he that received seed into the good ground is he that heareth the word, and understandeth it; which also beareth fruit, and bringeth forth, some an hundredfold, some sixty, some thirty. Another parable put he forth unto them, saying, The kingdom of heaven is likened unto a man which sowed good seed in his field: But while men slept, his enemy came and sowed tares among the wheat, and went his way'* (Matthew 13:14-25).

They fire arrows into peoples' lives and control people through demonic activities. Each time their victims try to escape, they force them to have sex in their dreams to defile their bodies. Such sexes in dreams make their victims unfit to break out of bondages.

> *'That the Lord sent a prophet unto the children of Israel, which said unto them, Thus saith the Lord God of Israel, I brought you up from Egypt, and brought you forth out of the house of bondage'* (Judges 6:8).

At other times, victims are fed in dreams to empower demons to work against them. Once such victims eat or drink anything in such dreams, he or she will begin to make mistakes until he or she enters into serious problems. Eating or having sex in the dream is not normal. They are serious weapons of defilement and destruction.

> *'And Ahab told Jezebel all that Elijah had done, and withal how he had slain all the prophets with the sword. Then Jezebel sent a messenger unto Elijah, saying, So let the gods do to me, and more also, if I make not thy life as the life of one of them by tomorrow about this time. And when he saw that, he arose, and went for his life, and came to Beer-sheba, which belongeth to Judah, and left his servant there. But he himself went a day's journey into the wilderness, and came and sat down under a juniper tree: and he requested for himself that he might die; and said, It is enough; now, O Lord, take away my life; for I am not better than my fathers. And as he lay and slept under a juniper tree, behold, then an angel touched him, and said unto him, Arise and eat. And he looked, and, behold, there was a cake baken on the coals, and a cruse of water at his head. And he did eat and drink, and laid him down again. And the angel of the Lord came again the second time, and touched him, and said, Arise and*

> *eat; because the journey is too great for thee. And he arose, and did eat and drink, and went in the strength of that meat forty days and forty nights unto Horeb the mount of God'* (I Kings 19:1-8).

These people(or even a single occultist) can bewitch a whole family, city or nation. They are everywhere and when you are uncompromising, they view you as hard-line opposition. They can do anything possible to confuse and bewitch you, or at least cause you to be imprisoned without you knowing the real powers behind your predicament.

> *'But there was a certain man, called Simon, which beforetime in the same city used sorcery, and bewitched the people of Samaria, giving out that himself was some great one: To whom they all gave heed, from the least to the greatest, saying, This man is the great power of God. And to him they had regard, because that of long time he had bewitched them with sorceries'* (Acts8:9-11).

These are enemies of your progress and unfriendly friends that you must dislodge through prayers. They can possess people in your family, village, residence, office and even within your country. When these possessed agents sense spiritually or physically that you are going to oppose them in near future or be greater than they are, they will bewitch your greatness, kill you or manipulate you to prison. It has happened severally in the past. It is still happening today and will continue to happen until Jesus returns to rid the earth of evil.

You could have been physically or spiritually imprisoned because of the greatness of your destiny. Naturally, when you are imprisoned, your destiny will not function. Your destiny will equally be imprisoned. And even though you are destined for greatness, you cannot do much when you are in prison. You need to come out.

Many people are born great. For these evil powers, the only way to stop such great people is to put them in prisons. There was once a great deliverance minister who was manipulated to make mistake in marriage. He married his worst enemy. And since then, his wife has never allowed him to minister. There is no greater prison than that. Prison takes people out of circulation and prevents them from being functional.

> *'And the king of Israel said, Take Micaiah, and carry him back unto Amon the governor of the city, and to Joash the king's son; And say, Thus saith the king, Put this fellow in the prison, and feed him with bread of affliction and with water of affliction, until I come in peace'* (I Kings 22:26-27).

Wicked people do not want to be challenged by people who are better than they are. They can kill, destroy and imprison great people to further their rules without rivals.

> *'And at that time Hanani the seer came to Asa king of Judah, and said unto him, Because thou hast relied on the king of Syria, and not relied on the Lord thy God, therefore is the host of the king of Syria escaped out of thine hand. Were not the Ethiopians and the Lubims a huge host, with very many chariots and horsemen? yet, because thou didst rely on the Lord, he delivered them into thine hand. For the eyes of the Lord run to and fro throughout the whole earth, to shew himself strong in the behalf of them whose heart is perfect toward him. Herein thou hast done foolishly: therefore*

> *from henceforth thou shalt have wars. Then Asa was wroth with the seer, and put him in a prison house; for he was in a rage with him because of this thing. And Asa oppressed some of the people the same time'* (2 Chronicles 16:7-10).

> *'Then he put out the eyes of Zedekiah; and the king of Babylon bound him in chains, and carried him to Babylon, and put him in prison till the day of his death'* (Jeremiah 52:11).

The fact is that many great people die in prisons. Most people who normally suffer and waste in prisons are stars who are supposed to be shinning in their different domains. Devil, seeing these great destinies, uses his agents on earth to lure them to prisons.

> *'I have seen servants upon horses, and princes walking as servants upon the earth'* (Ecclesiastes 10:7).

Jeremiah was a great prophet with great ministry, but an evil king imprisoned him. John the Baptist was a great prophet, the forerunner of Jesus whose birth was prophesied of by an angel of the Most High. However, the wicked Herod, an infidel, arrested him, imprisoned and later beheaded him.

The disciples of Jesus were not spared. They were arrested by ordinary religious men, and locked up in prisons. Peter who was a minister of the gospel was condemned and imprisoned. Paul the apostle was also arrested together with Silas and imprisoned, but they were released by forces of heaven when they prayed.

> *'And when they had laid many stripes upon them, they cast them into prison, charging the jailor to keep*

them safely: Who, having received such a charge, thrust them into the inner prison, and made their feet fast in the stocks. And at midnight Paul and Silas prayed, and sang praises unto God: and the prisoners heard them. And suddenly there was a great earthquake, so that the foundations of the prison were shaken: and immediately all the doors were opened, and every one's bands were loosed. And the keeper of the prison awaking out of his sleep, and seeing the prison doors open, he drew out his sword, and would have killed himself, supposing that the prisoners had been fled' (Acts 16:23-27).

There was the story of a onetime Nigerian president, who was very brutal and mercilessly. He was so insane that he determined to eliminate all his rivals. He killed every known person who opposed his rule, and ruled without rivals. Many people compromised and submitted to him, and very few individuals dared to resist him. He later imprisoned two great ex-soldiers who condemned his cruelty. This man's presidency was characterized by incessant murder, profanity, pride, perversion, internal conflicts and love for absolute power. However, when the militant and vibrant churches rose up and started praying against this tyrant, he died a shameful death while in power.

Among those he imprisoned were Shehu Yar'dua and Olusegun Obasanjo who were retired army generals and onetime president and vice president of Nigeria. While Yar'dua died in prison through food poison, Obasanjo survived and later became Nigerian president the second time; the first person to rule Nigeria twice. What was the secret behind this great feat? Obasanjo got born again while in prison and became a prisoner of hope. You too can become a prisoner of hope who can come out of prison to become a great person. The choice is yours and it can happen now. Those who had prison ministries preached to both Shehu Yar'dua an Obasanjo at the same time. Obasanjo made the right choice. It is your own time now to make a choice. May God help you to accept Jesus today and gain your eternal freedom forever – Amen.

> '*I call heaven and earth to record this day against you, that I have set before you life and death, blessing and cursing: therefore choose life, that both thou and thy seed may live: That thou mayest love the Lord thy God, and that thou mayest obey his voice, and that thou mayest cleave unto him: for he is thy life, and the length of thy days: that thou mayest dwell in the land which the Lord sware unto thy fathers, to Abraham, to Isaac, and to Jacob, to give them*' (Deuteronomy 30:19-20).

> '*And the Spirit and the bride say, Come. And let him that heareth say, Come. And let him that is athirst come. And whosoever will, let him take the water of life freely*' (Revelation 22:17).

Chapter

PRISON-BOUND CHARACTERS

There are copious evil characters and lifestyles that can lead you to either physical or spiritual imprisonment when nothing radical is done to destroy them. These characters may differ from person to person, nation to nation and tribe to tribe.

> *'I wrote unto the church: but Diotrephes, who loveth to have the preeminence among them, receiveth us not'* (3 John 1:9).

In the above reference, there was a man in a particular church called Diotrephes. He had domineering character and spirit, with demonic passion to rule and reign over everyone including his supposed masters. People like Diotrephes can be very destructive in families, political parties and even churches. They can use every weapon to fight their opponents, or go to extremes to win their opponents, even if it means breaking standing laws. Diotrephes saw John as a threat to his position in the church and refused to welcome the brethren.

He rejected John, his ministry and the evangelistic team. He went from house to house, person to person to tell all manner of malicious lies to twist hearts of brethren against the evangelistic team, and he excommunicated those who fail to buy into his lies. People, like Diotrephes, can kill and destroy, or despise authorities. *Domineering character and spirit* are not only evil; they are prison-bound. Many people are in prisons today because of seeking to be above others at all costs, through all evil means. Domineering spirit in a woman will not allow her to submit to her husband. She would press for equal rights.

Another imprisonment character is *evil-mindedness.* To be evil-minded is a very dangerous thing because an evil-minded person can go to any length to get whatever he or she wanted without considering unavoidable consequences. Evil-mindedness is morally reprehensible, sinful and wicked. An evil-minded person can be catastrophic at anytime, anywhere and in any slightest opportunity.

> *'Alexander the coppersmith did me much evil: the Lord reward him according to his works: Of whom be thou ware also; for he hath greatly withstood our words. At my first answer no man stood with me, but all men*

> *forsook me: I pray God that it may not be laid to their charge'* (2 Timothy 4:14-16).

Evil-minded people operate under highly classified codes. They possess evil minds, eyes, desires and devices. They engage in all manner of evil exploits, companionships, evil consultations and connections, evil counseling, debates, evil decrees, pervasions and evil emulations, and they populate nations with all manners of evil.

It is only an evil-minded person that can secretly wish to take other peoples' positions. They are perverse in nature and generally take much pleasure in committing sin, causing troubles in families, offices, schools and neighborhoods. They are always entangled in verbal strives, disputes and controversies. They consult evil people for evil and give evil and wrong advices to others. Their instructions and opinions are always wicked, and capable of inflaming betrayals and gang-ups against others. One thing evil-minded people are good at is premeditating and inventing evil.

Alexander the coppersmith was a typical example of an evil-minded person. According to Paul's letter to Timothy, Alexander's evil was indescribable and without comparison. He followed Paul to everywhere he went, in order to counter him with evil things to the extent that people began to avoid Paul. Paul prayed for the people Alexander deceived, but prayed that Alexander, a man who did much evil against him, be rewarded according to his works.

Evil character has ruined many people. If you are a victim of any evil character, you need to pray for yourself very well while you are still in prison. It will profit you more to receive deliverance before your release from prison, otherwise, the same evil characters can bring your back to prison or keep your great destiny barren.

> *'And when it was day, certain of the Jews banded together, and bound themselves under a curse, saying that they would neither eat nor drink till they had killed Paul. And they were more than forty which had made this conspiracy. And they came to the chief priests and elders, and said, We have bound ourselves under a great curse, that we will eat nothing until we have slain Paul. Now therefore ye with the council signify to the chief captain that he bring him down unto you tomorrow, as though ye would inquire something more perfectly concerning him: and we, or ever he come near, are ready to kill him'* (Acts 23:12-15).

Conspiracy and assassination are other prison-bound characters that are gravely evil. When you conspire against a fellow human, or a true child of God, you bring yourself under condemnation by the court of law to serve a prison sentence. Also people you conspired against or assassinated can place a curse upon you that is capable of rendering your life meaningless and prompting you to commit suicide.

> *'And one told David, saying, Ahithophel is among the conspirators with Absalom. And David said, O Lord, I pray thee, turn the counsel of Ahithophel into foolishness'* (2 Samuel 15:31).

> *'Aznd when Ahithophel saw that his counsel was not followed, he saddled his ass, and arose, and gat him home to his house, to his city, and put his household in order, and hanged himself, and died, and was buried in the sepulchre of his father'* (2 Samuel 17:23).

You may have been hired to conspire against a fellow man, or even shed innocent blood. These are prison-bound characters through which many lives have been wasted. You need to repent, confess the truth, and do restitution. Without doubt, your wicked ways must have brought untold heartbreaks, sufferings and sorrow to your victims and their families, and many peoples' destinies could be hanging on the balance of truth only you can reveal.

You need to be ready for restitution for all your crimes. Though God will forgive you as soon as you repent, but He would require that you make amends with all the people you have injured or wronged. Being released from prison will not be enough if you fail to restitute, because the people you offended will expect you to take full responsibilities of all your actions, even though you have become born again in the prison.

Restitution makes a person to pay back or be ready to pay back debts, or restore stolen or embezzled articles and confess covered up lies. This need to be done whether the people you offended are aware or not, for God knows.

> *'And the Lord sent Nathan unto David. And he came unto him, and said unto him, There were two men in one city; the one rich, and the other poor. The rich man had exceeding many flocks and herds: But the poor man had nothing, save one little ewe lamb, which he had bought and nourished up: and it grew up together with him, and with his children; it did eat of his own meat, and drank of his own cup, and lay in his bosom, and was unto him as a daughter And there came a traveler unto the rich man, and he spared to take of his own flock and of his own herd, to dress for the*

> *wayfaring man that was come unto him; but took the poor man's lamb, and dressed it for the man that was come to him. And David's anger was greatly kindled against the man; and he said to Nathan, As the Lord liveth, the man that hath done this thing shall surely die: And he shall restore the lamb fourfold, because he did this thing, and because he had no pity'* (2 Samuel 12:1-6).

Hatred for gospel preachers, or hardening of heart or speaking evil against the gospel does not bring any good. People who have lived their entire lives fighting God and His children have never achieved anything reasonable all through their lives.

> *'And he went into the synagogue, and spake boldly for the space of three months, disputing and persuading the things concerning the kingdom of God. But when divers were hardened, and believed not, but spake evil of that way before the multitude, he departed from them, and separated the disciples, disputing daily in the school of one Tyrannus'* (Acts 19:8-9).

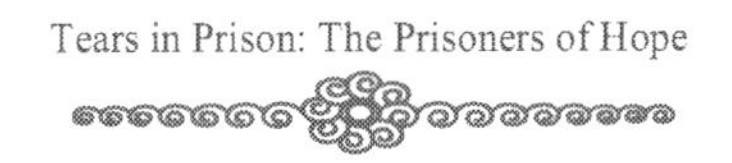

EXAMPLES OFPRISON-BOUND CHARACTERS

1. LAW BREAKING

This includes breaking the law of God, law of nature or outright disobedience of man's laws. In every family, school, office and anywhere we find ourselves in all nations of the world, laws exist to guide the place. Even God at the Garden of Eden gave Adam a commandment to keep.

> *'And the Lord God took the man, and put him into the garden of Eden to dress it and to keep it. And the Lord God commanded the man, saying, Of every tree of the garden thou mayest freely eat: But of the tree of the knowledge of good and evil, thou shalt not eat of it: for in the day that thou eatest thereof thou shalt surely die'* (Genesis 2:15-17).

Prison-bound characters influence people to disobey and break standing rules, despise dominion until they enter into troubles. Today, there are more lawbreakers who are not in prison. However, wherever you are, whether in or outside prison, spiritually, when you keep breaking laws, you incur yokes of disobedience upon your life (*See* Genesis 3:1-13). Lawbreakers all over the world, in or out of prison, are captives because they are bound spiritually.

2. MURDER

This is an act of killing or taking someone's life, with visible or invisible weapons; physically or spiritually.

> *'Whosoever hateth his brother is a murderer: and ye know that no murderer hath eternal life abiding in him'* (1John 3:15).

Cain was the first murderer in the Bible. He took his brother, Abel, to the field and killed him there. Murder is grievously evil. It is a prison-bound character that has wasted and is still wasting many peoples' lives in prison worldwide. A murderer who is in prison praying to be released should first deliver himself from demons that take over humans and influence them to commit murder. It will be better to be delivered of these demons while in prison than when released. Otherwise the same demons can still take control again.

> *'And Cain talked with Abel his brother: and it came to pass, when they were in the field, that Cain rose up against Abel his brother, and slew him. And the Lord said unto Cain, Where is Abel thy brother? And he said, I know not: Am I my brother's keeper? And he said, What hast thou done? the voice of thy brother's blood crieth unto me from the ground'* (Genesis 4:8-10).

Once these evil spirits are at work, a murderer can lose his or her consciousness until the deed is done. A young woman was once possessed by a murderous demon, and she lost all her consciousness and reasoning. She started seeing her young relative as a devil, until she decided to kill him. Fortunately enough, people came and rescued the boy from her. She was convinced that the boy was a devil until the spirit left her, and she discovered she had fallen under spiritual deceit. Murderous demons are very wicked and mean.

Another young man picked a knife and slaughtered his only brother. When people gathered, he argued that his brother was a goat. It was later when the evil spirit left him that he discovered that the person he saw as a goat was his only brother. He refused to eat for many days and later died in unfathomable sorrow and regrets. The spirit of murder can use any weapon to kill. Even Cain after killing his only brother still argued with God.

> *'And the Lord said unto Cain, Where is Abel thy brother? And he said, I know not: Am I my brother's keeper? And he said, What hast thou done? the voice of thy brother's blood crieth unto me from the ground'* (Genesis 4:9-10).

Many people under the influences of these demons have either killed their sons, daughters, parents, friends etc. Murder remains grievous prison-bound character that you must confront with all your strength, otherwise it would lead you to the grave.

3. POLYGAMOUS LIFESTYLE

Unknown to many people, this spirit is very dangerous and destructive. Many people have poisoned their wives and husbands in order to have free will to marry to another person of their choices.

> *'And it came to pass, that, when Abram was come into Egypt, the Egyptians beheld the woman that she was very fair. The princes also of Pharaoh saw her, and commended her before Pharaoh: and the woman was taken into Pharaoh's house. And he entreated Abram well for her sake: and he had sheep, and oxen, and he asses, and menservants, and maidservants, and she*

> *asses, and camels. And the Lord plagued Pharaoh and his house with great plagues because of Sarai Abram's wife'* (Genesis 12:14-17).

When a man begins to multiple wives to himself or a woman begins to run after men, there is trouble. Many divorce suits today are being motivated by this spirit. A woman ran into my office sometime to report her husband. She said that she got home that day and heard her husband fervently praying inside their bedroom. What was the man's prayer? His prayer was, *'O Lord, when will you kill this woman so that I can marry another wife?'* To him, his wife should die so he can marry another.

> *'Whosoever hateth his brother is a murderer: and ye know that no murderer hath eternal life abiding in him'* (1John 3:15).

Polygamous people can be very wicked. Polygamy is a sin of having more than one wife at the same time, secretly or openly. Polygamous families which seem to live peacefully now will still face their battles sooner or later.

Polyandry is the act of a woman having more than one husband and possibly having many children for them all. The Bible was clear that no one can serve two masters at a time. There are many prisoners who are serving jail terms because of evil consequences of polygamy.

> *'And Abraham said of Sarah his wife, She is my sister: and Abimelech king of Gerar sent, and took Sarah'* (Genesis 20:2).

Polygamy is a destructive weapon in the band of devil. It can separate a husband and wife and can cause tragic problems.

4. WICKEDNESS

This is when someone's wickedness is without measure. Wickedness is a prison-bound character, and when such wicked persons are not in prison yet, eventually they will surely get there. Many people carry out their wickedness before God without fear.

> *'And Judah took a wife for Er his firstborn, whose name was Tamar. And Er, Judah's firstborn, was wicked in the sight of the Lord; and the Lord slew him'* (Genesis 38:6-7).

To be wicked means to be cruel; lacking human feelings. Wicked people maltreat others without feelings of remorse pity. God Himself judges every act of wickedness, and a large number of people are in prison today as result of their wickedness. Wickedness is a grievous sin before God.

> *'And the Lord said, Because the cry of Sodom and Gomorrah is great, and because their sin is very grievous; I will go down now, and see whether they have done altogether according to the cry of it, which is come unto me; and if not, I will know. And the men turned their faces from thence, and went toward Sodom: but Abraham stood yet before the Lord'* (Genesis 18:20-22).

Wicked people always wish evil for people. They can go to any extent to waste lives without mercy or respect for life.

'And Haman said unto king Ahasuerus, There is a certain people scattered abroad and dispersed among the people in all the provinces of thy kingdom; and their laws are diverse from all people; neither keep they the king's laws: therefore it is not for the king's profit to suffer them. If it please the king, let it be written that they may be destroyed: and I will pay ten thousand talents of silver to the hands of those that have the charge of the business, to bring it into the king's treasuries.... The posts went out, being hastened by the king's commandment, and the decree was given in Shushan the palace. And the king and Haman sat down to drink; but the city Shushan was perplexed' (Esther 3:8-9, 15).

They take much pleasure in plotting and conspiring against people and destroying lives excites them.

5. **OPPRESSION**

An oppressor is an unjust and cruel person, who exercises excess power or authority over his subjects or people under him without any respect for life or to God. An oppressor is a prisoner already regardless of where they are now. Moreover, unless they repent, they must go to prison. Pharaoh was an oppressor. He afflicted the children of Israel with so much suffering and made them work without rest or pay. The children of Israel were forced to work or serve with rigor and their lives were battered with hard oppression. An oppressor is a spoiler, a destroyer and very wicked. They are prison candidates because they must also be oppressed in a time or in eternity.

'Woe to thee that spoilest, and thou wast not spoiled; and dealest treacherously, and they dealt not

> *treacherously with thee! when thou shalt cease to spoil, thou shalt be spoiled; and when thou shalt make an end to deal treacherously, they shall deal treacherously with thee'* (Isaiah 33:1).

Oppressors have one common type of heart that does not fear or regard God. They do not consider whether their victims are weak, poor, sick or hungry. They are always heartless, merciless and stubborn.

> *'And Pharaoh said, Who is the Lord, that I should obey his voice to let Israel go? I know not the Lord, neither will I let Israel go. And they said, The God of the Hebrews hath met with us: let us go, we pray thee, three days' journey into the desert, and sacrifice unto the Lord our God; lest he fall upon us with pestilence, or with the sword. And the king of Egypt said unto them, Wherefore do ye, Moses and Aaron, let the people from their works? get you unto your burdens'* (Exodus 5:2-4).

Oppressors increase labors and sufferings of their subjects or victims and make them work overtime without pay. They force people to suffer, cry and die in bondage.

> *'And the taskmasters hasted them, saying, Fulfill your works, your daily tasks, as when there was straw. And the officers of the children of Israel, which Pharaoh's taskmasters had set over them, were beaten, and demanded, Wherefore have ye not fulfilled your task in making brick both yesterday and today, as heretofore?... But he said, Ye are idle, ye are idle: therefore ye say, Let us go and do sacrifice to the Lord. Go therefore now, and work; for there shall no straw be given you, yet shall ye deliver the tale of bricks. And*

> *the officers of the children of Israel did see that they were in evil case, after it was said, Ye shall not minish ought from your bricks of your daily task'* (Exodus 5:13-14, 17-19).

Oppressors have no regard for God. Even in the face of suffering and death, they still oppress people without regarding God or any consequence. When God began to deal with Pharaoh, one would have expected Pharaoh to change his heart, but he was obstinate, immovable and foolishly stubborn. God destroyed Egyptian waters, streams, rivers, ponds, pools and they all became blood. Yet Pharaoh refused to bow to God and Moses. Frogs, lice and many other plagues were allowed by God to force Pharaoh to reason, but he continued to oppress Israel. Oppressors normally learn their lessons in a very hard way. Most oppressors need to be thrown into prisons before they could come back to their senses. If you are an oppressor, you can repent now and pray for deliverance and God will set you free.

6. **ANGER**

Anger simple means wrath, or strong vengeful indignation. It is destructive and can put someone into disaster without mercy. An angry person is one filled with vengeance.

> *'Simeon and Levi are brethren; instruments of cruelty are in their habitations. O my soul, come not thou into their secret; unto their assembly, mine honor, be not thou united: for in their anger they slew a man, and in their self-will they digged down a wall. Cursed be their anger, for it was fierce; and their wrath, for it was cruel: I will divide them in Jacob, and scatter them in Israel'* (Genesis 49:5-7).

An angry person can kill without proper reasoning out or considering imminent consequences. Moses was a great man, who was called and anointed by God. His birth and deliverance was all but miracle. He served Jethro, his father in-law, faithfully and was able to gather all the elders of Israel together for a meeting after his encounter with God. He approached Pharaoh and boldly demanded that he should let the children of Israel to go. He faced all the occult magicians of Egypt and defeated them. He refused to compromise with Pharaoh but demanded that the children of Israel be allowed to go and serve their God.

> *'And Pharaoh called for Moses and for Aaron, and said, Go ye, sacrifice to your God in the land. And Moses said, It is not meet so to do; for we shall sacrifice the abomination of the Egyptians to the Lord our God: lo, shall we sacrifice the abomination of the Egyptians before their eyes, and will they not stone us? We will go three days' journey into the wilderness, and sacrifice to the Lord our God, as he shall command us. And Pharaoh said, I will let you go, that ye may sacrifice to the Lord your God in the wilderness; only ye shall not go very far away: intreat for me. And Moses said, Behold, I go out from thee, and I will intreat the Lord that the swarms of flies may depart from Pharaoh, from his servants, and from his people, tomorrow: but let not Pharaoh deal deceitfully any more in not letting the people go to sacrifice to the Lord. And Moses went out from Pharaoh, and intreated the Lord. And the Lord did according to the word of Moses; and he removed the swarms of flies from Pharaoh, from his servants, and from his people; there remained not one. And Pharaoh hardened his*

> *heart at this time also, neither would he let the people go'* (Exodus 8:25-32).

Moses was a great deliverance minister whom God used to deliver a whole nation from decades old oppressions in Egypt by Pharaoh. Moses had a wonderful time with God. However, he had one stumbling block – anger. Anger stopped Moses from entering the Promised Land. This is a very serious thing. He was cut from his people and allowed to die alone outside the land of Canaan because of anger (*See* Numbers 20:7-13). You cannot take your anger for granted for it can ruin you forever.

Moses inherited anger from the tribes of Levi but did not pray against it. He was busy delivering others but he never bothered to deliver himself. He died and was buried outside the Promised Land alone in the mountain.

> *'And the Lord said unto him, This is the land which I sware unto Abraham, unto Isaac, and unto Jacob, saying, I will give it unto thy seed: I have caused thee to see it with thine eyes, but thou shalt not go over thither. So Moses the servant of the Lord died there in the land of Moab, according to the word of the Lord'* (Deuteronomy 34:4-5).

7. STEALING AND ROBBERY

Stealing is one of the greatest prison-bound characters worldwide. Many condemned criminals serving life imprisonments fall under this category. Covetousness is one of the key things that lure people into steal or robbery.

> *'But the children of Israel committed a trespass in the accursed thing: for Achan, the son of Carmi, the son of Zabdi, the son of Zerah, of the tribe of Judah, took of the accursed thing: and the anger of the Lord was kindled against the children of Israel. And Joshua sent men from Jericho to Ai, which is beside Beth-aven, on the east side of Bethel, and spake unto them, saying, Go up and view the country. And the men went up and viewed Ai. And they returned to Joshua, and said unto him, Let not all the people go up; but let about two or three thousand men go up and smite Ai; and make not all the people to labor thither; for they are but few. So there went up thither of the people about three thousand men: and they fled before the men of Ai. And the men of Ai smote of them about thirty and six men: for they chased them from before the gate even unto Shebarim, and smote them in the going down: wherefore the hearts of the people melted, and became as water'* (Joshua 7:1-5).

Achan must have been stealing in the past and going scot-free, until that particular day when he stole an accursed thing. Of course, he paid for it with his life. Stealing and robbery are identical twins, which can bring curses and destruction into your life and those of your family members. They are also capable of destroying your destiny and keeping you out of divine coverage.

> *'Now the sons of Eli were sons of Belial; they knew not the Lord. And the priests' custom with the people was, that, when any man offered sacrifice, the priest's servant came, while the flesh was in seething, with a fleshhook of three teeth in his hand; And he struck it into the pan, or kettle, or caldron, or pot; all that the fleshhook brought up the priest took for himself. So they did in Shiloh unto all the Israelites that came thither. Also before they burnt the fat, the priest's servant came, and said to the man that sacrificed, Give flesh to roast for the priest; for he will not have sodden flesh of thee, but raw. And if any man said unto him, Let them not fail to burn the fat presently, and then take as much as thy soul desireth; then he would answer him, Nay; but thou shalt give it me now: and if not, I will take it by force. Wherefore the sin of the young men was very great before the Lord: for men abhorred the offering of the Lord'* (1 Samuel 2:12-17).

Stealing is willfully taking other people's properties without their knowledge or consent, either by habitual or regular basis. It is also taking away by force or by unjust means what does not belong to you secretly, gradually or unexpectedly. Robbery and stealing are evil by all ramifications.

> *'And there was a man of mount Ephraim, whose name was Micah. And he said unto his mother, The eleven hundred shekels of silver that were taken from thee, about which thou cursedst, and spakest of also in mine ears, behold, the silver is with me; I took it. And his mother said, Blessed be thou of the Lord, my son'* (Judges 17:1-2).

Armed robbers can be very destructive. They can kill, steal and destroy. Most of them operate under influences of hard drugs and alcohol, and they always move under the directive of destructive demons. The bloods of innocent people they robbed, maimed or killed always cry against them. They can never be at peace. The only way out is to repent and cry to God for forgiveness, with deeper resolve never to be involved in robbery the rest of your life.

OVERCOMING PRISON-BOUND CHARACTERS

To overcome prison-bound characters, you must first answer the call of salvation by acknowledging your sins, repenting and forsaking them

> *'Come unto me, all ye that labor and are heavy laden, and I will give you rest. Take my yoke upon you, and learn of me; for I am meek and lowly in heart: and ye shall find rest unto your souls. For my yoke is easy, and my burden is light'* (Matthew 11:28-30).

Jesus Christ showed Nicodemus the only way to eternal life. He told him that he must be born again. Jesus in His own words said -

> *'… Verily, verily, I say unto thee, Except a man be born again, he cannot see the kingdom of God'* (John 3:3).

An armed robber who was condemned and crucified on a cross overcame his prison-bound characters when he acknowledged his sins before Jesus. He confessed them and received our Lord Jesus Christ as his Lord and personal savior, and instantly, he gained an eternal life in God's kingdom.

> *'And one of the malefactors which were hanged railed on him, saying, If thou be Christ, save thyself and us. But the other answering rebuked him, saying, Dost not thou fear God, seeing thou art in the same condemnation? And we indeed justly; for we receive the due reward of our deeds: but this man hath done nothing amiss. And he said unto Jesus, Lord, remember me when thou comest into thy kingdom.*

> *And Jesus said unto him, Verily I say unto thee, Today shalt thou be with me in paradise'* (Luke 23:39-43).

Abel exhibited godly character when he made up his mind to serve God in fear and reverence. He offered to God a righteous sacrifice of faith. Abraham also manifested godly character when he gave Lot the opportunity to choose first a desired land before him, instead of fighting over things of this world. Joseph was able to come out of prison because he rejected free offer of sexual sin from one of the most beautiful women of his generation. He remained faithful to God till the time of sudden promotion, and as a prime minister in Egypt, he never oppressed his enemies. Rahab, together with her family, were saved from mass destruction because Rahab overcame her prison-bound character with wisdom. Daniel stood his ground and rejected idol worship and all the evil men after his life were totally destroyed.

> *'But Daniel purposed in his heart that he would not defile himself with the portion of the king's meat, nor with the wine which he drank: therefore he requested of the prince of the eunuchs that he might not defile himself'* (Daniel 1:8).

The three wise men from the east overcame prison-bound characters when they used their hard earned wealth to honor the king of kings. They traveled all the way from the East to worship Jesus. They prayed and waited until the star of Jesus appeared to guide them where the king of kings was born.

> *'Now when Jesus was born in Bethlehem of Judaea in the days of Herod the king, behold, there came wise men from the east to Jerusalem,... And when they were come into the house, they saw the young child*

with Mary his mother, and fell down, and worshipped him: and when they had opened their treasures, they presented unto him gifts; gold, and frankincense, and myrrh. And being warned of God in a dream that they should not return to Herod, they departed into their own country another way' (Matthew 2:1-2, 11-12)

CONSEQUENCES OF PRISON-BOUND CHARACTERS

- They can drive you out of comfort zones and make you enemy of God (*See* Genesis 3:14-24).

- They can bring curses to your destiny, and can make you a fugitive and vagabond on earth (*See* Genesis 4:9-15).

- Prison-bound characters can bring your entire investment on earth to total destruction and waste your life in the end (*See* Genesis 7:11-24).

- They can bring disagreement, misunderstanding, confusion, and waste of whole life's efforts (*See* Genesis 11:6-9).

- They can separate a man from his beloved wife, children, and inheritance and make life miserable (*See* Genesis 12:15-16).

- Prison-bound characters can bring sufferings, plagues and all manner of family problems (*See* Genesis 1217).

- They can bring God's judgment and termination of lives (*See* Genesis 38:7-10).

- Prison-bound characters can change good to bad; bring suffering, destruction, divine punishment, untimely deaths, defeats and lots of all good things (Exodus 7:19-25, 8:5-7, 16-32, 19:1-35, 10:1-29, 12:29-36, 14:5-9, 23-31).

- They can bring people to condemnation, blotting out their names from the book of life (Exodus 32:32-33, Deuteronomy 4:29; 12:28-32).

- They can bring God's fire of judgment against God's ministers (Leviticus 10:1-2).
- They can cause people to be stoned to death (Leviticus 24:10-23).
- They can bring strange fire into the congregation of God's people to consume them to death (Numbers 11:1-3).
- Unchecked prison-bound characters can bring leprosy and delay the journey of God's people (Numbers 12:10-16).
- They can take you away from God's plan and promises and rest. They can bring defeat and loss of life (Numbers 14:11-12, 20-23 ,45,26:1-2,63-65, Deuteronomy 1:22-46,2:13-15, Deuteronomy 9:4-29,20:1).
- They can waste peoples' lives and bury them in shame (Numbers 16:31-34).
- Prison-bound characters can terminate ministries or limit ministers to certain levels that are far below levels of their calling (Numbers 20:12-13, 27:12-18, Deuteronomy 4:21-26).
- They can bring serpentine bites, together with incurable and shameful deaths (Numbers 31:1-2, 7-24, Deuteronomy 7:1-4, 9:4-29).
- They can blot out a whole nation from the surface of the earth (Deuteronomy 25:19, Psalms 9:17).
- They can bring God's anger upon people (Deuteronomy 29:12-29).

- They can deliver you to your enemies for destruction and you suffer everywhere you go (Judges 2:14, 20-28,3:7-8, 12-14,4:1-3,5:8, 6:14, 20-25,35, 10:6-18,13:1, 17:1).

- They can open rooms for evil spirits to hunt you, or cause divisions, treachery, cruelty, blood shedding, war and destructions (Judges 9:22-57).

- Prison-bound characters can bring family destruction and cause you to spend eternity with devil (1 Samuel 3:11-18, 4:10-22).

- They can put a people under the leadership of evil and selfish leaders (1 Samuel 8:6-18, 22,14:52).

- Termination of ministry or divine assignment, lack of divine communication with God, and closed heaven are all consequences of prison-bound characters (1 Samuel 13:11-15, 14-36-37,1 Chronicles 10:1-14, 15:10-23,34-36, 16:14-23).

- Prison-bound characters can attract God's sword of destruction in a family, causing premature deaths and unanswered prayers (2 Samuel 12:1-13, 2 Chronicles 6:36, 7:12-22).

- They can bring destructive pestilence and mass deaths (2 Samuel 24:5,25,1 Chronicles 21:5-28; 2 Chronicles 6:36, 7:12-22).

- They can also cause shameful defeats by very weak enemies (1 Kings 14:25-29).

- They can cause evil pronouncements and attract death of family members (2 Kings 16:3-7, 11-14).

- Prison-bound characters can bring curses of evil inheritance upon families; born and unborn. (1 Kings 21:17-24, 22:34-40, 2 Chronicles 7:12-22, 18:33-34,2 Kings 9:30-37, 2 Chronicles 16:19-23).

- They can bring shameful deaths with great sufferings, and without cure (2 Kings 1:1-8, 2 Chronicles 22:5-9, 16:2-12).

- Prison-bound characters can cause you to inherit another man's problems for generations (2 Kings 5:25-27, 15:5-7, 32-38).

- They can fuel life imprisonment sentences (2 Kings 17:3-24, 2 Chronicles 36:6-10).

- People with prison-bound characters sow much and harvest little; they eat much but have not enough (Haggai 1:5-6,9-11,Malachi 1:14).

- Their prayers are never answered(Zechariah 7:13, 11:15-17, Malachi 4:2-3).

- These evil characters can instigate deaths by hanging and destruction of entire family (Esther 7:1-10, 8:1-17, 10:3).

Every wise prisoner would do everything possible to overcome these evil and prison-bound characters. It is a dangerous thing to keep God out of your plans, engaging in useless striving, impatience, drunkenness, envy, hatred, lying, conspiracy, cheating, defilement, immorality, lust, harlotry, rape, supporting and planning evil, mocking God, covering sin, forsaking God, pride, depending on charms, oppressing the poor, harboring unforgiving spirit and being crafty. All these things prison-bound characters are evil.

DEATH OF PRISONERS OF HOPE

Death of any prisoner of hope is never a defeat, failure or an end. It is always a victorious beginning of eternal life with God. Normally, when a true child of God dies, he or she wakes up before God, who welcomes him or her.

Therefore, if for any reason God decides to call any prisoner of hope to eternity from the prison, believers should not be extremely sorrowful or deeply disappointed with God.

The greatest favor you can do to any dying person is to make sure he or she dies in Christ. Death of a true child of God; a prisoner of hope, is the beginning of true life and not the end of life. The Scripture calls it the resurrection of the dead.

FACTS ABOUT RESURRECTION

The Holy Spirit witnesses to all true believers that death is never an end but a beginning of life. Even in the days of Abraham, he believed in resurrection. When he was about to offer his only begotten son Isaac, he believed strongly that God is able to raise him back to life.

> *'By faith Abraham, when he was tried, offered up Isaac: and he that had received the promises offered up his only begotten son, Of whom it was said, That in Isaac shall thy seed be called: Accounting that God was able to raise him up, even from the dead; from whence also he received him in a figure'* (Hebrews 11:17-19).

The Old Testament saints believed the doctrine of resurrection and they all testified to it. Though this body you carry now may have come under attacks of Satan and his agents, and hardships in prison are too severe; the demonic mosquitoes, merciless bed bugs and marine spirit cockroaches all eating your body in the prison, but be assured that at the time of resurrection after death, they will have no power over you.

> *'For I know that my redeemer liveth, and that he shall stand at the latter day upon the earth: And though after my skin worms destroy this body, yet in my flesh shall I see God: Whom I shall see for myself, and mine eyes shall behold, and not another; though my reins be consumed within me'* (Job 19:25-27).

After physical death, our redeemer appears to welcome all prisoners of hope with resurrected bodies. The grave cannot restrain us from meeting our God. Pains and torments of death will all cease after physical death. Suffering will not continue as well. It is a well-known fact that there are those who will not taste the grave. While the saints transcend the grave to heaven, the sinners go to hell.

> *'And many of them that sleep in the dust of the earth shall awake, some to everlasting life, and some to shame and everlasting contempt'* (Daniel 12:2)

> *'But God will redeem my soul from the power of the grave: for he shall receive me'* (Psalms 49:15).

When all the dead get up from the grave at resurrection, separation of sinners from the saints will take place. Jesus Christ, speaking about the resurrection of the dead, said -

> *'Verily, verily, I say unto you, The hour is coming, and now is, when the dead shall hear the voice of the*

> *Son of God: and they that hear shall live. For as the Father hath life in himself; so hath he given to the Son to have life in himself; And hath given him authority to execute judgment also, because he is the Son of man. Marvel not at this: for the hour is coming, in the which all that are in the graves shall hear his voice, And shall come forth; they that have done good, unto the resurrection of life; and they that have done evil, unto the resurrection of damnation'* (John 5:25-29).

The dead will cease to hear earthly voices, but spiritually will hear the voice of the Son of God. All prisoners of hope who died will be separated and unite with Christ at the time of resurrection.

> *'Jesus saith unto her, Thy brother shall rise again. Martha saith unto him, I know that he shall rise again in the resurrection at the last day'* (John 11:23-24).

Four days after Lazarus was buried, Jesus proved that resurrection of the dead is real. Though prisoners of hope die, they will surely transcend the grave to heaven. Between the time of death and resurrection, believers'(*prisoners of hope*) souls go to heaven immediately to be with the Lord while the souls of dead sinners go to hell. Both sinners and saints will remain spiritually conscious and can hear and see.

> *'And Jesus said unto him, Verily I say unto thee, Today shalt thou be with me in paradise'* (Luke 23:43).

There will be distinction between resurrections of sinners and saints. In the resurrection, while believers will be resurrected to eternal life, the sinners will be subjected to judgment and eternal damnation. It is important to understand what the resurrection to life is all about. It is the first resurrection, which is also the resurrection of the just, the righteous and all prisoners of hope. All the above phrases have the same implication.

> *'But when thou makest a feast, call the poor, the maimed, the lame, the blind: And thou shalt be blessed; for they cannot recompense thee: for thou shalt be recompensed at the resurrection of the just'* (Luke 14:13-14).

> *'But every man in his own order: Christ the firstfruits; afterward they that are Christ's at his coming'* (1 Corinthians 15:23).

The just will be resurrected to be with the Lord forever and ever in the eternity. So while friends and relatives cry for prisoners of hope who die, they stand before Christ in heaven rejoicing. Many prisoners of hope in prisons today will surely be released and allowed to go back into the world to fulfill their destinies. But if for any reason anyone dies, he or she will forever be with the Lord. We that are alive should prayerfully remain faithful to God so as to join them in heaven.

I read a tracts so many years ago written by Dr. M.L. Rossvally. In that tract he wrote, 'Twice or trice in my life, God in His mercy touched my heart and twice before my conversion I was under deep conviction. During the American war, I was a surgeon in the United State Army and after the battle of Gettysburg, there were many hundreds of wounded soldiers in my hospital. Among them were twenty-eight soldiers who were severely wounded.

Most of them were to have their legs amputated. Some had already lost arms and others both arms and legs.

Among the twenty-eight soldiers was a young man who had been recruited into the service for only three months, and being too young to qualify as a combat soldier, he enlisted as a drummer. When my assistant surgeon and steward wanted to administer chloroform to him before the amputation, he turned away his head and politely refused to receive it. When the steward reminded him it was the doctor's orders, he said, '*Send the doctor to me*'.

When I went to his bedside I said, 'Youngman, why did you refuse the administration chloroform? When I found you on the battlefield you were so far gone that I thought it hardly worthwhile to pick you up. But when you opened those large blue eyes I thought you had a mother somewhere who might at that moment be thinking of her boy. I did not want you to die on the battlefield, so I ordered you to be brought here. Now you have lost so much blood that you are too weak to endure an operation without chloroform. Therefore, you had better let me give you some.

He laid his hand on mine, and looking into my eyes, said, '*Doctor, one Sunday afternoon in the Sabbath school when I was nine and a half years old, I gave my heart to Christ. I learnt to trust him then. I have been trusting in Him ever since, and I know I can still trust him now. He is my strength and my stimulant. He will support me while you amputate my arm and leg*'. I then asked him if he would allow me to give him a little brandy.

Again he looked straight into my face and said, '*Doctor, when I was about five years old my mother knelt by my side and said, 'Charlie, I am now praying to Jesus that you may never know the taste of strong drink. Your father died as a drunkard and went down to drunkard's grave, and I promised God, if it was His will that you should grow up, that you would be a young man against the bitter cup'. I have not tasted intoxicating liquor of any kind and as I am, in all probability would you make me drink in my last hours on earth?'*

I cannot forget the look in Charlie's face. At that time, I hated Jesus, but I respected Charlie's loyalty to his Savior. When finally something touched my heart, I did for Charlie what I had never done for any other soldier. I asked him if he wished to see a chaplain. *'Oh, yes sir'*, was his answer.

When the chaplain came, he recognized Charlie at once, having met him often at prayer meetings. Taking his hand he said, *'Well Charlie, I am sorry to see you in this sad condition'.'Oh, I am all right, sir'*, he answered. *'The doctor offered me chloroform, but I declined it. Then he offered me brandy, which I also declined. And now, if my Savior calls me, I can go to him in my right mind'. 'You may not die, Charlie'*, said the Chaplain. *'But if the Lord should call you anyway, is there anything I can do for you when you are gone?'*

'Chaplain, please put your hand under my pillow and take my little Bible. In it, you will find my mother's address. Please send it to her and write her a letter and tell her that since the day I left home I have never let a day pass without reading a portion of God's Word and praying daily that God would bless my dear mother, whether am on match to the battlefield or in the hospital'.

'Is there anything else I can do for you, my lad', asked the Chaplain. *'Yes, please write a letter to the Superintendent of Sand Street Sunday School, Brooklyn, N.Y and tell him that I have never forgotten the kind words, many prayers and good advice he gave me, they have followed me through the dangers of battle. And*

now, in my dying hour I asked my dear Savior to bless my dear old superintendent, that is all, sir'.

Turning towards me, Charlie said '*Now doctor, I am ready, and I promise you that I will not groan while you take out my arm and leg, if you will not offer me chloroform'*. I promised, but I had not the courage to take the knife in my hand to perform the operation without first going into the next room and taking a little stimulant to nerve myself to perform my duty.

While I was cutting through Charlie Carlson, he never groaned, but when I took the saw to separate the bone, the lad took the corner of his pillow on his mouth, and all that I could hear him utter was '*O Jesus, blessed Jesus, stand by me now!*' He kept his promise and never groaned. That night I could not sleep, for whichever way I turned, I saw those soft blue eyes, and when I closed my eyes, the words, '*Blessed Jesus, stand by me now*' kept ringing in my ears. Between twelve and one O'clock, I left my house and visited the hospital; a thing I had never done before unless when specially called. I had a strong desire to see Charlie.

Upon my arrival at the hospital I was informed by the night steward that sixteen soldiers had died and been carried down to the mortuary. 'How is Charlie Carlson, is he among the dead?, I asked. 'No sir', answered the steward. 'He is sleeping like sweet baby. When I came up to the bed where he laid, one of the nurses informed me that about nine o'clock that morning, two members of the USA Christian commission came through to the hospital to read and sing a hymn. They were accompanied by the Chaplain who knelt by Charlie Carlson's bed and offered a fervent and soul-stirring prayer after which they sang, while still upon their knees, the sweetest of all hymns 'Jesus lover of my soul', in which Charlie joined.

I could not understand how a boy who had undergone such excruciating pains could sing. Five days after I had amputated that dear boy's arm and leg, he sent for me. It was from him on that fateful day I had the first gospel sermon. *'Doctor'*, he said. *'My time has come. I do not expect to see another sunrise, but thank God I am ready to go. But before I die, I desire to thank you with all my heart for your kindness to me. Doctor, you are a Jew and you do not believe in Jesus, but will you please stand here and see me die, trusting my Savior to the last moment of my life?'*

I tried to stay, but I could not, for I had not the courage to stand by and watch a Christian boy die rejoicing in the love of Jesus whom I had been taught to hate. So I hurriedly left the room. About twenty minutes later, a steward who found me sitting in my private office covering my face with my hands, said, *'Doctor, Charlie Carlson wishes to see you'*.

'I have just seen him', I answered, 'And I cannot see him again. *'But doctor, he says he must see you once more before he dies'*. So I made up my mind to see him, and perhaps say an endearing word and let him die, but I was determined that no word of his would influence me in the least, so far as his Jesus was concerned. When I entered the hospital, I saw he was sinking fast, so I sat down by his bed. Asking me to take his hand, he said, *'Doctor, I love you because you are a Jew, the best friend I have found in this world was a Jew'*.

I asked him who that was. He answered, *'Jesus Christ to whom I want to introduce you to before I die. And now, will you promise me, doctor, that you will never forget what I am about to say to you?'* I promised and he said, *'Five days ago, while you amputated my arm and leg, I prayed to Lord Jesus Christ to convert your soul*. Those words went deep into my heart. I could not understand how, when I was causing him the most intense pain, he could forget all about himself and think of nothing but his Savior and my unconverted soul. All I could say to him was 'Well, my dear boy, you will soon be alright'. And with those words, I left him and twelve minutes later he fell asleep, as safe in the arms of Jesus.

Hundreds of soldiers died in my hospital during that war but I followed only one to his grave, and that one was Charlie Carlson, the drummer boy. I rode three miles to see him buried. I had him dressed in a new uniform and placed in an officer's coffin with a United States' flag over it.

That dear boy's words made deep impression upon me. I was rich at that time, so far as money was concerned. But I would have given every penny I possessed if I could have felt toward Christ as Charlie did. But that feeling cannot be bought with money. Alas! I could not forget the boy himself. I now know that at that time, I was under deep conviction of sin, but I fought against Christ with all the hatred of an orthodox Jew for nearly ten years, until finally the dear boy's prayer was answered and God converted my soul.

About eighteen months after my confession, I attended a prayer meeting one evening in the city of Brooklyn. It was one of those meetings when Christians testify to the loving kindness of their Savior. After several of them had spoken an elderly lady rose up and said, '*Dear friends, this may be the last time that I may be privileged to testify for Christ. My family physician told me yesterday that my right lung is nearly gone, and that the left lung is very much affected. So at the best, I have but a short while to be with you, but what is left of me belongs to Jesus*'.

'Oh! It is a great joy to know that I shall meet my boy with Jesus in heaven. My son was not only a soldier for his country but also a soldier for Christ. He was wounded at Gettysburg, and he fell into the hands of a Jewish doctor, who amputated his arm and leg, and he died five days later. The chaplain of the regiment wrote me a letter and sent me my boy's bible. In that letter, I was informed that my Charlie in his dying hour sent for the Jewish doctor and said to him, 'Doctor, before I die I wish to tell you that five days ago while you amputated my arm and leg, I prayed to Lord Jesus Christ to convert your soul'.

When I heard this lady's testimony, I could sit still no longer. I left my seat, crossed to the room and taking her by the hand, said, *'God bless you, my dear sister. Your boy's prayers has been heard and answered. I am the Jewish doctor for whom your Charlie prayed and his Savior is now my Savior'.*[4]

This story is a perfect example of death of prisoners of hope. Our journey does not end at death or in the grave. We are going beyond the grave. If it pleases God to call you to glory from the prison, make sure you are a prisoner of hope. Do not allow anyone to die by your side today without introducing him or her to the Savior, Lord Jesus Christ. Pray, preach and try as much as possible to give hope to fellow prisoners.

> *'For God so loved the world, that he gave his only begotten Son, that whosoever believeth in him should not perish, but have everlasting life'* (John 3:16).
>
> *'For whosoever shall call upon the name of the Lord shall be saved'* (Romans 10:13).

[4] **Dr. M. L. ROSSVALLY.**

Announce to them that Jesus loves them and cares for them, no matter the pains, suffering and rejection. Always pray that your teaching and preaching will bring deep conviction upon everyone around you. Lead people to confess Jesus, regardless of their faith, creed, or religion. Whosoever, of any religion, tribe or nationality that shall call upon the name of Jesus shall be saved.

Start preaching right now; talk to everyone including fellow prisoners. The mission of Christ on earth is not to condemn but to convince, convict and convert.

> *'For God sent not his Son into the world to condemn the world; but that the world through him might be saved… And when he is come, he will reprove the world of sin, and of righteousness, and of judgment…So when they continued asking him, he lifted up himself, and said unto them, He that is without sin among you, let him first cast a stone at her. And again he stooped down, and wrote on the ground. And they which heard it, being convicted by their own conscience, went out one by one, beginning at the eldest, even unto the last: and Jesus was left alone, and the woman standing in the midst'* (John 3:17,16:8, 8:7-9).

The verdict of human judges or courts in your country is not enough to condemn you, if only you will believe and confess Christ. The only people in prison upon whom courts' verdicts will stand are those that believed not.

> *'He that believeth on him is not condemned: but he that believeth not is condemned already, because he hath not believed in the name of the only begotten Son of God…. He that believeth on the Son hath*

everlasting life: and he that believeth not the Son shall not see life; but the wrath of God abideth on him' (John 3:18, 36).

Stand upon the above Scriptures, reverse every human court's conviction, and destroy their condemnation upon your life. Begin to cancel every evil utterance, negative words and human judgments delivered on your head. The prison is not your final destination. Tell everyone that you are no longer in darkness. Arise and shine, and darkness gives way.

'And this is the condemnation, that light is come into the world, and men loved darkness rather than light, because their deeds were evil' (John 3:19).

Accept Jesus now and renounce evil works. Love Jesus, and believe in Him. Enter into His light, and walk therein. Having confessed all your sins, believe that He has already forgiven you all. Reject guilt and condemnation and never believe devil's lies.

'Therefore I say unto you, What things soever ye desire, when ye pray, believe that ye receive them, and ye shall have them' (Mark 11:24).

Settle all your differences with people in prison and begin to relate to them as fellow prisoners of hope. Love one another, care for one another and pray with one another. Your prayers will be answered. Let no prisoner of hope be afraid of death. Rather, be concerned that if any should die, he or she dies in Christ as a prisoner of hope, not as sinner.

One of my sons in the Lord, Late Pastor Okwudili Cornelius Nnaemeka understood eternity very well. It was difficult to come across him without hearing the message of salvation from him. He preaches in season and out of season, in health and in sickness.

> *'And Jesus came and spake unto them, saying, All power is given unto me in heaven and in earth. Go ye therefore, and teach all nations, baptizing them in the name of the Father, and of the Son, and of the Holy Ghost: Teaching them to observe all things whatsoever I have commanded you: and, lo, I am with you always, even unto the end of the world. Amen'* (Matthew 28:18-20).

He was a master in personal evangelism and as far as he was concerned, there is no limitation in preaching about Jesus. He had strong conviction that was unshakable. To him, everyone must be given an opportunity to hear the gospel without restriction or discrimination. On his dying bed, he preached to a nurse that was supposed to attend to him, until he passed on to glory. To him, it does not matter whether he was in pains or not. What mattered to him more was that the nurse's soul.

> *'I am debtor both to the Greeks, and to the Barbarians; both to the wise, and to the unwise. So, as much as in me is, I am ready to preach the gospel to you that are at Rome also. For I am not ashamed of the gospel of Christ: for it is the power of God unto salvation to everyone that believeth; to the Jew first, and also to the Greek'* (Romans 1:14-16).

His death was a great shock to most of us who were very close to him. But our greatest joy was that he died a prisoner of hope. Before his death as a soul winner, he experienced thorough conversion and devoted most of his time, talent, strength and money to the furtherance of the gospel. His life alone helped the spread of gospel in my town. Most people accepted Christ on hearing that Okwudili had become born again. He was a soul winner who understood the need and the call on his life. He was a compassionate soul winner and his passion for Christ made him sacrifice family respect and the pride of acclaimed academic excellence.

> *'But when he saw the multitudes, he was moved with compassion on them, because they fainted, and were scattered abroad, as sheep having no shepherd'* (Matthew 9:36).

> *'I say the truth in Christ, I lie not, my conscience also bearing me witness in the Holy Ghost, That I have great heaviness and continual sorrow in my heart. For I could wish that myself were accursed from Christ for my brethren, my kinsmen according to the flesh'* (Romans 9:1-3).

During those days, our compassion for lost souls made us sacrifice so much, in order to go into effectual and fervent prayers, together with long tireless journeys of preaching and inviting sinners to the Savior. We endured hardship, denied ourselves many sleep, shed tears and fasted for many days not for our personal prosperities, but to rescue people from bondages of sin. Okwudili's death threw me off-balance, pained me to the marrow and made me ran away the moment he was being taken to the grave, believing that he will wake up as I prayed in a lonely place. But thanks God that he is resting in the bosom of Lord Jesus. He died as a prisoner of hope, waiting for us to finish our own battles here on earth. Preaching the gospel to the living is an obligation for it is a debt we all owe to God.

'I charge thee therefore before God, and the Lord Jesus Christ, who shall judge the quick and the dead at his appearing and his kingdom; Preach the word; be instant in season, out of season; reprove, rebuke, exhort with all longsuffering and doctrine. For the time will come when they will not endure sound doctrine; but after their own lusts shall they heap to themselves teachers, having itching ears; And they shall turn away their ears from the truth, and shall be turned unto fables. But watch thou in all things, endure afflictions, do the work of an evangelist, make full proof of thy ministry. For I am now ready to be offered, and the time of my departure is at hand. I have fought a good fight, I have finished my course, I have kept the faith' (2 Timothy 4:1-7).

Sometime ago, a prisoner of hope named Irving passed away. As his life was living him, he said, *"O the depth of peace and joy in Jesus Christ'*. For prisoners of hope, life after earthly life is very wonderful. The moment a true child of God, a prisoner of hope, leaves this world, he or she enters into the New Jerusalem; the eternal city prepared for them that loved Jesus. If you are born again, whether you are in prison or out there, you are already a citizen of heaven. True prisoners of hope are just strangers here on earth because our home is heaven. Our Father is in heaven, our Savior is there, our treasures and inheritances are all waiting for us in heaven.

Many prisoners of hope at the points of death saw the glorious beyond, rejoiced and testified of it. One prisoner of hope when dying said, *'The battle is fought, the victory is won! I am sweeping through the gates washed in the blood of the Lamb'*. It is a joyful thing to die as prisoners of hope. As much as possible, do not permit anyone around you to die without this experience.

> *'Having the glory of God: and her light was like unto a stone most precious, even like a jasper stone, clear as crystal; And had a wall great and high, and had twelve gates, and at the gates twelve angels, and names written thereon, which are the names of the twelve tribes of the children of Israel: On the east three gates; on the north three gates; on the south three gates; and on the west three gates. And the wall of the city had twelve foundations, and in them the names of the twelve apostles of the Lamb…. And the building of the wall of it was of jasper: and the city was pure gold, like unto clear glass. And the foundations of the wall of the city were garnished with all manner of precious stones. The first foundation was jasper; the second, sapphire; the third, a chalcedony; the fourth, an emerald; The fifth, sardonyx; the sixth, sardius; the seventh, chrysolite; the eighth, beryl; the ninth, a topaz; the tenth, a chrysoprasus; the eleventh, a jacinth; the twelfth, an amethyst. And the twelve gates were twelve pearls; every several gate was of one pearl: and the street of the city was pure gold, as it were transparent glass… And the city had no need of the sun, neither of the moon, to shine in it: for the glory of God did lighten it, and the Lamb is the light thereof'* (Revelation 21:11-14, 18-21,23).

One striking thing to dream about heaven is its beauty, which cannot be stained by sin. It is a place filled with blazing and brilliant glory of God. No wonder, when one prisoner of hope was dying, he cried out, *'Perhaps, I am too anxious. Can this be death? Why, it is better than living! Tell them I died happy in Jesus'*. It is a joyful experience to die as a prisoner of hope. Heaven has been perfectly designed with millions of intersecting layers of avenues that can easily contain billions and billions of people.

> *'And had a wall great and high, and had twelve gates, and at the gates twelve angels, and names written thereon, which are the names of the twelve tribes of the children of Israel: On the east three gates; on the north three gates; on the south three gates; and on the west three gates. And the wall of the city had twelve foundations, and in them the names of the twelve apostles of the Lamb. And he that talked with me had a golden reed to measure the city, and the gates thereof, and the wall thereof. And the city lieth foursquare, and the length is as large as the breadth: and he measured the city with the reed, twelve thousand furlongs. The length and the breadth and the height of it are equal. And he measured the wall thereof, an hundred and forty and four cubits, according to the measure of a man, that is, of the angel'* (Revelation 21:12-17).

You may be hungry now in prison and eating unbalanced diet. Do not worry, for it will not be so in heaven. In heaven, prisoners of hope will know no suffering, hunger or thirst. You may be going through pains now, or devastated by hardship, or abandoned by loves ones, or being harass by the jailors, but in heaven, Jesus will wipe away all your tears.

You will drink from the waters of life and eat from the tree of life that yields different type of fruit. The leaves of the tree of life will bring perfect and permanent healing to nations of the world.

> *'And he shewed me a pure river of water of life, clear as crystal, proceeding out of the throne of God and of the Lamb. In the midst of the street of it, and on either side of the river, was there the tree of life, which bare twelve manner of fruits, and yielded her fruit every month: and the leaves of the tree were for the healing of the nations. And there shall be no more curse: but the throne of God and of the Lamb shall be in it; and his servants shall serve him: And they shall see his face; and his name shall be in their foreheads. And there shall be no night there; and they need no candle, neither light of the sun; for the Lord God giveth them light: and they shall reign forever and ever'* (Revelation 22:1-5).

Our joy, health, hope and peace will be fully restored and made perfect. A prisoner of hope who was passing away saw heaven and said, *'Glory to God. I see the heavens open before me. What shall I say? Christ is altogether lovely. His glorious angels are come for me. And my mansion is all ready. Now I go home into paradise'*. I pray that your dreams will change to see heaven instead of dreaming of evil pursuers. If God will give you the vision of heaven now, your whole affection will change.

> *'For since the beginning of the world men have not heard, nor perceived by the ear, neither hath the eye seen, O God, beside thee, what he hath prepared for him that waiteth for him'* (Isaiah 64:4).

At times when I read about heaven, or imagine heaven, I feel like dying. Nevertheless, we must fulfill our assignment before death. You will not die, in the mighty name of Jesus.

> *'For David, after he had served his own generation by the will of God, fell on sleep, and was laid unto his fathers, and saw corruption'* (Acts 13:36).

We have a destiny to fulfill before death. Life in the prison is very bad because the suffering is ruthless. However, I want to tell you something, no matter what you are going through on earth now, a memory of a stay in heaven can make you to forget your present sufferings, in the hope of a glorious destiny after death. The sort hardship endured in Nigerian prisons and most Africa countries are enormously appalling.

Chapter

OPPORTUNITIES IN THE PRISON

All over the world, prisons can be places of great opportunities. However, there be many disadvantages too, but prisoners who receive Christ as their Lord and Savior, and prayerfully trust God will come out of prisons better people. Lots of prisoners in the Bible made it to the top after prison sentences. You too can make it regardless of those difficult challenges you are facing now. Trust God.

> *'Then Pharaoh sent and called Joseph, and they brought him hastily out of the dungeon: and he shaved himself, and changed his raiment, and came in unto Pharaoh... And the thing was good in the eyes of Pharaoh, and in the eyes of all his servants. And Pharaoh said unto his servants, Can we find such a one as this is, a man in whom the Spirit of God is? And Pharaoh said unto Joseph, Forasmuch as God hath shewed thee all this, there is none so discreet and wise as thou art: Thou shalt be over my house, and according unto thy word shall all my people be ruled: only in the throne will I be greater than thou. And Pharaoh said unto Joseph, See, I have set thee over all the land of Egypt. And Pharaoh took off his ring from his hand, and put it upon Joseph's hand, and arrayed him in vestures of fine linen, and put a gold chain about his neck; And he made him to ride in the second chariot which he had; and they cried before him, Bow the knee: and he made him ruler over all the land of Egypt. And Pharaoh said unto Joseph, I am Pharaoh, and without thee shall no man lift up his hand or foot in all the land of Egypt'* (Genesis 41:14, 37-44).

Learn to trust God. When you trust Him, He is able to make you walk out of this prison a better and favored person, regardless of any brutal judgment hanging on your head. It is obvious that you will surely meet horrible people in prisons who serve devil, but there are equally good prisoners. There are prisoners of hope in virtually every prison in the world. A young man called Jamie Lawrence came out of prison to become an English premier league star.

The world is full of demonic distractions, worldliness and destructive programs. However, you need to take enough time in prison to get yourself prepared to face the world. In western countries, you can study or school inside prison. Therefore, utilize academic opportunities in prison, if they exist where you are now, to equip yourself profitably. In Africa, prisoners learn fundamental technical works that can benefit them after prison. You can rebuild your future even while in prison. Prayer is also a great investment. There are many things in the world waiting to destroy every prisoner released from the prison. These destructive elements can only get you easily when you fail to equip yourself now in prison.

However, prisoners who fail or ignore to deal with their prison-bound evil characters before leaving prison yards usually fall victim to evil powers controlling the world. The Bible exposed them as lusts of flesh. Demons behind lusts of flesh are wicked and when you fail to deal with them, they can pull you back into prison. This is because they are more operational in the spiritual than in the physical.

Lust of the flesh is having uncontrollable desires for sexual immorality or yielding to satisfactions of evil desires of the flesh. While in prison, you may lust after someone in your heart but practically be restricted. But in the world, people lust after people and then go further to practice sexual immoralities. Many people have been caught in rapes, impregnating their house helps, or daughters and even distributing HIV to their unsuspecting victims.

> *'And upon all the ships of Tarshish, and upon all pleasant pictures. And the loftiness of man shall be bowed down, and the haughtiness of men shall be*

made low: and the Lord alone shall be exalted in that day' (Isaiah 2:16-17).

'Ye have heard that it was said by them of old time, Thou shalt not commit adultery: But I say unto you, That whosoever looketh on a woman to lust after her hath committed adultery with her already in his heart. And if thy right eye offend thee, pluck it out, and cast it from thee: for it is profitable for thee that one of thy members should perish, and not that thy whole body should be cast into hell. And if thy right hand offend thee, cut it off, and cast it from thee: for it is profitable for thee that one of thy members should perish, and not that thy whole body should be cast into hell' (Matthew 5:27-30).

Through prayers and determination, it is easier for any prisoner to deal with the lust of flesh while in prison than in the world. Demons that are behind lusts of flesh can easily be cast out in the prison than in the world. The world can offer you lust of flesh and provide you the opportunity to practice it, but not so, with prison, which has physical restrictions.

'But put ye on the Lord Jesus Christ, and make not provision for the flesh, to fulfill the lusts thereof' (Romans 13:14).

'Now these things were our examples, to the intent we should not lust after evil things, as they also lusted. Neither be ye idolaters, as were some of them; as it is written, The people sat down to eat and drink, and rose up to play. Neither let us commit fornication, as some of them committed, and fell in one day three and twenty thousand. Neither let us tempt Christ, as some

of them also tempted, and were destroyed of serpents. Neither murmur ye, as some of them also murmured, and were destroyed of the destroyer. Now all these things happened unto them for ensamples: and they are written for our admonition, upon whom the ends of the world are come' (1 Corinthians 10:6-11)

Prisoners have less battle to fight in terms of dealing with demons behind sins. However, in the world, before you can even contemplate, evil opportunities avail themselves to you so you can carry out evil imaginations. These evil opportunities avail themselves right in your bedrooms, offices, kitchen, neighborhood, and even in your church. There is more idolatry, eating, drinking, playing, fornication, temptation and all manner of demonic entertainments in the world than in prisons.

'Who hath woe? Who hath sorrow? Who hath contentions? Who hath babbling? Who hath wounds without cause? Who hath redness of eyes? They that tarry long at the wine; they that go to seek mixed wine. Look not thou upon the wine when it is red, when it giveth his color in the cup, when it moveth itself aright. At the last it biteth like a serpent, and stingeth like an adder. Thine eyes shall behold strange women, and thine heart shall utter perverse things. Yea, thou shalt be as he that lieth down in the midst of the sea, or as he that lieth upon the top of a mast. They have stricken me, shalt thou say, and I was not sick; they have beaten me, and I felt it not: when shall I awake? I will seek it yet again' (Proverbs 23:29-35).

In the world today, it is easier for friends, enemies, neighbors or circumstances to force you into immorality, idolatry, drinking, and all sorts of evil than in prison. Every necessary means can be employed to get you back into the world. Marine spirits have released billions of sexual demons and all manner of sicknesses and diseases into the world. These marine demons and their powers are less effective in prisons because men and women are not allowed to stay together. Prisoners can only imagine these wicked things, but in the world, wickedness is surplus and free of charge. It is no longer news that sex clubs, nude clubs and all manner of evil and malicious gatherings go on in the open without reproof. Any sin you cannot overcome while in prison is capable of destroying you or bringing you back to prison, and even waste your life.

> *'And when the woman saw that the tree was good for food, and that it was pleasant to the eyes, and a tree to be desired to make one wise, she took of the fruit thereof, and did eat, and gave also unto her husband with her; and he did eat. And the eyes of them both were opened, and they knew that they were naked; and they sewed fig leaves together, and made themselves aprons. And they heard the voice of the Lord God walking in the garden in the cool of the day: and Adam and his wife hid themselves from the presence of the Lord God amongst the trees of the garden. And the Lord God called unto Adam, and said unto him, Where art thou? And he said, I heard thy voice in the garden, and I was afraid, because I was naked; and I hid myself'* (Genesis 3:6-10).

> *'When I saw among the spoils a goodly Babylonish garment, and two hundred shekels of silver, and a wedge of gold of fifty shekels weight, then I coveted them, and took them; and, behold, they are hid in the*

> *earth in the midst of my tent, and the silver under it'* (Joshua 7:21).

Eve saw the forbidden fruit and her mind believed Satan's deceit that it was good for the body. Her eye saw that it was a pleasant tree to be desired to make one wise. However, regardless of how wild your eyes or mind is in prison, there are things you will never see or have access to until you are released. Lot also became a victim of deceitful eyes. There is not much difference between the world today and Sodom and Gomorrah of the days of Lot. Local and international fashion designers of our world today are very wicked carrying out satanic agendas. They have even penetrated into the church and its leadership worldwide.

It is easier to live a holy life in prison than in the world. If you cannot serve God while in prison, you cannot think or assume you can do it when you are released. In the world today, and even in the church, we have earring and jewel competitions, and ornaments of gold and painting competitions. Perm and jerry curls competitions exist even among male pastors. There are also wigs, artificial hairs, female trousers, chains, rings (*some in the legs, nose, and tongue*) competitions. Most ladies in Pentecostal churches even go to churches half naked.

> *'Turn away mine eyes from beholding vanity; and quicken thou me in thy way'* (Psalm 119:37).

> *'Let thine eyes look right on, and let thine eyelids look straight before thee. Ponder the path of thy feet, and let all thy ways be established. Turn not to the right hand nor to the left: remove thy foot from evil'* (Proverbs 4:25-27).

Hundreds, thousand and millions of so-called Christians and religious people are bowing down to devil physically. So many others dine daily with devil. It is not enough for you to open your month and promise God many things you will do for Him when you come out of prison. If you cannot serve God, live holy and relate well with other prisoners now, you cannot do it when you are released. So many people in the world today are bowing down to devil to meet up with evil demands of the world.

> *'Then the devil taketh him up into the holy city, and setteth him on a pinnacle of the temple, And saith unto him, If thou be the Son of God, cast thyself down: for it is written, He shall give his angels charge concerning thee: and in their hands they shall bear thee up, lest at any time thou dash thy foot against a stone. Jesus said unto him, It is written again, Thou shalt not tempt the Lord thy God. Again, the devil taketh him up into an exceeding high mountain, and sheweth him all the kingdoms of the world, and the glory of them'* (Matthew 4:5-8).

The queen of heaven has captured the world. The wealth and kingdoms of the world are being controlled by devil himself. It is only militant Christians that can wrestle to recover their possessions from devil. If you are not one, it will be very difficult to contend with devil and defeat him.

> *'Then all the men which knew that their wives had burned incense unto other gods, and all the women that stood by, a great multitude, even all the people that dwelt in the land of Egypt, in Pathros, answered Jeremiah, saying, As for the word that thou hast spoken unto us in the name of the Lord, we will not*

hearken unto thee. But we will certainly do whatsoever thing goeth forth out of our own mouth, to burn incense unto the queen of heaven, and to pour out drink offerings unto her, as we have done, we, and our fathers, our kings, and our princes, in the cities of Judah, and in the streets of Jerusalem: for then had we plenty of victuals, and were well, and saw no evil. But since we left off to burn incense to the queen of heaven, and to pour out drink offerings unto her, we have wanted all things, and have been consumed by the sword and by the famine' (Jeremiah 44:15-18).

You cannot allow yourself to be influence by the thought that your age mates in the world have all successfully gone ahead of you. When you refuse to accept Christ while in the prison now, you will definitely be forced to compete with them out of pride of life when you are released. Some of your age mates can be car owners and controllers of companies now, but if you do not understand very well the purpose of God for your life, you may proudly get off track. In prison, you have less evil powers to contend with. However, you may be physically very hungry in prison now, but you can do better spiritually than the richest person in the world. Pride is very destructive and can waste lives without mercy. You cannot afford to let pride destroy you.

'Son of man, take up a lamentation upon the king of Tyrus, and say unto him, Thus saith the Lord God; Thou sealest up the sum, full of wisdom, and perfect in beauty. Thou hast been in Eden the garden of God; every precious stone was thy covering, the sardius, topaz, and the diamond, the beryl, the onyx, and the jasper, the sapphire, the emerald, and the carbuncle,

and gold: the workmanship of thy tabrets and of thy pipes was prepared in thee in the day that thou wast created. Thou art the anointed cherub that covereth; and I have set thee so: thou wast upon the holy mountain of God; thou hast walked up and down in the midst of the stones of fire. Thou wast perfect in thy ways from the day that thou wast created, till iniquity was found in thee. By the multitude of thy merchandise they have filled the midst of thee with violence, and thou hast sinned: therefore I will cast thee as profane out of the mountain of God: and I will destroy thee, O covering cherub, from the midst of the stones of fire. Thine heart was lifted up because of thy beauty, thou hast corrupted thy wisdom by reason of thy brightness: I will cast thee to the ground, I will lay thee before kings, that they may behold thee' (Ezekiel 28:12-17).

'Whose adorning let it not be that outward adorning of plaiting the hair, and of wearing of gold, or of putting on of apparel; But let it be the hidden man of the heart, in that which is not corruptible, even the ornament of a meek and quiet spirit, which is in the sight of God of great price. For after this manner in the old time the holy women also, who trusted in God, adorned themselves, being in subjection unto their own husbands' (1 Peter 3:3-5).

'Pride goeth before destruction, and an haughty spirit before a fall' (Proverbs 16:18).

So many other vices which are not always emphasized include carnal festivals, worldly entertainments, cares, enjoyment and worldly pursuits. These things are not found in the prison. That is why prison is a good fighting position against evil through prayers much more than in the world.

> *'For the time past of our life may suffice us to have wrought the will of the Gentiles, when we walked in lasciviousness, lusts, excess of wine, revellings, banquetings, and abominable idolatries: Wherein they think it strange that ye run not with them to the same excess of riot, speaking evil of you'* (1 Peter 4:3-4).

> *'For as in the days that were before the flood they were eating and drinking, marrying and giving in marriage, until the day that Noe entered into the ark, And knew not until the flood came, and took them all away; so shall also the coming of the Son of man be'* (Matthew 24:38-39).

You need to develop a godly character now while in prison. Take a solid decision now to serve God, and live your entire life for Him. Start doing now all you wish to do when you are released. Take a decision for God now and begin to practice it as if you are out of the prison already. Develop a prayer life that is constant and consistent. Choose a day or days for special prayer and fasting. Study your Bible all the time and if you have to stay a little longer in prison, read the Bible over and over from Genesis to Revelation, whether you understand it or not, keep reading and do not be discouraged at all.

To me, prisoners who are serious with the Lord can be more spiritual than most people in the world. Devil has used freedom and liberty which exist in the world to waste many lives and destinies. When you prayerfully discover your destiny in the prison, you will easily make it in the world. Ask God through prayers why you were born. You need to know what you can do best, or what your potentials are. You can achieve much on earth by discovering your potentials even now that you are in prison.

When you take time in prayers to discover your potential, you can make it better because it is like provisions for every vision. Vision without potential is like burden. Your potentials can remove your burden and make life easy for you. When you prayerfully discover your potentials, you will live a life without struggle, and frustrations will phase out in your life.

Everyone on earth has potentials but few people discover them. In most cases, it requires battling or applying pressure to discover your potentials. It does not come on a platter of gold. Even though you have it within you, but you have to fight and prayerfully discover it. Education is very good and can sharpen your creativity, but your potentials distinguish you.

What it takes for the seed in you to become a big tree is within you. You only need the force of prayer to bring it to life. Without discovering your potentials and prayerfully receiving God's grace to live for God, you will not make it in the world. Our present world and generation have grown without God. Parental trainings, security and godly fears have all disappeared.

In the world today, teenagers lose their virginity without guilt or shame and get HIV at the same time. Babies are born HIV positives, and helpful drugs are scarce. The impact that these diseases have brought to the world is nothing less than a global social revolution and yet so many people around the world are still not bothered that there is problem.

According to December, 2004, UNAIDS/WHO Statistics,

- *More than 20 million people have died of Aids since 1981.*

- *Africa has 12 million Aids orphans.*

- *By December, 2004, women accounted for 47% of all people living with HIV worldwide.*

- *Young people (15-24 years old) accounted for half of all new HIV infections worldwide. More than 6,000 become infected with HIV every day.*

- *Of the 6.5 million people in developing and transitional countries who need life saving Aids drugs, fewer than 1 million are receiving them. Most of these people are rushing to eternity without Christ.*

THE DAY OF JUDGMENT IS COMING

God has set a day aside to judge the world. On the judgment day, all sinners who ever lived and died in ungodliness will be resurrected at the second resurrection, after the battle of Gog and Magog at the close of the millennium, to be judged and condemned to eternal hell.

> '*And I saw a great white throne, and him that sat on it, from whose face the earth and the heaven fled away; and there was found no place for them. And I saw the dead, small and great, stand before God; and the books were opened: and another book was opened, which is the book of life: and the dead were judged out of those things which were written in the books, according to their works. And the sea gave up the dead which were in it; and death and hell delivered up the dead which were in them: and they were judged every man according to their works. And death and hell were cast into the lake of fire. This is the second death. And whosoever was not found written in the book of life was cast into the lake of fire*' (Revelation 20:11-15).

In that day, all sinners who ever lived and died in sin will stand before the high Judge, who sits upon the great white throne, to give accounts of all their deeds on earth. The book of the record will be opened on that day by the impartial Judge, and every evil work done by every sinner will be brought into judgment and every secret thing exposed.

> '*Because he hath appointed a day, in the which he will judge the world in righteousness by that man whom he hath ordained; whereof he hath given assurance unto all men, in that he hath raised him from the dead*' (Acts 17:31).

> *'For the eyes of the Lord run to and fro throughout the whole earth, to shew himself strong in the behalf of them whose heart is perfect toward him. Herein thou hast done foolishly: therefore from henceforth thou shalt have wars'* (2 Chronicles 16:9).

All evil works and secrets are recorded in that book, and every evil intent or purpose will be exposed. Every person, small and great, will be judged according to their works.

> *'But I say unto you, That every idle word that men shall speak, they shall give account thereof in the day of judgment'* (Matthew 12:36).

> *'Neither is there any creature that is not manifest in his sight: but all things are naked and opened unto the eyes of him with whom we have to do'* (Hebrews 4:13).

Before we go further, let us see the order of events in the divine program.

THE RAPTURE OF THE CHURCH

The rapture of the church simply means the '*catching up*' of all true Christians in Christ to meet with the Lord in the sky.

> *'But I would not have you to be ignorant, brethren, concerning them which are asleep, that ye sorrow not, even as others which have no hope. For if we believe that Jesus died and rose again, even so them also which sleep in Jesus will God bring with him. For this we say unto you by the Word of the Lord, that we which are alive and remain unto the coming of the Lord shall not prevent them which are asleep. For the Lord himself shall descend from heaven with a shout, with the voice of the archangel, and with the trump of God: and the dead in Christ shall rise first: Then we which are alive and remain shall be caught up together with them in the clouds, to meet the Lord in the air: and so shall we ever be with the Lord. Wherefore comfort one another with these words'* (1 Thessalonians 4:13-18).

At the rapture, every true believer living righteously and walking in the light of Christ will be "*caught up*" in the sky to be with Christ. Moreover, true saints who also died in Christ will be resurrected and taken up to the sky to join the Lord at the same time.

> *'But every man in his own order: Christ the firstfruits; afterward they that are Christ's at his coming.... Behold, I shew you a mystery; We shall not all sleep, but we shall all be changed, In a moment, in the twinkling of an eye, at the last trump: for the trumpet shall sound, and the dead shall be raised incorruptible, and we shall be changed. For this corruptible must put on incorruption, and this mortal must put on*

> *immortality. So when this corruptible shall have put on incorruption, and this mortal shall have put on immortality, then shall be brought to pass the saying that is written, Death is swallowed up in victory. O death, where is thy sting? O grave, where is thy victory? The sting of death is sin; and the strength of sin is the law. But thanks be to God, which giveth us the victory through our Lord Jesus Christ. Therefore, my beloved brethren, be ye steadfast, unmovable, always abounding in the work of the Lord, forasmuch as ye know that your labor is not in vain in the Lord'* (1 Corinthians 15:23, 51-58)

The rapture will take place in a twinkling of an eye, without any prior notice. Prophecies, which are to be fulfilled before the rapture, are being fulfilled before our very eyes.

> *'Now the Spirit speaketh expressly, that in the latter times some shall depart from the faith, giving heed to seducing spirits, and doctrines of devils; Speaking lies in hypocrisy; having their conscience seared with a hot iron; Forbidding to marry, and commanding to abstain from meats, which God hath created to be received with thanksgiving of them which believe and know the truth'* (1 Timothy 4:1-3).

One of the strangest stories I have ever read about is the story of an American woman, who first altered her female organs to transform herself into a man, and later as a man got pregnant with a child. This is an abominable thing before God and man.

The rapture can take place any moment and anyone who is not ready to meet with the Lord remains in a terribly delicate and fearful position. At the rapture, all the righteous and just people who died will be resurrected.

> *'And I saw thrones, and they sat upon them, and judgment was given unto them: and I saw the souls of them that were beheaded for the witness of Jesus, and for the word of God, and which had not worshipped the beast, neither his image, neither had received his mark upon their foreheads, or in their hands; and they lived and reigned with Christ a thousand years. But the rest of the dead lived not again until the thousand years were finished. This is the first resurrection. Blessed and holy is he that hath part in the first resurrection: on such the second death hath no power, but they shall be priests of God and of Christ, and shall reign with him a thousand years'* (Revelation 20:4-6).

The righteous saints who suffered one thing or another for the sake of Jesus and the Word of God, and yet remained faithful until death will be resurrected first. This is called the first resurrection; the resurrection of the just or the righteous. It is at this time that Christ will finally take the saints to Himself, changing their bodies from mortality to immortality.

> *'For our conversation is in heaven; from whence also we look for the Savior, the Lord Jesus Christ: Who shall change our vile body, that it may be fashioned like unto his glorious body, according to the working whereby he is able even to subdue all things unto himself'* (Philippians 3:20-21).

The time of the rapture is a time before the tribulation when Christ will take all the saints out of this world so that they will not suffer with the sinners who will be left in the world at that time.

> *'And take heed to yourselves, lest at any time your hearts be overcharged with surfeiting, and drunkenness, and cares of this life, and so that day come upon you unawares. For as a snare shall it come on all them that dwell on the face of the whole earth. Watch ye therefore, and pray always, that ye may be accounted worthy to escape all these things that shall come to pass, and to stand before the Son of man'* (Luke 21:34-36).

It is very obvious that we are living in the last days of this age, and every wise believer should not compete with the people of the world or be complacent with standards of this world. We are warned to be ready always for Christ is coming for His bride. After the rapture, Christ will reward believers, who remained faithful to Him and His Father.

> *'We are confident, I say, and willing rather to be absent from the body, and to be present with the Lord. Wherefore we labor, that, whether present or absent, we may be accepted of him. For we must all appear before the judgment seat of Christ; that every one may receive the things done in his body, according to that he hath done, whether it be good or bad'* (2 Corinthians 5:8-10).

THE GREAT TRIBULATION

Christians and sinners who joke with their destinies will surely miss the rapture. Those who miss the rapture will remain on earth to experience the great tribulation for seven years. Like I said before, the rapture can take place any moment from now, and immediately after, follows the great tribulation for the remaining people on earth. For seven years, all careless believers and sinner will suffer greatly on earth.

> *'For thus saith the Lord; We have heard a voice of trembling, of fear, and not of peace. Ask ye now, and see whether a man doth travail with child? Wherefore do I see every man with his hands on his loins, as a woman in travail, and all faces are turned into paleness? Alas! For that day is great, so that none is like it: it is even the time of Jacob's trouble; but he shall be saved out of it'* (Jeremiah 30:5-7).

It is going to be a terrible time of trouble and fear for the people who would remain on earth. It is a period of wrath, judgment, indignation, desolation, trail, overturning and days of tribulation. Both God and devil will release their wrath upon the people on earth. Within this period of seven years, also called Daniels seventieth week, people on earth will terribly suffer.

In Daniel's prophecy, the '*Seventieth week*' refers to the seven years of great tribulation after rapture.

> *'And the ten horns out of this kingdom are ten kings that shall arise: and another shall rise after them; and he shall be diverse from the first, and he shall subdue three kings. And he shall speak great words against the*

> *most High, and shall wear out the saints of the most High, and think to change times and laws: and they shall be given into his hand until a time and times and the dividing of time. But the judgment shall sit, and they shall take away his dominion, to consume and to destroy it unto the end. And the kingdom and dominion, and the greatness of the kingdom under the whole heaven, shall be given to the people of the saints of the most High, whose kingdom is an everlasting kingdom, and all dominions shall serve and obey him'* (Daniel 7:24-27).

> *'Fulfill her week, and we will give thee this also for the service which thou shalt serve with me yet seven other years'* (Genesis 29:27).

At the beginning of the great tribulation, a red horse having the color of blood will appear to bring war and fear upon the earth. Peace will disappear and lots of people will be killed. There will be mass destructions and panic as nations will rise against each other.

> *'And when he had opened the second seal, I heard the second beast say, Come and see. And there went out another horse that was red: and power was given to him that sat thereon to take peace from the earth, and that they should kill one another: and there was given unto him a great sword'* (Revelation 6:3-4).

Another horse with a black color signifying famine during this period will also appear to starve people to death. The richest people on earth at that time will eat what prisoners eat in African prisons. There will be extreme suffering, poverty and global rationing of food. Many people will die out of hunger, and many others will become food for wild animals that will be turned loose to cause terrible deaths on earth.

> *'And when he had opened the third seal, I heard the third beast say, Come and see. And I beheld, and lo a black horse; and he that sat on him had a pair of balances in his hand. And I heard a voice in the midst of the four beasts say, A measure of wheat for a penny, and three measures of barley for a penny; and see thou hurt not the oil and the wine. And when he had opened the fourth seal, I heard the voice of the fourth beast say, Come and see. And I looked, and behold a pale horse: and his name that sat on him was Death, and Hell followed with him. And power was given unto them over the fourth part of the earth, to kill with sword, and with hunger, and with death, and with the beasts of the earth'* (Revelation 6:5-8).

The great tribulation will be very frightening, as people, who are not taken away during the rapture, will witness the full wrath of God's punishment. The earth will quake in many unexpected places. The sun will become black and the moon as blood. The stars will fall to the earth, creating fearful sights.

> *'And I beheld when he had opened the sixth seal, and, lo, there was a great earthquake; and the sun became black as sackcloth of hair, and the moon became as blood; And the stars of heaven fell unto the earth, even as a fig tree casteth her untimely figs, when she is shaken of a mighty wind. And the heaven departed as a scroll when it is rolled together; and every mountain and island were moved out of their places'* (Revelation 6:12-14).

At that time, the atmospheric heaven will suddenly be rolled away. Mountains and Island will move violently out of their positions. Cities, villages and islands will leave their former places like soldiers in war fronts. It will be a period of horror and panic, as terrible fears will grip hearts of men as seas, cities and mountains change positions to bring chaos and catastrophe on earth.

> *'And the kings of the earth, and the great men, and the rich men, and the chief captains, and the mighty men, and every bondman, and every free man, hid themselves in the dens and in the rocks of the mountains; And said to the mountains and rocks, Fall on us, and hide us from the face of him that sitteth on the throne, and from the wrath of the Lamb: For the great day of his wrath is come; and who shall be able to stand?'* (Revelation 6:15-17).

As these things take place on earth, no wise people including scientists will be able to control the situation. At that time believers who were ruptured will be enjoying with Christ in the sky. The trees and all green vegetations will be consumed by the fire of judgment.

> *'And the seven angels which had the seven trumpets prepared themselves to sound. The first angel sounded, and there followed hail and fire mingled with blood, and they were cast upon the earth: and the third part of trees was burnt up, and all green grass was burnt up. And the second angel sounded, and as it were a great mountain burning with fire was cast into the sea: and the third part of the sea became blood; And the third part of the creatures which were in the sea, and*

had life, died; and the third part of the ships were destroyed' (Revelation 8:6-9).

Great mountains will be cast away into the sea and the third part of the sea will be converted to blood. Ships will be destroyed and death will not spare any inhabitant of the sea. The waters will be poisoned and anyone that drinks it will drink poisonous water. Real darkness will be all over the world and the scientists will not be able to control the natural environment.

'And the third angel sounded, and there fell a great star from heaven, burning as it were a lamp, and it fell upon the third part of the rivers, and upon the fountains of waters; And the name of the star is called Wormwood: and the third part of the waters became wormwood; and many men died of the waters, because they were made bitter. And the fourth angel sounded, and the third part of the sun was smitten, and the third part of the moon, and the third part of the stars; so as the third part of them was darkened, and the day shone not for a third part of it, and the night likewise. And I beheld, and heard an angel flying through the midst of heaven, saying with a loud voice, Woe, woe, woe, to the inhabiters of the earth by reason of the other voices of the trumpet of the three angels, which are yet to sound!' (Revelation 8:10-13).

There will be distressing judgment all over the earth, as the bottomless pit will be opened. The bottomless pit is an intermediate place of punishment for fallen angels and demons. In a great fury, these demons will emerge from the pit as locust in large numbers coming out amidst great smoke. These horrible locusts will possess powers to sting like scorpions.

> '*And the fifth angel sounded, and I saw a star fall from heaven unto the earth: and to him was given the key of the bottomless pit. And he opened the bottomless pit; and there arose a smoke out of the pit, as the smoke of a great furnace; and the sun and the air were darkened by reason of the smoke of the pit. And there came out of the smoke locusts upon the earth: and unto them was given power, as the scorpions of the earth have power. And it was commanded them that they should not hurt the grass of the earth, neither any green thing, neither any tree; but only those men which have not the seal of God in their foreheads. And to them it was given that they should not kill them, but that they should be tormented five months: and their torment was as the torment of a scorpion, when he striketh a man. And in those days shall men seek death, and shall not find it; and shall desire to die, and death shall flee from them. And the shapes of the locusts were like unto horses prepared unto battle; and on their heads were as it were crowns like gold, and their faces were as the faces of men. And they had hair as the hair of women, and their teeth were as the teeth of lions. And they had breastplates, as it were breastplates of iron; and the sound of their wings was as the sound of chariots of many horses running to battle. And they had tails like unto scorpions, and there were stings in their tails: and their power was to hurt men five months*' (Revelation 9:1-6,10).

They will only be allowed to use their evil powers to sting men and torment them for five months without killing them.

Death itself will be warned and forbidden not to kill anyone within these five months period. This will allow the locusts the opportunity to really torment the people that will left on earth with their poisonous venous. These are not ordinary locusts that you know. However, they will be Satan himself in form of locusts.

> *'And they had a king over them, which is the angel of the bottomless pit, whose name in the Hebrew tongue is Abaddon, but in the Greek tongue hath his name Apollyon. One woe is past; and, behold, there come two woes more hereafter. And the sixth angel sounded, and I heard a voice from the four horns of the golden altar which is before God, Saying to the sixth angel which had the trumpet, Loose the four angels which are bound in the great river Euphrates. And the four angels were loosed, which were prepared for an hour, and a day, and a month, and a year, for to slay the third part of men. And the number of the army of the horsemen were two hundred thousand thousand: and I heard the number of them. And thus I saw the horses in the vision, and them that sat on them, having breastplates of fire, and of jacinth, and brimstone: and the heads of the horses were as the heads of lions; and out of their mouths issued fire and smoke and brimstone. By these three was the third part of men killed, by the fire, and by the smoke, and by the brimstone, which issued out of their mouths. For their power is in their mouth, and in their tails: for their tails were like unto serpents, and had heads, and with them they do hurt'* (Revelation 9:11-19).

The name of the leader of these demons is *Abaddon*, which means *'destroyer or destruction'*. In Greek, it will be called

Apollyon, which also means *'The one who is destroying'*. During this time, that beast called antichrist will manifest.

When he shows up, the antichrist will present himself to the world as the deliverer of all humanity. In that way, he will form one world government, and with some level of success bring temporary peace on earth three and half years before the main great tribulation. The last half of the *'week'*, that is the last half of the seven years (*3 1/2 years, or 42 months or 1,260 days*) will be so severe under the wrath of antichrist, who will break his covenant in the midst (middle) of the *week* with nations especially with Israel.

> *'And he shall confirm the covenant with many for one week: and in the midst of the week he shall cause the sacrifice and the oblation to cease, and for the overspreading of abominations he shall make it desolate, even until the consummation, and that determined shall be poured upon the desolate'* (Daniel 9:27).

> *'And deceiveth them that dwell on the earth by the means of those miracles which he had power to do in the sight of the beast; saying to them that dwell on the earth, that they should make an image to the beast, which had the wound by a sword, and did live. And he had power to give life unto the image of the beast, that the image of the beast should both speak, and cause that as many as would not worship the image of the beast should be killed. And he causeth all, both small and great, rich and poor, free and bond, to receive a mark in their right hand, or in their foreheads: And that no man might buy or sell, save he that had the mark, or the name of the beast, or the number of his*

name. Here is wisdom. Let him that hath understanding count the number of the beast: for it is the number of a man; and his number is Six hundred threescore and six' (Revelation 13:14-18).

Out of fear, many people will submit to the antichrist, and worship him as God. He will kill all those who would resist his government. He will curse God, and openly blaspheme against Him. He will war against the saints who would remain on earth.

Millions of people on earth will be killed violently and many more will be tormented. The antichrist will demand that all who accept him as god to receive the mark of the beasts in their right hands or in their foreheads. Those who refuse to comply will be denied of their rights, benefits and entitlements. None of them will be allowed to buy or sell except they accept the mark, the name of the beast or the number of his name – 666. However, all those who take on the mark, name or number of the beast will be tormented by the wrath of God and will also spend eternity in the burning lake of fire.

'And the first went, and poured out his vial upon the earth; and there fell a noisome and grievous sore upon the men which had the mark of the beast, and upon them which worshipped his image.... And the third angel followed them, saying with a loud voice, If any man worship the beast and his image, and receive his mark in his forehead, or in his hand, The same shall drink of the wine of the wrath of God, which is poured out without mixture into the cup of his indignation; and he shall be tormented with fire and brimstone in the presence of the holy angels, and in the presence of

> *the Lamb: And the smoke of their torment ascendeth up forever and ever: and they have no rest day nor night, who worship the beast and his image, and whosoever receiveth the mark of his name. Here is the patience of the saints: here are they that keep the commandments of God, and the faith of Jesus'* (Revelation 16:2,14:9-12).

Immediately after deceiving majority of the people on earth, the antichrist will mount the throne to rule forever. However, the wrath of God will come upon him from heaven. It will be the most foolish decision to cooperate with devil no matter your suffering on earth. After the very short period of fake peace from the antichrist to the world, God will strike.

> *'And I heard a great voice out of the temple saying to the seven angels, Go your ways, and pour out the vials of the wrath of God upon the earth. And the first went, and poured out his vial upon the earth; and there fell a noisome and grievous sore upon the men, which had the mark of the beast, and upon them, which worshipped his image. And the second angel poured out his vial upon the sea; and it became as the blood of a dead man: and every living soul died in the sea'* (Revelation 16:1-3).

There will be grievous sores upon men and women who take the mark of the beast or worship the image of the beast. The full wrath of God shall surely be poured on the beasts and his followers. The Lord will pour malignant sores on all the beast's worshippers. The sea will also be turned to blood and the whole sea will be affected. The springs of waters and the rivers will all be polluted.

'And I heard a great voice out of the temple saying to the seven angels, Go your ways, and pour out the vials of the wrath of God upon the earth. And the first went, and poured out his vial upon the earth; and there fell a noisome and grievous sore upon the men, which had the mark of the beast, and upon them, which worshipped his image. And the second angel poured out his vial upon the sea; and it became as the blood of a dead man: and every living soul died in the sea. And the third angel poured out his vial upon the rivers and fountains of waters; and they became blood. And I heard the angel of the waters say, Thou art righteous, O Lord, which art, and wast, and shalt be, because thou hast judged thus. For they have shed the blood of saints and prophets, and thou hast given them blood to drink; for they are worthy. And I heard another out of the altar say, Even so, Lord God Almighty, true and righteous are thy judgments. And the fourth angel poured out his vial upon the sun; and power was given unto him to scorch men with fire. And men were scorched with great heat, and blasphemed the name of God, which hath power over these plagues: and they repented not to give him glory' (Revelation 16:1-9).

To quench a thirst at that time, people will be forced to drink blood. Fountains of waters and rivers will all be under judgment universally. The sun will be too hot that everyone on earth will be scorched by it. God's judgment will also hit the seat of the beast and his evil kingdom.

At that time, the deceived and all unrepentant people on the earth trusting the fake powers of the antichrist will still refuse to repent of their deeds.

> *'And the fifth angel poured out his vial upon the seat of the beast; and his kingdom was full of darkness; and they gnawed their tongues for pain, And blasphemed the God of heaven because of their pains and their sores, and repented not of their deeds. And the sixth angel poured out his vial upon the great river Euphrates; and the water thereof was dried up, that the way of the kings of the east might be prepared'* (Revelation 16:10-12).

As they gather to fight, they will be disgraced in the battlefield. This will be called the final *battle of Armageddon*.

THE BATTLE OF ARMAGEDDON

- *(Revelation 19:15-21). After this, there will be another program called the imprisonment of Satan.*

- *(Revelation 20:1-3). Thereafter, another program that will last for one thousand years called - the millennial kingdom, takes place.*

- *(Revelation 20:4-7). The next item in the program of God is called the final judgment.*

FINAL DAY OF RECKONING

This is the great Day of Judgment; for all the dead and living sinners. All dead sinners will surely face the dreadful judgment of God.

> *'And I saw the dead, small and great, stand before God; and the books were opened: and another book was opened, which is the book of life: and the dead were judged out of those things which were written in the books, according to their works. And the sea gave up the dead, which were in it; and death and hell delivered up the dead, which were in them: and they were judged every man according to their works. And death and hell were cast into the lake of fire. This is the second death. And whosoever was not found written in the book of life was cast into the lake of fire'* (Revelation 20:12-15).

All dead sinners remain under judgment termed *awaiting trial* in hell. They will be resurrected to be finally judged by Jesus. At this time, all the dead will be raised and judged.

THE WORST PRISON YARD

In the last pages of this book, I will be discussing about the *second death.* Death itself means separation. Physical death, which is of course the *first death,* is the separation of soul and spirit from the body, while *second death* is the final and eternal separation from God.

> *'And death and hell were cast into the lake of fire. This is the second death. And whosoever was not found written in the book of life was cast into the lake of fire'* (Revelation 20:14-15).

Sinners who died without Christ will face the second death, which is also the spiritual death. They will be finally separated from God forever. What a tragedy!

> *'When the Son of man shall come in his glory, and all the holy angels with him, then shall he sit upon the throne of his glory: And before him shall be gathered all nations: and he shall separate them one from another, as a shepherd divideth his sheep from the goats: And he shall set the sheep on his right hand, but the goats on the left'* (Matthew 25:31-33).

The separation of sinners from the righteous will be done by Jesus Christ, the impartial Judge. The righteous will go to His right hand, and the sinners to His left hand. After the separation, Jesus will address each side. On His right hand will be true believers whose names are written in the Book of life. This group of people is to die once, which is physical death, and afterwards live eternal life in paradise.

All unbelievers and sinners will stand at the left hand of Jesus. These are all unjust and unrighteous people who despised every opportunity given to them to repent on earth and give their lives to Christ Jesus. Jesus will rebuke and place an eternal curse on them. They will be cast into the everlasting fire prepared for Satan and all his angles.

> *'Then shall he say also unto them on the left hand, Depart from me, ye cursed, into everlasting fire, prepared for the devil and his angels: For I was an hungred, and ye gave me no meat: I was thirsty, and ye gave me no drink: I was a stranger, and ye took me not in: naked, and ye clothed me not: sick, and in prison, and ye visited me not. Then shall they also answer him, saying, Lord, when saw we thee an hungred, or athirst, or a stranger, or naked, or sick, or in prison, and did not minister unto thee? Then shall he answer them, saying, Verily I say unto you, Inasmuch as ye did it not to one of the least of these, ye did it not to me. And these shall go away into everlasting punishment: but the righteous into life eternal'* (Matthew 25:41-46).

Satan and all sinners will go into everlasting punishment that will never end. They will be judged and punished. Every record of sin against every unbeliever, in every generation and every age since the world began, will be exposed before God.

> *'The wicked shall be turned into hell, and all the nations that forget God'* (Psalms 9:17).

> *'For Tophet is ordained of old; yea, for the king it is prepared; he hath made it deep and large: the pile thereof is fire and much wood; the breath of the Lord, like a stream of brimstone, doth kindle it'* (Isaiah 30:33).

However clever the wicked are, they must surely all die someday, and at the appointed time they will all be judged. Even those whose bodies were eaten up or consumed by veracious fishes will all be gathered together, resurrected and judged. The lake of fire will swallow Satan, all his angels, the beast, all murderers, whoremongers, sorcerers, idolaters and all liars. The lake of fire will be the worst prison yard in the entire universe. You should never ever wish to end up in this prison.

> *'But the fearful, and unbelieving, and the abominable, and murderers, and whoremongers, and sorcerers, and idolaters, and all liars, shall have their part in the lake which burneth with fire and brimstone: which is the second death'* (Revelation 21:8).

There was a young man from my village called Clement. He used to be my friend and also a relative. He was physically strong, very intelligent, smart and clever. He was the first 419[5]fraudster I ever know; a millionaire that my town never ever had. You cannot beat him in crime for he was expert in calculation and a very clever dribbler. We went to Pentecostal church together, ate together and prayed together. But he was so ambitious and vowed to be successful at all cost. He left home and went fully into fraud in the city. As a result of his new lifestyle, he went from one prison to another until he got used to prison life. He used to mock us in those days saying that heaven is like struggling during a rush hour to catch a bus in Lagos, Nigeria. He said that when it is time to go to heaven, he will push down the weak ones and enter the bus first, like he usually do in

[5] 419 – Refers to all financial crimes and advanced fee frauds punishable under the Nigerian criminal code of Law – 'Code 419', in the Nigerian Constitution.

Lagos. He even boasted that no one should border burying him when he dies, since the Lagos State Local government will be forced to pick his body and bury him by the time he begins to decay and smell.

> *'The same shall drink of the wine of the wrath of God, which is poured out without mixture into the cup of his indignation; and he shall be tormented with fire and brimstone in the presence of the holy angels, and in the presence of the Lamb: And the smoke of their torment ascendeth up forever and ever: and they have no rest day nor night, who worship the beast and his image, and whosoever receiveth the mark of his name'* (Revelation 14:10-11).

He refused to belong to any group meeting or church. But the day death came to his doorsteps, he cried like a baby. Surely, he must have recognized his folly and felt the pains of death. Pains of death are different from pains of hell fire. Jesus Christ himself warned us against the danger of hell fire.

> *'And if thy hand offend thee, cut it off: it is better for thee to enter into life maimed, than having two hands to go into hell, into the fire that never shall be quenched: Where their worm dieth not, and the fire is not quenched. And if thy foot offend thee, cut it off: it is better for thee to enter halt into life, than having two feet to be cast into hell, into the fire that never shall be quenched: Where their worm dieth not, and the fire is not quenched. And if thine eye offend thee, pluck it out: it is better for thee to enter into the kingdom of God with one eye, than having two eyes to be cast into*

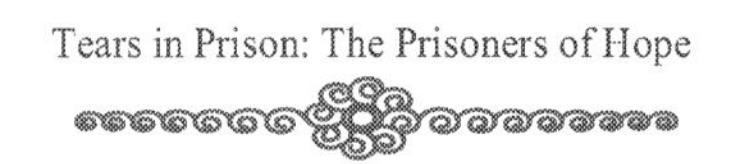

> *hell fire: Where their worm dieth not, and the fire is not quenched'* (Mark 9:43-48).

There was a man who lived all his life fighting God and His Word. He was an avowed enemy of God. His name was Crowell. He too realized his mistakes too late. He said, *'The devil is ready to seduce us, and I have been seduced'.*[6] Sir Thomas Scotch believed in God's judgment only when it was too late for him. In his last words, he cried in anguish, *'Until this moment, I thought there was neither a God nor hell. Now I know and feel that they are, both, and am doomed to perdition by the just judgment of the almighty'.*[7] The rich man in the book of Luke realized his mistakes only in hell fire and he cried out in torments,

> *'….Father Abraham, have mercy on me, and send Lazarus, that he may dip the tip of his finger in water, and cool my tongue; for I am tormented in this flame'* (Luke 16:23-24).

Whether you believe it or not, one day you will surely die. And after death comes judgment. Tom Paine lived his life fighting against God and even put his hatred against God in writing. He was born in Thedford, England, in 1737 and witnessed the revival by George Whitefield. Few hours before his death, an eyewitness heard him cry, *'O Lord, help me! O God Help me! Jesus Christ, help me! O, God! What have I done to suffer so much?'*[8]Moments later, he was repossessed by demons and he said, *'But there is not God!'* Yet again, he said, *'Yet if there be, what would become of me hereafter?'*

---

[6] Smith E. Airen, *Mystery of The Holy Spirit* – (Church Media Service: Lagos), 2008, pg. 428.
[7] Ibid, pg. 428.
[8] Ibid, pg. 427.

When the elderly woman who was attending to him was leaving the room, Tom Paine said, *'Stay with me, for God's sake! For I cannot bear to be left alone! It is hell to be left alone'*. By the time he gave up the Ghost, his last words were, *'My God, My God, why hast thou forsaken me?'*[9] Thomas Hobbes, the great atheist cried in his dying hour before he died, *'I am taking a fearful leap into the dark'*.[10]What a soul will suffer in hell fire cannot be compared to the whole suffering on earth gathered together and heaped upon one person's head.

> *'And if thy right eye offend thee, pluck it out, and cast it from thee: for it is profitable for thee that one of thy members should perish, and not that thy whole body should be cast into hell'* (Matthew 5:29).

The above Scripture is a very serious warning from Jesus Christ himself. Regardless of whatever struggles, suffering and pain you are going through in prison now, never pray or wish to die without Christ. Do not postpone your decision to receive salvation from Christ today for tomorrow may be too late. Today is a day of grace, mercy and salvation. Grab it and seek for God's favor. You can be forgiven and blessed once again.

> *'Seek ye the Lord while he may be found, call ye upon him while he is near'* (Isaiah 55:6).

> *'(For he saith, I have heard thee in a time accepted, and in the day of salvation have I succored thee: behold, now is the accepted time; behold, now is the day of salvation)'* (2 Corinthians 6:2).

---

[9] Smith E. Airen, *Mystery of The Holy Spirit* – (Church Media Service: Lagos), 2008, pg. 427

[10] Ibid, pg. 428

Charles IX of France lamented, *'What blood, what murders, what evil counsels have I followed! I am lost! I see it well!'*[11]You may not have another or better opportunity than the opportunity you have now. Give your life to Christ now, beloved. Always remember that all unrepentant sinners will be separated from God forever, and banished to the lake of fire forever. Now that you can take the water of life freely and drink from the cup of salvation, do not fail yourself. Jesus Christ has paid for all your sins and guilt so you can be free.

> *'If ye then be risen with Christ, seek those things which are above, where Christ sitteth on the right hand of God. Set your affection on things above, not on things on the earth'* (Colossians 3:1-2).
>
> *'But he that is joined unto the Lord is one spirit'* (1 Corinthians 6:17).

Set your affection on things above and let your ambitions be affected by the Word of God. Do not set your affection on things on earth, or people. Get rid of anything that opposes or is in collision with God's Word for your life. Sacrifice them to God in the altar of the Lord. And all will be well with you.

[11] Smith E. Airen, *Mystery of The Holy Spirit* – (Church Media Service: Lagos), 2008, pg. 428

Chapter

WARFARE SECTION

TO BE DISCHARGED AND ACQUITTED

'And, behold, the angel of the Lord came upon him, and a light shined in the prison: and he smote Peter on the side, and raised him up, saying, Arise up quickly. And his chains fell off from his hands. And the angel said unto him, Gird thyself, and bind on thy sandals. And so he did. And he saith unto him, Cast thy garment about thee, and follow me. And he went out, and followed him; and wist not that it was true which was done by the angel; but thought he saw a vision. When they were past the first and the second ward, they came unto the iron gate that leadeth unto the city; which opened to them of his own accord: and they went out, and passed on through one street; and forthwith the angel departed from him' (Acts 12:7-10)

Prayers to be discharged and acquitted are prayers designed to vindicate accused persons who are yet to be tried and judged. Such prayers are necessitated by the fact that many peoples' cases have been pushed aside and often neglected for years without being called up or addressed. In such cases, persons who are involved are remanded in prisons beyond the time stipulated by the law. Joseph too was arrested and unjustly imprisoned without any fair trial.

'And it came to pass, when she saw that he had left his garment in her hand, and was fled forth, That she called unto the men of her house, and spake unto them, saying, See, he hath brought in an Hebrew unto us to mock us; he came in unto me to lie with me, and I cried with a loud voice: And it came to pass, when he heard that I lifted up my voice and cried, that he left his garment with me, and fled, and got him out. And she laid up his garment by her, until his lord came home. And she spake unto him according to these words, saying, The Hebrew servant, which thou hast brought unto us, came in unto me to mock me: And it came to pass, as I lifted up my voice and cried, that he left his garment with me, and fled out. And it came to pass, when his master heard the words of his wife, which she spake unto him, saying, After this manner did thy servant to me; that his wrath was kindled' (Genesis 39:13-19).

'Wherein they think it strange that ye run not with them to the same excess of riot, speaking evil of you: Who shall give account to him that is ready to judge the quick and the dead' (1 Peter 4:4-5).

'Doth our law judge any man, before it hear him, and know what he doeth?' (John 7:51).

Potiphar ordered Joseph's imprisonment without giving him any fair trial (*See* Psalms 105:17-20, Genesis 39:20). Today, there are thousands of prisoners like Joseph in prisons across world. As an accused person waiting for judgment, if you do not pray these prayers to be discharged and acquitted, you may end your life in prison or stay longer than necessary.

However, if you are guilty of offenses you are accused of, you still need to pray these prayers to be discharged and acquitted to obtain quick and fair trial. As a prisoner of hope, give your life to Christ before praying these prayers below. Effectual prayers can reduce your stay in prison, and get you discharged and acquitted. You can be extraordinarily favored, vindicated and yet granted divine pardon. Start praying now, and do not stop praying until you are released and sent back to your rightful position in your family.

PRAYERS TO BE DISCHARGED AND ACQUITTED

1. Father Lord, help me not to overstay in this place, in the name of Jesus.

2. Any power assigned to prolong my stay in this place, be frustrated now, in the name of Jesus.

3. O Lord, arise in your power and discharge me from this place, in the name of Jesus.

4. I command magistrates and judges handling my case to favor me now, in the name of Jesus.

5. Lord Jesus, discharge and acquit me by Your power, in the name of Jesus.

6. Let forces of darkness delaying my judgment die, in the name of Jesus.

7. Holy Ghost fire, burn to ashes every yoke of bondage in my life, in the name of Jesus.

8. Blood of Jesus, flow into the courtroom and influence my judgment for good, in the name of Jesus.

9. Any evil personality assigned to convert my judgment to failure, die, in the name of Jesus.

10. Fire of God, consume every false report written against me, in the name of Jesus.

11. Let all officials assigned to decide my case favor me, in the name of Jesus.

12. I command divine influence to overshadow every evil case against me, in the name of Jesus.

13. Let any lawyer working in this case against me receive confusion, in the name of Jesus.

14. Let my enemies make great mistakes in court that will favor me, in the name of Jesus.

15. Holy Ghost fire, consume every document designed to implicate me, in the name of Jesus.

16. O Lord, arise and deliver me from wicked people, in the name of Jesus.

17. Anything that will happen for me to be released out of this place, happen now, in the name of Jesus.

18. Lord Jesus, discharge and acquit me to Your own glory, in the name of Jesus.

19. I fire back every arrow of imprisonment fired against me in this place, in the name of Jesus.

20. Any work of native doctors and herbalists working against me, fail woefully, in the name of Jesus.

21. Father Lord, take over my case and release me miraculously, in the name of Jesus.

22. I walk out of this place a free man(or woman) forever and ever, in the name of Jesus.

TO REVERSE YOUR JUDGMENT

> *'Then Pharaoh sent and called Joseph, and they brought him hastily out of the dungeon: and he shaved himself, and changed his raiment, and came in unto Pharaoh… And Pharaoh said unto Joseph, Forasmuch as God hath shewed thee all this, there is none so discreet and wise as thou art: Thou shalt be over my house, and according unto thy word shall all my people be ruled: only in the throne will I be greater than thou. And Pharaoh said unto Joseph, See, I have set thee over all the land of Egypt. And Pharaoh took off his ring from his hand, and put it upon Joseph's hand, and arrayed him in vestures of fine linen, and put a gold chain about his neck; And he made him to ride in the second chariot which he had; and they cried before him, Bow the knee: and he made him ruler over all the land of Egypt. And Pharaoh said unto Joseph, I am Pharaoh, and without thee shall no man lift up his hand or foot in all the land of Egypt'* (Genesis 41:14, 39-44).

Joseph's reactions to his betrayal, maltreatment and misfortune were all remarkably different as compared to the way many prisoners would react today. It is common among prisoners today to be filled with deeply rooted bitterness, hatred, anger, ill feelings, strong desires for revenge and other negative and wicked feelings. Such prisoners can never forgive people who offended them or caused them to be put in prison.

But the truth is that when you determinedly refuse to forgive and let go, you also throw away your chances of having any relationship with God, and your prayers will become meaningless and cannot be answered (*See* Matthew 18:23-35, 7:1-2, James 2:13). God commanded that you should forgive your offenders as God also forgives you of your own grievous sins (*See* Matthew 5:39-46, 6:12-15, Matthew 18:21-22, Luke 6:35-37, Romans 12:14, 17, 19, 21, Mark 11:25-26).

Moses forgave the Israelites (*See* Exodus 32:7-14, 31-33).

Joseph forgave his brothers (*See* Genesis 45:5-15, 50:19-21).

David forgave Saul (*See* 1 Samuel 24:1-22, 9: 1-13).

Solomon forgave Adonijah (*See* 1 Kings 1:41-53).

The prophet forgave Jeroboam (*See* 1 Kings 13:1-6)

Stephen forgave his persecutors (*See* Acts 7:54-60).

Jesus forgave His executioners (*See* Luke 23: 34).

When you are innocent and an unjust judgment is passed against you, forgive those concerned and pray the prayers provided in this book. If you remain true to Christ, and faithful to God like Joseph, all injustices against you will be reversed or overturned at the fullness of time (*See* Genesis 39:4-6, Ecclesiastes 9:10, 1 Corinthians 15:58, 4:2, Titus 2:9, 10, 1 Peter 2:18, Psalms 75:6-7, Daniel 3:30).

Complaining, murmuring, feelings of bitterness, petitioning, regretting, fighting back or planning for revenge without prayers will never help you. You may even do other things that do not contradict the law, but without effective prayers all your efforts will amount to nothing. These prayers will reverse every evil verdict or delays to your freedom and set you free miraculously. No occult manipulation, evil gang-up, or even your enemies' plans against you will stand as you pray these prayers.

> *'Behold, they shall surely gather together, but not by me: whosoever shall gather together against thee shall fall for thy sake. Behold, I have created the smith that bloweth the coals in the fire, and that bringeth forth an instrument for his work; and I have created the waster to destroy. No weapon that is formed against thee shall prosper; and every tongue that shall rise against thee in judgment thou shalt condemn. This is the heritage of the servants of the Lord, and their righteousness is of me, saith the Lord'* (Isaiah 54:15-17).

Your enemies do not have the final say. God has the final say.

PRAYERS TO REVERSE YOUR JUDGMENT

1. Any evil conclusion or verdict against my life, be reversed immediately, in the name of Jesus.
2. Fire of God, burn to ashes evil handwritings assigned to implicate me, in the name of Jesus.
3. O Lord, arise, take over my case and let it end to my favor, in the name of Jesus.
4. Blood of Jesus, flow into this place and change my verdict, in the name of Jesus.
5. Every occult agreement affecting my case, I reverse you now, in the name of Jesus.
6. You that power delaying my judgment, I cut you off, in the name of Jesus.
7. Anointing to leave this prison victoriously, fall upon me now, in the name of Jesus.
8. Heavenly Father, meet me in the court and reverse my case, in the name of Jesus.
9. Every determined enemy working against my deliverance, scatter, in the name of Jesus.
10. I fire back every arrow of detention fired into my life, in the name of Jesus.
11. O Lord, arise and perfect my freedom by force, in the name Jesus.
12. Any evil conclusion or conviction against my destiny, fail woefully, in the name of Jesus.

13. I cancel every occult manipulation to pervert my judgment, in the name of Jesus.

14. Let the police and lawyers handling my case end my case to my favor, in the name of Jesus.

15. You my destiny, refuse to be caged by your enemies, in the name of Jesus.

16. Let all demons following me to pervert my judgment die, in the name of Jesus.

17. Every evil decision against me, be reversed immediately, in the name of Jesus.

18. You the facts that will set me free, what are you waiting for? Manifest now, in the name of Jesus.

19. Lord Jesus, envelop my life with divine freedom, in the name of Jesus.

20. O Lord, arise and frustrate all my enemies in police and the court, in the name of Jesus.

21. I command every change that will bring about my freedom to come now, in the name of Jesus.

I REFUSE TO DIE IN PRISON

> *'Then spake the chief butler unto Pharaoh, saying, I do remember my faults this day: Pharaoh was wroth with his servants, and put me in ward in the captain of the guard's house, both me and the chief baker: And we dreamed a dream in one night, I and he; we dreamed each man according to the interpretation of his dream. And there was there with us a young man, an Hebrew, servant to the captain of the guard; and we told him, and he interpreted to us our dreams; to each man according to his dream he did interpret. And it came to pass, as he interpreted to us, so it was; me he restored unto mine office, and him he hanged'* (Genesis 41:9-13).

Millions of prisoners all over the world go through lots of human sufferings daily. Thousands have died without witnessing justice. One of the purposes of this book is to make your case different. Whether you have fallen sick in prison, dejected, hated, oppressed or about to die, you need to pray these prayers to live beyond the prison bars.

Have you lost hope already or have you given up life? Please cheer up today; repent of all your sins and start praying these prayers. Even when it has become apparent that your relatives have forgotten you, and had shared all your properties concluding that you will not come out alive, pray these prayers with all diligence and you will not die, but be discharged and acquitted soon.

> *'Now about that time Herod the king stretched forth his hands to vex certain of the church. And he killed James the brother of John with the sword. And because he saw it pleased the Jews, he proceeded further to take Peter also. (Then were the days of unleavened bread.) And when he had apprehended him, he put him in prison, and delivered him to four quaternions of soldiers to keep him; intending after Easter to bring him forth to the people. Peter therefore was kept in prison: but prayer was made without ceasing of the church unto God for him'* (Acts 12:1-5).

> *'And a certain man was there, which had an infirmity thirty and eight years. When Jesus saw him lie, and knew that he had been now a long time in that case, he saith unto him, Wilt thou be made whole? The impotent man answered him, Sir, I have no man, when the water is troubled, to put me into the pool: but while I am coming, another steppeth down before me. Jesus saith unto him, Rise, take up thy bed, and walk. And*

immediately the man was made whole, and took up his bed, and walked: and on the same day was the Sabbath' (John 5:5-9)

Jesus healed all manner of diseases (*See* Matthew 4:23-25). He fed five thousand hungry followers (*See* Matthew 14: 15-21). He cast out spirit of lunatic, raised Lazarus from dead, raised the only son of a widow who was being carried out of the city for burial, calmed great storms that rose against his disciples, opened prison doors for Daniel, Joseph, Peter, Paul and Silas, and took a thief to paradise from the cross (*See* Matthew 17:14-18, John 11:1-3, 11-45, Luke 7:11-17, Luke 8:22-25, Acts 12:1-17, Daniel 6:1-28, Luke 23:40-43). There is nothing that Jesus cannot do. Your case is a simple one before Him.

Your prayers here will not only deliver you from physical death, it will deliver you also from spiritual death. You will come out of prison alive and be promoted and honored with abundant life, if only you can let Jesus be in charge of your life today.

PRAYERS TO REFUSE TO DIE IN PRISON

1. Every arrow of spiritual death fired into my life, I fire you back to your sender, in the name of Jesus.

2. I command every spirit of death that has entered into my life to die, in the name of Jesus.

3. I break and loose myself from every covenant of death, in the name of Jesus.

4. I refuse to surrender to death assigned to waste my destiny, in the name of Jesus.

5. Holy Ghost fire, burn to ashes every seed of death planted into my life, in the name of Jesus.

6. Blood of Jesus, erase every mark of death in any area of my life, in the name of Jesus.

7. Fire of God, burn to ashes every agent of death in my life, in the name of Jesus.

8. O Lord, arise and deliver me from the grip of death, in the name of Jesus.

9. Let the power of God take me away from every evil arrest, in the name of Jesus.

10. Heavenly father, deliver me from the mouth of hungry lions, in the name of Jesus.

11. Every yoke of death in my life, break to pieces, in the name of Jesus.

12. Any evil power pursuing me from the grave, die, in the name of Jesus.

13. Demons from dark rooms of my father's house, be frustrated to death, in the name of Jesus.

14. O Lord, arise and scatter every evil gang-up against me, in the name of Jesus.

15. Let the fire of death inside me be quenched now, in the name of Jesus.

16. Every arrow of sickness and disease in my life, come out and be broken, in the name of Jesus.

17. You my life, escape from every sword of death, in the name of Jesus.

18. Powers that killed other people here in prison, I am not your candidate, release me now, in the name of Jesus.

19. Environmental demons assigned to waste my life, be wasted, in the name of Jesus.

20. Every messenger of death attacking me in this place, I reject your message, in the name of Jesus.

TO HAVE YOUR CASE STRUCK OUT

'And it came to pass, when she saw that he had left his garment in her hand, and was fled forth, That she called unto the men of her house, and spake unto them, saying, See, he hath brought in an Hebrew unto us to mock us; he came in unto me to lie with me, and I cried with a loud voice: And it came to pass, when he heard that I lifted up my voice and cried, that he left his garment with me, and fled, and got him out. And she laid up his garment by her, until his lord came home. And she spake unto him according to these words, saying, The Hebrew servant, which thou hast brought unto us, came in unto me to mock me: And it came to pass, as I lifted up my voice and cried, that he left his garment with me, and fled out. And it came to pass, when his master heard the words of his wife, which she spake unto him, saying, After this manner did thy servant to me; that his wrath was kindled' (Genesis 39:13-19).

'Wherein they think it strange that ye run not with them to the same excess of riot, speaking evil

of you: Who shall give account to him that is ready to judge the quick and the dead' (1 Peter 4:4-5).

'Doth our law judge any man, before it hear him, and know what he doeth?' (John 7:51).

When Joseph saw himself in a new environment, he remained faithful to his God. For those who walk by sight, a change in physical environment can easily lead them to change their attitude, character, or even change their religion or God. But Joseph remained faithful to God while in Potiphar's house. He rejected an invitation from a demon-possessed woman to commit fornication.

'And it came to pass after these things that his master's wife cast her eyes upon Joseph; and she said, Lie with me. But he refused, and said unto his master's wife, Behold, my master wotteth not what is with me in the house, and he hath committed all that he hath to my hand; There is none greater in this house than I; neither hath he kept back anything from me but thee, because thou art his wife: how then can I do this great wickedness, and sin against God? And it came to pass, as she spake to Joseph day by day that he hearkened not unto her, to lie by her, or to be with her. And it came to pass about this time that Joseph went into the house to do his business; and there was none of the men of the house there within. And she caught him by his garment,

> *saying, Lie with me: and he left his garment in her hand, and fled, and got him out'* (Genesis 39:7-12).

When he was accused wrongly and unjustly imprisoned, he remained calm and trusted God. He must have prayed a lot instead of complaining, murmuring or feeling bitter towards people around him. Many prisoners fight their battles carnally and always lose. You need to pray and believe God for your release and it will surely come to pass.

> *'Moreover the word of the Lord came unto Jeremiah the second time, while he was yet shut up in the court of the prison, saying, Thus saith the Lord the maker thereof, the Lord that formed it, to establish it; the Lord is his name; Call unto me, and I will answer thee, and shew thee great and mighty things, which thou knowest not'* (Jeremiah 33:1-3).

Millions of prisoners across the world have lost all hopes because there were unjustly accused and imprisoned. But if you would faithfully pray the prayers in this book trusting God, you will be delivered regardless of presently dire conditions you are in.

> *'When Jesus saw him lie, and knew that he had been now a long time in that case, he saith unto him, Wilt thou be made whole? The impotent man answered him, Sir, I have no man, when the water is troubled, to put me into the pool: but while I am*

> *coming, another steppeth down before me.'* (John 5:6-7).

Giving your life to Christ and remaining faithful to His Word is a key that can open doors for you and draw numerous answers to your prayers. God told Jeremiah that if he prays, He (*God*) will deliver him and show him greater things than he ever knew. He prayed and God used him to write Jeremiah chapters 34 to 52, with the five chapters of the book of Lamentations. God can do all things, and there is nothing God cannot do. Nothing!

PRAYERS TO HAVE YOUR CASE STRUCK OUT

1. Father Lord, influence my case to be struck out of the court in my favor, in the name of Jesus.

2. Any power assigned to destroy me with this case, I cut your head off, in the name of Jesus.

3. Blood of Jesus, take away my case from police and the court mysteriously, in the name of Jesus.

4. Fire of God, burn to ashes every document filed against me, in the name of Jesus.

5. I command the magistrate or judge in charge of my case to strike it out to my favor, in the name of Jesus.

6. Let all evidence lined up against me, be reversed to favor me, in the name of Jesus.

7. Any problem assigned to waste my time in vain, be wasted, in the name of Jesus.

8. Lord Jesus, arise and terminate every case against my life, in the name of Jesus.

9. Let all evil conspiracies against me be reversed to my favor, in the name of Jesus.

10. Every evil gang up against my life, scatter in shame, in the name of Jesus.

11. Any evil personality that has vowed to waste my life through this case, fail woefully, in the name of Jesus.

12. Let all false witnesses gathered against me be nullified, in the name of Jesus.

13. O Lord, arise and deliver me from this case of destruction, in the name of Jesus.

14. Let every case file produced against me disappear forever, in the name of Jesus.

15. O hand of God, rewrite my case to my favor, in the name of Jesus.

16. Let every satanic agenda against me in this case fail woefully, in the name of Jesus.

17. Lord Jesus, delete evil handwriting drawn against my destiny, in the name of Jesus.

18. Any evil program going on against my life, be terminated, in the name of Jesus.

19. O Lord, arise and deliver me from every evil verdict prepared against me, in the name of Jesus.

TO RECEIVE PARDON

'And at midnight Paul and Silas prayed, and sang praises unto God: and the prisoners heard them. And suddenly there was a great earthquake, so that the foundations of the prison were shaken: and immediately all the doors were opened, and every one's bands were loosed. And the keeper of the prison awaking out of his sleep, and seeing the prison doors open, he drew out his sword, and would have killed himself, supposing that the prisoners had been fled. But Paul cried with a loud voice, saying, Do thyself no harm: for we are all here. Then he called for a light, and sprang in, and came trembling, and fell down before Paul and Silas, And brought them out, and said, Sirs, what must I do to be saved? And they said, Believe on the Lord Jesus Christ, and thou shalt be saved, and thy house. And they spake unto him the word of the Lord, and to all that were in his house. And he took them the same hour of the night, and washed their stripes; and was baptized, he and all his, straightway. And when he had brought them into his house, he set meat before them, and rejoiced, believing in God with all his

house. And when it was day, the magistrates sent the serjeants, saying, Let those men go. And the keeper of the prison told this saying to Paul, The magistrates have sent to let you go: now therefore depart, and go in peace. But Paul said unto them, They have beaten us openly uncondemned, being Romans, and have cast us into prison; and now do they thrust us out privily? Nay verily; but let them come themselves and fetch us out. And the serjeants told these words unto the magistrates: and they feared, when they heard that they were Romans. And they came and besought them, and brought them out, and desired them to depart out of the city. And they went out of the prison, and entered into the house of Lydia and when they had seen the brethren, they comforted them, and departed' (Acts 16:25-40)

Prayers for pardon after being found guilty, judged and condemned are very necessary. When you truly repent of all your offenses, confess them and forsake all your sins, God will make a way for you to be released without negotiations. There is nothing God cannot do.

'When a man's ways please the Lord, he maketh even his enemies to be at peace with him' (Proverbs 16:7).

When God pardons a prisoner, no man or woman has power to bring such person under condemnation (*See* Romans 8:31-39). With the prayers in this book, you can pray your name into the list of people that will be pardoned in a shortest time. It has never been an obligation under any law that you must finish serving your prison terms. Rise up today, repent truly and pray for pardon, release and rehabilitation, and God in His infinite mercies will hear your prayers.

Joseph did not finish his prison terms. Daniel, Peter, Paul and Silas all came out before their jail terms were over. The secret is repentance, salvation, obedience to God's Word and prayers. Beloved, I counsel you to start praying today while believing God for His pardon and all will be well with you.

PRAYERS TO RECEIVE PARDON

1. Wind of Holy Ghost, bring divine mercy upon my life today, in the name of Jesus.

2. Any power working against my pardon, die, in the name of Jesus.

3. Blood of Jesus, plead on my behalf, in the name of Jesus.

4. Let the voice of my heavenly Father declare my freedom by force, in the name of Jesus.

5. Evil powers of my father's house working against my freedom, die, in the name of Jesus.

6. Every stumbling block to my freedom, disappear by force, in the name of Jesus.

7. Lord Jesus, speak death to every enemy of my freedom, in the name of Jesus.

8. Let forces of darkness gathering against my freedom scatter by force, in the name of Jesus.

9. O Lord, arise and deliver me from every demonic postponement, in the name of Jesus.

10. I command every satanic roadblock in my life to be removed forever, in the name of Jesus.

11. You that evil personality delaying my freedom, die, in the name of Jesus.

12. I decree that the transfer that will affect my pardon will not be delayed, in the name of Jesus.

13. Any evil assignment standing against my deliverance, be terminated, in the name of Jesus.

14. Fire of God, burn to ashes every document filed against my freedom, in the name of Jesus.

15. Every enemy of my pardon, you are wicked, die, in the name of Jesus.

16. Any wicked transfer designed to delay my freedom, I stop you now, in the name of Jesus.

17. O Lord, send to me men and women that will affect my freedom from prison, in the name of Jesus.

18. I command any person's retirement that will cause my pardon to manifest to occur, in the name of Jesus.

19. Any evil vow made to waste my life, break, in the name of Jesus.

20. Spirit of bribery and corruption sitting upon my life, be exposed to death, in the name of Jesus.

21. Father Lord, move away every mountain standing against my liberation, in the name of Jesus.

22. Every evil mouth speaking against me, be closed forever, in the name of Jesus.

23. O Lord, raise up great people that will command my freedom, in the name of Jesus.

TO DISCOVER YOURSELF

'And it came to pass after these things, that the butler of the king of Egypt and his baker had offended their lord the king of Egypt. And Pharaoh was wroth against two of his officers, against the chief of the butlers, and against the chief of the bakers. And he put them in ward in the house of the captain of the guard, into the prison, the place where Joseph was bound. And the captain of the guard charged Joseph with them, and he served them: and they continued a season in ward. And they dreamed a dream both of them, each man his dream in one night, each man according to the interpretation of his dream, the butler and the baker of the king of Egypt, which were bound in the prison. And Joseph came in unto them in the morning, and looked upon them, and, behold, they were sad. And he asked Pharaoh's officers that were with him in the ward of his lord's house, saying, Wherefore look ye so sadly today? And they said unto him, We have dreamed a dream, and there is no interpreter of it. And Joseph said unto them, Do not interpretations belong to God? Tell me them, I

pray you. And the chief butler told his dream to Joseph, and said to him, In my dream, behold, a vine was before me; And in the vine were three branches: and it was as though it budded, and her blossoms shot forth; and the clusters thereof brought forth ripe grapes: And Pharaoh's cup was in my hand: and I took the grapes, and pressed them into Pharaoh's cup, and I gave the cup into Pharaoh's hand. And Joseph said unto him, This is the interpretation of it: The three branches are three days: Yet within three days shall Pharaoh lift up thine head, and restore thee unto thy place: and thou shalt deliver Pharaoh's cup into his hand, after the former manner when thou wast his butler' (Genesis 40:1-13).

In the above account, the chief butler discovered his destiny while serving his prison terms. The problem with so many prisoners today is that they undermine possibilities of discovering God's purposes for their lives on earth while in prison. Though Satan has labored a lot to waste your life, he will not succeed, in the name of Jesus.

'For David, after he had served his own generation by the will of God, fell on sleep, and was laid unto his fathers, and saw corruption' (Acts 13:36).

'But Daniel purposed in his heart that he would not defile himself with the portion of the king's meat, nor with the wine which he drank: therefore

he requested of the prince of the eunuchs that he might not defile himself' (Daniel 1:8).

'If the foundations be destroyed, what can the righteous do?' (Psalms 11:3).

Ending up in a prison does not make you a loser. You can come out of prison and still make it in life. Nelson Mandela spent twenty-seven (27) years in prison. Like Joseph in the Bible, he came out to become the first black president of South Africa. Olusegun Obasanjo was once a prisoner. He came out also to become the only president who has ruled Nigeria a second time. So who has lied to you that being in prison is the end of your life? Many people have come out of prison to become great leaders of their time. You can become a great leader in your generation tomorrow if you do the right thing today.

Instead of destruction, when you pray, you will be promoted, delivered and converted to an instrument of deliverance for many other people. Whatever you are going through now, if you can open your heart for Jesus Christ and ask Him to come in and be in charge of your life, you will be delivered and set free. This book is designed to produce leaders that will liberate the world.

PRAYERS TO DISCOVER YOURSELF

1. O Lord, why am I here on earth? Show me now, in the name of Jesus.
2. Any power attacking my eyes and ears, stop and die, in the name of Jesus.
3. Fire of God, pass through my ears and cause me to hear God's voice, in the name of Jesus.
4. Blood of Jesus, cleanse me and reveal my real self to me and to the world, in the name of Jesus.
5. Heavenly Father, take me to my place of inheritance on earth, in the name of Jesus.
6. Let evil forces blocking my view scatter and die, in the name of Jesus.
7. Father Lord, arise and take me away from fake life of fantasy, in the name of Jesus.
8. Father Lord, You designed my original destiny, please cause it to manifest now, in the name of Jesus.
9. Any evil power attacking my potentials, I command you to die now, in the name of Jesus.
10. Any disease preventing me from discovering myself, die without mercy, in the name of Jesus.
11. You my dream life, change to my favor, in the name of Jesus.
12. O Lord, arise and reveal to me why you created me, in the name of Jesus.

13. Let all evil forces of darkness assigned to divert my destiny receive death, in the name of Jesus.

14. Heavenly Father, guide me into my divinely appointed destiny, in the name of Jesus.

15. Any power hiding me from good things, expose me by force, in the name of Jesus.

16. You altars of my father's house, release my arrested destiny and disappear, in the name of Jesus.

17. Any ancestral limitation over my life, catch fire and be consumed completely, in the name of Jesus.

18. I recover my destiny from dark rooms of satanic kingdoms, in the name of Jesus.

19. You my true destiny, wherever you are, appear now, in the name of Jesus.

20. Every agent of confusion in my life, surrender to me today and die, in the name of Jesus.

21. Anointing to manifest and prevail, fall upon me, in the name of Jesus.

22. Any power standing against my progress, receive destruction, in the name of Jesus.

FOR DELIVERANCE WHILE IN PRISON

'But upon mount Zion shall be deliverance, and there shall be holiness; and the house of Jacob shall possess their possessions' (Obadiah 1:17).

'How God anointed Jesus of Nazareth with the Holy Ghost and with power: who went about doing good, and healing all that were oppressed of the devil; for God was with him' (Acts 10:38).

'Shall the prey be taken from the mighty, or the lawful captive delivered? But thus saith the Lord, Even the captives of the mighty shall be taken away, and the prey of the terrible shall be delivered: for I will contend with him that contendeth with thee, and I will save thy children. And I will feed them that oppress thee with their own flesh; and they shall be drunken with their own blood, as with sweet wine: and all flesh shall know that I the Lord am thy Savior and thy Redeemer, the mighty One of Jacob' (Isaiah 49:24-26).

There is no level of bondage Jesus cannot break if you give Him the chance. One good thing to note about Christ's deliverances is that He delivers from both physical and spiritual bondages regardless of levels of damage devil has inflicted already. When all possessed people came to Him, and people with all manner of sicknesses, diseases and madness, He healed and delivered them all (*See* Matthew 4:23-25).

Others went to Him with palsy, fever, blindness, deafness, withered hands, poverty, hunger, unclean spirits, leprosy, plagues, issue of blood, fear and all evil works, He delivered them all without negotiating with Satan (*See* Matthew 8:5-13, 14, 15, 9:27-31, Mark 7:31-37, Mark 3:1-5, 8:1-9, Luke 17:11-19, Mark 3:10, 11, 5:25-34, Matthew 14:22-32).

Any evil power that has vowed to swallow you will not have victory over you. Through these prayers here, you can revoke all evil verdicts; remove evil embargoes and limitations, and walk out of every bondage. No evil decree or judgment can stand against the delivering power of Jesus Christ.

PRAYERS FORDELIVERANCE WHILE IN PRISON

1. Deliverance fire of God, take me away from bondage, in the name of Jesus.

2. Any serpent of confinement keeping me here in prison, die, in the name of Jesus.

3. O Lord, arise and deliver me from captivity, in the name of Jesus.

4. Any power keeping me away from my helpers, release me by force, in the name of Jesus.

5. Every chain of bondage holding me down, break to pieces, in the name of Jesus.

6. Lord Jesus, take me back to my inheritance, in the name of Jesus.

7. Any evil padlock assigned to waste my life, break and release me, in the name of Jesus.

8. I decree that I will find favor before those who will influence my deliverance, in the name of Jesus.

9. Any invisible yoke holding me down, break and release me, in the name of Jesus.

10. Everlasting God, give me everlasting deliverance, in the name of Jesus.

11. O Lord, break every protocol and deliver me from this place, in the name of Jesus.

12. Powers of darkness assigned to keep me here forever, be wasted, in the name of Jesus.

13. Blood of Jesus, speak me out of this bondage, in the name of Jesus.

14. By the power in the Word of God, I receive my deliverance, in the name of Jesus.

15. You that power that has vowed to waste me in this prison, be wasted, in the name of Jesus.

16. Any evil sacrifice offered to keep me here, be exposed and destroyed, in the name of Jesus.

17. I revoke every evil verdict pronounced against me, in the name of Jesus.

18. Let decrees of devil against me be reversed, in the name of Jesus.

19. You my life, what are you doing in detention? Come out now, in the name of Jesus.

20. O Lord, deliver me spiritually and physically, in the name of Jesus.

FOR FAVOR

'Then Nebuchadnezzar spake, and said, Blessed be the God of Shadrach, Meshach, and Abed-nego, who hath sent his angel, and delivered his servants that trusted in him, and have changed the king's word, and yielded their bodies, that they might not serve nor worship any god, except their own God. Therefore I make a decree, That every people, nation, and language, which speak anything amiss against the God of Shadrach, Meshach, and Abed-nego, shall be cut in pieces, and their houses shall be made a dunghill: because there is no other God that can deliver after this sort. Then the king promoted Shadrach, Meshach, and Abed-nego, in the province of Babylon' (Daniel 3:28-30).

Seeing yourself in prison does not mean you have come to the end of your life. History has proven that prisoners often have more opportunities of being favored by God than those who are physically free. When you gain an understanding of God's purpose for allowing you to be in prison at this time of your life, you can make good use of your time in prison well. You can pray and call upon God for unmerited favor.

By the time you finally come out of prison, your prayers would have prepared a better place for you. Obasanjo came out of prison to become a President, king maker and an international figure. It did not matter what people said about him. He went ahead and achieved what many politicians, soldiers and other leaders have not achieved in their lifetime.

Do not give up. Take your time to pray for God's favor upon your life. Once you are through, your time will come. As long as you are still in this prison, do not stop praying and doing what is good before God and man. By the time you are discharged, you will rise above your equals, and far above your masters.

PRAYERS TO RECEIVE FAVOR

1. Any power aborting God's favor upon me life, die, in the name of Jesus.
2. O Lord, command favor into my life, in the name of Jesus.
3. Every antichrist favor in my life, catch fire and burn to ashes, in the name of Jesus.
4. Any womb that is swallowing my favor, open now, in the name of Jesus.
5. Lord Jesus, speak favor into my destiny, in the name of Jesus.
6. Holy Ghost fire, burn to ashes every wicked thing being done against my life, in the name of Jesus.
7. Unmerited favor of God, manifest in my life today, in the name of Jesus.
8. O Lord, grant me favor before the entire inmates, in the name of Jesus.
9. Let favor and peace reign in my life forever, in the name of Jesus.
10. I receive favor from my right, left and centre, in the name of Jesus.
11. Blood of Jesus, speak favor into my life, in the name of Jesus.
12. Let the miracle working power of God bring favor into my life today, in the name of Jesus.

13. O Lord, baptize me with Your favor, in the name of Jesus.

14. You my enemies, whether you like it or not, favor me, in the name of Jesus.

15. You my life, begin to attract God's favor and mercy, in the name of Jesus.

16. Father Lord, make me a candidate of Your favor and divine mercy, in the name of Jesus.

17. Fire of God, burn to ashes every demon diverting Your favor upon my life, in the name of Jesus.

18. Lord Jesus, put people that will favor me in high positions, in the name of Jesus.

19. Any reshuffling that will bring favor into my life, take place now, in the name of Jesus.

20. I break the backbone of hatred any person have for my life, in the name of Jesus.

21. Any evil personality working against me, be frustrated, in the name of Jesus.

FOR DIVINE HEALTH

'And said, If thou wilt diligently hearken to the voice of the Lord thy God, and wilt do that which is right in his sight, and wilt give ear to his commandments, and keep all his statutes, I will put none of these diseases upon thee, which I have brought upon the Egyptians: for I am the Lord that healeth thee' (Exodus 15:26).

When you genuinely repent and remain a true child of God, you will enjoy the benefits and blessings meant for covenant children of God. No sickness, pestilence, inflammation, fever, ulcer, boils, cancer, itching, swellings, plagues, heart failure, disease etc will prevail over you.

'And it shall come to pass, if thou shalt hearken diligently unto the voice of the Lord thy God, to observe and to do all his commandments which I command thee this day, that the Lord thy God will set thee on high above all nations of the earth: And all these blessings shall come on thee, and overtake thee, if thou shalt hearken unto the voice of the Lord thy God. Blessed shalt thou be in the city, and blessed shalt thou be in the field. Blessed

shall be the fruit of thy body, and the fruit of thy ground, and the fruit of thy cattle, the increase of thy kine, and the flocks of thy sheep. Blessed shall be thy basket and thy store. Blessed shalt thou be when thou comest in, and blessed shalt thou be when thou goest out. The Lord shall cause thine enemies that rise up against thee to be smitten before thy face: they shall come out against thee one way, and flee before thee seven ways. The Lord shall command the blessing upon thee in thy storehouses, and in all that thou settest thine hand unto; and he shall bless thee in the land which the Lord thy God giveth thee. The Lord shall establish thee an holy people unto himself, as he hath sworn unto thee, if thou shalt keep the commandments of the Lord thy God, and walk in his ways. And all people of the earth shall see that thou art called by the name of the Lord; and they shall be afraid of thee. And the Lord shall make thee plenteous in goods, in the fruit of thy body, and in the fruit of thy cattle, and in the fruit of thy ground, in the land which the Lord sware unto thy fathers to give thee. The Lord shall open unto thee his good treasure, the heaven to give the rain unto thy land in his season, and to bless all the work of thine hand: and thou shalt lend unto many nations, and thou shalt not borrow. And the Lord shall make thee the head, and not the tail; and thou shalt be above only, and thou shalt not be beneath; if that thou hearken unto the commandments of the Lord thy God, which I command thee this day, to observe and to do them: And thou shalt not go aside from any of the words which I command thee this day, to the right hand, or to the left, to go after other gods to serve them' (Deuteronomy 28:1-14).

As a child of God, nothing evil or wicked can stand before the mighty Spirit of God, which dwells in you. Your body is the temple of the Holy Ghost, and for that reason, He cannot allow any sickness to defile His temple. When you call Him for healing, He is committed to keep His temple free from sin, sickness and all satanic works.

'But if the Spirit of him that raised up Jesus from the dead dwell in you, he that raised up Christ from the dead shall also quicken your mortal bodies by his Spirit that dwelleth in you... Likewise the Spirit also helpeth our infirmities: for we know not what we should pray for as we ought: but the Spirit itself maketh intercession for us with groanings which cannot be uttered. And he that searcheth the hearts knoweth what is the mind of the Spirit, because he maketh intercession for the saints according to the will of God' (Romans 8:11, 26-27).

'How God anointed Jesus of Nazareth with the Holy Ghost and with power: who went about doing good, and healing all that were oppressed of the devil; for God was with him' (Acts 10:38).

Have faith in God and His Word as you pray these prayers. God's Word is His will. God's powers cannot condole any sickness and do not honor impossibilities. As a Christian, you have been given dynamic power, authority and dominion over every ill health.

> *'And Jesus came and spake unto them, saying, All power is given unto me in heaven and in earth. Go ye therefore, and teach all nations, baptizing them in the name of the Father, and of the Son, and of the Holy Ghost: Teaching them to observe all things whatsoever I have commanded you: and, lo, I am with you always, even unto the end of the world. Amen'* (Matthew 28:18-20).

> *'For by him were all things created, that are in heaven, and that are in earth, visible and invisible, whether they be thrones, or dominions, or principalities, or powers: all things were created by him, and for him: And he is before all things, and by him all things consist'* (Colossians 1:16-17).

> *'Then he called his twelve disciples together, and gave them power and authority over all devils, and to cure diseases. And the apostles, when they were returned, told him all that they had done. And he took them, and went aside privately into a desert place belonging to the city called Bethsaida. They answering said, John the Baptist; but some say, Elias; and others say, that one of the old prophets is risen again. He said unto them, But*

> *whom say ye that I am? Peter answering said, The Christ of God'* (Luke 9:1, 10, 19-20).

It is not God's will for sickness and disease to feed on you. Cast them out by force. You have access to the Spirit of God to cast out demons. (*See* Romans 8:11, 1 Corinthians 6:19, Mark 16:17, 18, Luke 10:18-20, 9:1, John 14:12-14, Matthew 18:18-19). You can start praying and you will see every sickness and disease abandon your life forever.

PRAYERS FOR DIVINE HEALTH

1. I command every sickness in my body to die and come back no more, in the name of Jesus.

2. Fire of God, burn to ashes every evil deposit in my life, in the name of Jesus.

3. Every infirmity that entered into my life in the dream, come out and die, in the name of Jesus.

4. Any food I ate in dreams troubling my life, I cast you out now, in the name of Jesus.

5. You my lost health, I recover you by force, in the name of Jesus.

6. Any power attacking my health, I chase you out by force, in the name of Jesus.

7. Every strange movement in my life, be arrested unto death, in the name of Jesus.

8. You my life, reject every sickness and disease now, in the name of Jesus.

9. Any evil personality harassing me sexually in the dream, be destroyed, in the name of Jesus.

10. Blood of Jesus, flow into my foundation and heal me perfectly, in the name of Jesus.

11. Let my blood receive sound healing, in the name of Jesus.

12. I release every organ of my body from every sickness and disease, in the name of Jesus.

13. I eat the fruit of sound health, in the name of Jesus.

14. O hand of God, feed me with the food of champions, in the name of Jesus.

15. Let the waters of life enter into my body, soul and Spirit, in the name of Jesus.

16. I fire back every arrow of sickness and disease fired against my life, in the name of Jesus.

17. Any problem that is eating up my health, I terminate your existence, in the name of Jesus.

18. Blood of Jesus speak destruction unto every disease, sickness and infirmities in my life, in the name of Jesus.

19. Let the anger of God destroy every demon against my health and my life, in the name of Jesus.

20. Any power blocking my health and deliverance, give way by force, in the name of Jesus.

21. Any satanic serpent eating up my health, vomit it and die, in the name of Jesus.

22. Any evil altar promoting bad health in my life, catch fire, in the name of Jesus.

23. Every problem in the garden of my life, die with your supporters, in the name of Jesus.

FOR DIVINE PROVISION

'And the word of the Lord came unto him, saying, Arise, get thee to Zarephath, which belongeth to Zidon, and dwell there: behold, I have commanded a widow woman there to sustain thee. So he arose and went to Zarephath. And when he came to the gate of the city, behold, the widow woman was there gathering of sticks: and he called to her, and said, Fetch me, I pray thee, a little water in a vessel, that I may drink. And as she was going to fetch it, he called to her, and said, Bring me, I pray thee, a morsel of bread in thine hand. And she said, As the Lord thy God liveth, I have not a cake, but an handful of meal in a barrel, and a little oil in a cruse: and, behold, I am gathering two sticks, that I may go in and dress it for me and my son, that we may eat it, and die. And Elijah said unto her, Fear not; go and do as thou hast said: but make me thereof a little cake first, and bring it unto me, and after make for thee and for thy son. For thus saith the Lord God of Israel, The barrel of meal shall not waste, neither shall the cruse of oil fail, until the day that the Lord sendeth rain upon the earth. And she went and

> *did according to the saying of Elijah: and she, and he, and her house, did eat many days. And the barrel of meal wasted not, neither did the cruse of oil fail, according to the word of the Lord, which he spake by Elijah'* (1 Kings 17:8-16).

One of the core problems with many prisoners today is lack of faith and courage. Faith and courage are fundamental for change. Prayer and faith when combined together can do great things. Faith is the key that unlocks doors of heavenly resources and prayer is the hand that turns the key. Without faith, prayer is as good as useless, unprofitable and a waste of time.

> *'If any of you lack wisdom, let him ask of God, that giveth to all men liberally, and upbraideth not; and it shall be given him. But let him ask in faith, nothing wavering. For he that wavereth is like a wave of the sea driven with the wind and tossed. For let not that man think that he shall receive any thing of the Lord. A double-minded man is unstable in all his ways'* (James 1:5-8).

Do not allow physical limitations to discourage you in your prayers for divine provision in prison. Pray with all your heart whenever you pray. God can use anything or anyone He chooses to provide all your needs while in prison. Hagar and her son Ishmael were cut off from their only source of livelihood and were abandoned in the wilderness. However, when Ishmael started crying, God responded with divine provision and help.

> *'And the water was spent in the bottle, and she cast the child under one of the shrubs. And she went, and sat her down over against him a good way off, as it were a bowshot: for she said, Let me not see the death of the child. And she sat over against him, and lift up her voice, and wept. And God heard the voice of the lad; and the angel of God called Hagar out of heaven, and said unto her, What aileth thee, Hagar? fear not; for God hath heard the voice of the lad where he is. Arise, lift up the lad, and hold him in thine hand; for I will make him a great nation. And God opened her eyes, and she saw a well of water; and she went, and filled the bottle with water, and gave the lad drink'* (Genesis 21:15-19).

These prayers can help you recover all your lost provisions; unlock your financial blessings, take away poverty and attract God's favors. Prayer is an investment. It is like an open cheque or key to heaven's bank.

> *'Not because I desire a gift: but I desire fruit that may abound to your account. But I have all, and abound: I am full, having received of Epaphroditus the things which were sent from you, an odor of a sweet smell, a sacrifice acceptable, well pleasing to God. But my God shall supply all your need according to his riches in glory by Christ Jesus'* (Philippians 4:17-19).

As you pray these prayers with all diligence, God will go beyond prison and provide all your needs. A throne of blessing can be prepared for a prisoner outside the prison. It has happened so many times. As you insist on praying for change, let it happen to you, in the name of Jesus.

PRAYERS FOR DIVING PROVISION

1. O Lord my God, arise and supply all my needs, in the name of Jesus.

2. Any satanic roadblock blocking my supplies, be dismantled, in the name of Jesus.

3. Let every demonic hindrance to my supplies clear away now, in the name of Jesus.

4. Any satanic store keeping back my supplies, release them now, in the name of Jesus.

5. I command every good thing that has been eluding me to manifest now, in the name of Jesus.

6. Father Lord, restore all my lost blessings by Your mercy, in the name of Jesus.

7. You that strongman keeping my blessings away from me, die, in the name of Jesus.

8. You my financial hindrances, be removed by force, in the name of Jesus.

9. I command spirit of favor to fall upon my life now, in the name of Jesus.

10. Every yoke of poverty upon my life, break by force, in the name of Jesus.

11. Every good thing I need in this prison, begin to appear by force, in the name of Jesus.

12. I break and loose myself from environmental poverty, in the name of Jesus.

13. Every enemy of my provision, you must die, in the name of Jesus.

14. O Lord, bring all my needs in this place by Your power, in the name of Jesus.

15. Every spirit of starvation in my life, die immediately, in the name of Jesus.

16. Let my blessings be too hot to be kept away from me, in the name of Jesus.

17. Every demon against my divine provisions, die, in the name of Jesus.

18. Any evil hand stealing my blessings, I cut you off, in the name of Jesus.

19. I reject every embarrassment of poverty in this place, in the name of Jesus.

FOR DIVINE DIRECTION

> *'Now when they had gone throughout Phrygia and the region of Galatia, and were forbidden of the Holy Ghost to preach the word in Asia, After they were come to Mysia, they assayed to go into Bithynia: but the Spirit suffered them not. And they passing by Mysia came down to Troas. And a vision appeared to Paul in the night; There stood a man of Macedonia, and prayed him, saying, Come over into Macedonia, and help us. And after he had seen the vision, immediately we endeavored to go into Macedonia, assuredly gathering that the Lord had called us for to preach the gospel unto them'* (Acts 16:6-10).

Prison can also be symbolic of a wilderness where God may have purposely allowed you into after being separated from the world or busy life so He can give you clear guidance. Consider what God revealed to Hosea - *'Therefore, behold, I will allure her, and bring her into the wilderness, and speak comfortably unto her'* (Hosea 2:14). God is after your heart. So if prison is the best place He can get your attention, He would permit it. Who knows what could have happened if you had stayed a day longer than the day you were arrested?

Who knows if you would have been a dead person if you did? You need to see a reason to thank God, and prayerfully discover God's purpose for your life on earth.

Choices you make in life determine the direction you follow and your destiny thereafter. God promised to guide all His children so they can always avoid costly mistakes in life.

> *'The meek will he guide in judgment: and the meek will he teach his way'* (Psalms 25:9).

> *'And thine ears shall hear a word behind thee, saying, This is the way, walk ye in it, when ye turn to the right hand, and when ye turn to the left'* (Isaiah 30:21).

You have to prayerfully commit your ways to God for true and profitable guidance. If you have not been born again yet, you do not have plenty of time. Give your life to Jesus immediately. Acknowledge all your sins, confess and forsake them. Until your heart is cleansed and purged, you will remain in darkness about God's purpose for your life. If you really desire God's guidance, you have to pray like Jesus did.

> *'And in the morning, rising up a great while before day, he went out, and departed into a solitary place, and there prayed'* (Mark 1:35).

> *'And it came to pass in those days, that he went out into a mountain to pray, and continued all*

> *night in prayer to God. And when it was day, he called unto him his disciples: and of them he chose twelve, whom also he named apostles'* (Luke 6:12-13).

> *'And when he had sent the multitudes away, he went up into a mountain apart to pray: and when the evening was come, he was there alone'* (Matthew 14:23).

When you identify with God while you are here in this prison, He will identify with you now and hereafter. He will guide you into His perfect will and deliver you from all troubles. These prayers here will not only help you in this prison alone, you will be divinely directed, helped and empowered to know God's timetable for you on earth. Arise now, pray and shine for your light is come and the glory of God has risen upon you.

PRAYERS FOR DIVING DIRECTION

1. Father Lord, identify with me in this place of confinement, in the name of Jesus.

2. OLord, let Your presence be with me in this place, in the name of Jesus.

3. Spirit of the Living God, guide me to God's perfect will, in the name of Jesus.

4. Any power assigned to divert my destiny in this place, die, in the name of Jesus.

5. I bind every evil spirit working against me in this place, in the name of Jesus.

6. Father Lord, cause me to relax in Your will in this place, in the name of Jesus.

7. Every satanic barrier to my success in this place, be rolled away, in the name of Jesus.

8. Any satanic network designed to waste my time in this place, be shattered, in the name of Jesus.

9. I receive my divine assignment in this place with joy, in the name of Jesus.

10. Every demonic delay against the work of God for my life in this place, be terminated, in the name of Jesus.

11. I reject every bad company designed to waste my life, in the name of Jesus.

12. I break and loose myself from every yoke of confusion, in the name of Jesus.

13. I destroy every unprofitable association in this place, in the name of Jesus.

14. Father Lord, help me to discover Your will for me in this place, in the name of Jesus.

15. You my life, I connect you to the divine will of God in this place, in the name of Jesus.

16. O Lord, arise and engage me profitable in this place, in the name of Jesus.

17. Fire of God, burn to ashes every evil yoke wasting prisoners in this place, in the name of Jesus.

18. You the strongman of this place, I am not your candidate, I pull you down, in the name of Jesus.

19. I break and loose myself from spiritual captivity resident in this place, in the name of Jesus.

TO RECEIVE POWER TO SERVE

> *'Therefore, my beloved brethren, be ye steadfast, unmovable, always abounding in the work of the Lord, forasmuch as ye know that your labor is not in vain in the Lord'* (1 Corinthians 15:58).

> *'Therefore seeing we have this ministry, as we have received mercy, we faint not; But have renounced the hidden things of dishonesty, not walking in craftiness, nor handling the word of God deceitfully; but by manifestation of the truth commending ourselves to every man's conscience in the sight of God'* (2 Corinthians 4:1-2).

Lord Jesus Christ is our role model in the ministry of soul winning. The purpose of everything He did on earth was to prepare men's hearts to receive salvation, and be restored back to privilege relationship with God. Across the world, prisoners die daily without receiving grace to meet with God, their creator. Therefore, you that are born again now, as a prisoner, you need to be concerned about other prisoners who are not born again Christians.

> *'I am debtor both to the Greeks, and to the Barbarians; both to the wise, and to the unwise. So, as much as in me is, I am ready to preach the gospel to you that are at Rome also. For I am not ashamed of the gospel of Christ: for it is the power of God unto salvation to everyone that believeth; to the Jew first, and also to the Greek'* (Romans 1:14-16).

> *'For the Son of man is come to save that which was lost. How think ye? if a man have an hundred sheep, and one of them be gone astray, doth he not leave the ninety and nine, and goeth into the mountains, and seeketh that which is gone astray? And if so be that he find it, verily I say unto you, he rejoiceth more of that sheep, than of the ninety and nine which went not astray'* (Matthew 18:11-13).

The brother to the prodigal son was selfish and self-centered that he could not even reason for a moment like his father over his brother, who was thought dead but came back alive; was lost but found (*See* Luke 15:25-32). When you know what the saving power of Christ can do for you and you choose to do nothing to use it, you cannot claim to be a Christian or a follower of Christ (*See* 2 Kings 5:1-4, Matthew 9:36, Mark 2:1-4, Galatians 4:19-20, Acts 9:26-28, 18:24-28). As a Christian in prison, you need to take a step to start a Christian fellowship in prison. Pray for God's grace and love to multiply true fellowship in the prison which includes:

1. *Loving and comforting one another (See 1 Corinthians 13:1-3, 1 Thessalonians 4:18).*
2. *Greeting one another (See 1 Peter 5:14, Romans 16:16).*
3. *Bearing one another's burden (See Galatians 6:2).*
4. *Praying together (See James 5:16).*
5. *Ministering to others (See 1 Peter 4:10).*
6. *Forgiving one another (See Colossians 3:13, Ephesians 4:32).*
7. *Teaching one another (See Colossians 3:16).*
8. *Submitting to one another (See 1 Peter 5:5, Ephesians 5:21).*
9. *Preferring one another over self (See Romans 12:10).*
10. *Edifying one another (See Romans 14:19, 1 Thessalonians 5:11).*

REWARD FOR SERVING GOD

God rewards His children who obey His Word and remain faithful to His purposes. These are those loyal to God's kingdom on earth. God also gives honor, glory, crown of righteousness and joy of service to those who serve Him in truth and in Spirit (*See* Matthew 25:21-23. 2 Timothy 4:8, Revelation 2:10). Pray for His grace to serve Him in prison and everywhere you are at all times.

PRAYERS TO RECEIVE POWER TO SERVE

1. I release myself unto God for every day service, in the name of Jesus.

2. Every sin and filthiness in my root, be uprooted by force, in the name of Jesus.

3. I command every work of devil in my life to come to an end, in the name of Jesus.

4. Fire of God, burn to ashes all evil forces against my services to God, in the name of Jesus.

5. Every serpent in the garden of my life, come out and die, in the name of Jesus.

6. Every satanic property in my life, catch fire, in the name of Jesus.

7. Let all footholds and satanic seats in my life be dismantled, in the name of Jesus.

8. I withdraw my service and commitment to devil today and forever and ever, in the name of Jesus.

9. I withdraw every invitation I have given to devil into my life, in the name of Jesus.

10. Let the power of prayer and evangelism possesses me now, in the name of Jesus.

11. I command my body, soul and Spirit to respond to divine service of God, in the name of Jesus.

12. Let the nine gifts of the Holy Spirit begin to work in my life, in the name of Jesus.

13. Father Lord, help me to operate with discerning gifts, in the name of Jesus.

14. I receive the ability to operate with dynamic power and declaration gifts, in the name of Jesus.

15. Father Lord, empower me to challenge every satanic counterfeits in my life, in the name of Jesus.

16. I receive God's power and grace, purity and discipline into my life, in the name of Jesus.

17. Let the nine fruits of the Spirit and holiness characterizes my life, in the name of Jesus.

18. Excellent Spirit of God, possess me forever, in the name of Jesus.

19. Power for fervent prayers, saintly purposes, purity and sound principles, and posses me, in the name of Jesus.

FOR THE CONVICTED

'Then the presidents and princes sought to find occasion against Daniel concerning the kingdom; but they could find none occasion nor fault; forasmuch as he was faithful, neither was there any error or fault found in him. Then said these men, We shall not find any occasion against this Daniel, except we find it against him concerning the law of his God. Then these presidents and princes assembled together to the king, and said thus unto him, King Darius, live forever. All the presidents of the kingdom, the governors, and the princes, the counselors, and the captains, have consulted together to establish a royal statute, and to make a firm decree, that whosoever shall ask a petition of any God or man for thirty days, save of thee, O king, he shall be cast into the den of lions. Now, O king, establish the decree, and sign the writing, that it be not changed, according to the law of the Medes and Persians, which altereth not. Wherefore king Darius signed the writing and the decree. Now when Daniel knew that the writing was signed, he went into his house; and his windows being open in his chamber toward

Jerusalem, he kneeled upon his knees three times a day, and prayed, and gave thanks before his God, as he did aforetime' (Daniel 6:4-10, 18-22).

Many prisoners have died before their time because of the of horror human judgments. Human judgments cannot stand the test of time when you have a genuine relationship with God and understand the power and efficacy of prayers.

'Peter therefore was kept in prison: but prayer was made without ceasing of the church unto God for him. And when Herod would have brought him forth, the same night Peter was sleeping between two soldiers, bound with two chains: and the keepers before the door kept the prison. And, behold, the angel of the Lord came upon him, and a light shined in the prison: and he smote Peter on the side, and raised him up, saying, Arise up quickly. And his chains fell off from his hands. And the angel said unto him, Gird thyself, and bind on thy sandals. And so he did. And he saith unto him, Cast thy garment about thee, and follow me. And he went out, and followed him; and wist not that it was true which was done by the angel; but thought he saw a vision. When they were past the first and the second ward, they came unto the iron gate that leadeth unto the city; which opened to them of his own accord: and they went out, and passed on through one street; and forthwith the angel departed from him. And when

> *Peter was come to himself, he said, Now I know of a surety, that the Lord hath sent his angel, and hath delivered me out of the hand of Herod, and from all the expectation of the people of the Jews... And at midnight Paul and Silas prayed, and sang praises unto God: and the prisoners heard them. And suddenly there was a great earthquake, so that the foundations of the prison were shaken: and immediately all the doors were opened, and every one's bands were loosed'* (Acts 12:5-11, 16:25-26).

Judgments in human courts are temporal to those who know their God; those who believe ineffectiveness of prayers. As a son of God, heir and member of Christ's body, a new creature, beloved of God, temple of God, peculiar treasure and sheep of the great shepherd, your stay in prison is temporal. You are an ambassador of Christ in the prison. You will be freed Halleluiah!

> *'Now then we are ambassadors for Christ, as though God did beseech you by us: we pray you in Christ's stead, be ye reconciled to God'* (2 Corinthians 5:20).

(*See also* John 1:12, Ephesians 5:30, 2 Corinthians 5:17, John 16:27, Matthew 12:49, 50, Psalms 105:14-15, Revelation 1:5-6, Romans 8:17, 32, Deuteronomy 32:9, Isaiah 40:31, John 10:11-15).

When you do the right thing, fulfilling your purpose in prison, you will be released. When you handle these prayers with all seriousness, the prison's strongman cannot keep you a second beyond the time for your release. You need to make sure you do God's work by serving other prisoners.

> *'For David, after he had served his own generation by the will of God, fell on sleep, and was laid unto his fathers, and saw corruption'* (Acts 13:36).

You are coming out soon to evangelize and take your place in the whole world, in the name of Jesus – Amen.

PRAYERS FOR THE CONVICTED

1. Any power that wants me to overstay in this prison, die, in the name of Jesus.

2. O Lord, empower me to be profitable for Your kingdom here in prison, in the name of Jesus.

3. Father Lord, show me Yourself in this prison, in the name of Jesus.

4. You the strongman of this prison, I bind you and cast you out, in the name of Jesus.

5. Fire of God, burn every destructive spirit inside me, in the name of Jesus.

6. Any agent of Satan assigned to destroy me in this prison, be disgraced, in the name of Jesus.

7. Every evil tongue that will rise against me in this prison, be divided, in the name of Jesus.

8. You that power wasting other prisoners here, you will not waste me, in the name of Jesus.

9. Father Lord, give me a daily assignment in this prison, in the name of Jesus.

10. Blood of Jesus, speak death unto every problem against me here, in the name of Jesus.

11. Any evil plan to destroy me in this prison, be exposed and disgraced, in the name of Jesus.

12. O Lord, deliver me miraculously from this prison, in the name of Jesus.

13. You spirit of self-destruction, regrets and worry, I cast you out now, in the name of Jesus.

14. I cast you out every wicked spirit inside me, in the name of Jesus.

15. Holy Ghost fire, burn to ashes every killer of prisoners coming after me, in the name of Jesus.

16. Any evil throne in this prison working against me, scatter, in the name of Jesus.

17. Let every environmental power in this prison be paralyzed, in the name of Jesus.

18. Let that food poison prepared against me in this prison ferment and sour, in the name of Jesus.

19. O Lord, spare my life in this prison, in the name of Jesus.

20. Blood of Jesus, flow into this prison and deliver me perfectly, in the name of Jesus.

AGAINST EVIL POWERS OF YOUR FATHER'S HOUSE

Now there cried a certain woman of the wives of the sons of the prophets unto Elisha, saying, Thy servant my husband is dead; and thou knowest that thy servant did fear the Lord: and the creditor is come to take unto him my two sons to be bondmen. And Elisha said unto her, What shall I do for thee? Tell me, what hast thou in the house? And she said, Thine handmaid hath not anything in the house, save a pot of oil' (2 Kings 4:1-2).

'Then there was a famine in the days of David three years, year after year; and David inquired of the Lord. And the Lord answered, It is for Saul, and for his bloody house, because he slew the Gibeonites' (2 Samuel 21:1).

'Thou shalt not bow down thyself to them, nor serve them: for I the Lord thy God am a jealous God, visiting the iniquity of the fathers upon the children unto the third and fourth generation of them that hate me' (Exodus 20:5).

Evil powers of one's father's house, when not properly dealt with, are capable of rendering activities of such person useless. The sins of Ahab and Jezebel put their family into bondage (*See* 2 Kings 9:30-37, 10:1, 6-8, 10, 11). Evil covenants can affect born and unborn children, from generation to generation (*See* Joshua 9:15, 22, 23, 27,2 Samuel 21:1-9). Powers of darkness in family foundations are capable of ruining or destroying all efforts of the members of such families to succeed in life. They can bring fear, sleepless nights, marital crises, and all manner of strange problems.

> *'Remember, O Lord, what is come upon us: consider, and behold our reproach. Our inheritance is turned to strangers, our houses to aliens. We are orphans and fatherless, our mothers are as widows. We have drunken our water for money; our wood is sold unto us. Our necks are under persecution: we labor, and have no rest. We have given the hand to the Egyptians, and to the Assyrians, to be satisfied with bread. Our fathers have sinned, and are not; and we have borne their iniquities'* (Lamentations 5:1-7).

The same power brought to zero the excellence of the tribe of Reuben and wasted lives of their youths.

> *'And Jacob called unto his sons, and said, Gather yourselves together, that I may tell you that which shall befall you in the last days. Gather yourselves together, and hear, ye sons of Jacob; and hearken unto Israel your father. Reuben, thou art my firstborn, my might, and the beginning of my strength, the excellency of dignity, and the*

> *excellency of power: Unstable as water, thou shalt not excel; because thou wentest up to thy father's bed; then defiledst thou it: he went up to my couch'* (Genesis 49:1-4).
>
> *'Let Reuben live, and not die; and let not his men be few'* (Deuteronomy 33:6).

This is the time for you to fight all the evil powers of your father's house. Those wicked powers are capable of causing premature deaths, rejection, hatred and poverty. These prayers here can enter into darkrooms of your father's house and dislodge every demon. The dragon of your father's house and every evil investment will be wasted if you handle these prayers with all seriousness.

Pray fervently and break the backbone of evil powers of your father's house over your life.

PRAYERS AGAINST EVIL POWERS OF YOUR FATHER'S HOUSE

1. You evil powers of my father's house working against me, die, in the name of Jesus.

2. Every yoke of bondage of my father's house, break, in the name of Jesus.

3. By the anointing of the Holy Ghost, I break every chain of imprisonment upon me, in the name of Jesus.

4. Every enemy of my deliverance from my place of birth, be disgraced and die, in the name of Jesus.

5. I command the strongman of my father's house to be frustrated, in the name of Jesus.

6. Any evil conspiracy in my father's house, spiritual or physical, scatter, in the name of Jesus.

7. Blood of Jesus flow into my father's house and destroy our bondage, in the name of Jesus.

8. Let every agenda of strongman of my father's house be frustrated, in the name of Jesus.

9. Every yoke of shame, reproach and disgrace upon my father's house, be destroyed, in the name of Jesus.

10. Any evil link between my ancestor's altar, and me be cut off, in the name of Jesus.

11. Let all problems in my life emanating from my father's house be eliminated, in the name of Jesus.

12. Lord Jesus, walk into the dark rooms of my father's house and deliver me, in the name of Jesus.

13. Let the ground open and swallow all problems in my life, in the name of Jesus.

14. Every good thing I have lost while in this prison, I recover you double, in the name of Jesus.

15. Any serpent of darkness in my father's house, I cut you into pieces, in the name of Jesus.

16. Any stubborn personality from my father's house, I break your backbone, die, in the name of Jesus.

17. Let every strongman over my life from my father's house die, in the name of Jesus.

18. Every inherited covenant from my father's house, expire, in the name of Jesus.

19. Let the camp of all my enemies catch fire and burn to ashes, in the name of Jesus.

20. You the dragon of my father's house, die, in the name of Jesus.

TO RECEIVE VICTORY IN COURT

'Moreover the word of the Lord came unto Jeremiah the second time, while he was yet shut up in the court of the prison, saying, Thus saith the Lord the maker thereof, the Lord that formed it, to establish it; the Lord is his name; Call unto me, and I will answer thee, and shew thee great and mighty things, which thou knowest not' (Jeremiah 33:1-3).

'And the keeper of the prison told this saying to Paul, The magistrates have sent to let you go: now therefore depart, and go in peace. But Paul said unto them, They have beaten us openly uncondemned, being Romans, and have cast us into prison; and now do they thrust us out privily? nay verily; but let them come themselves and fetch us out. And the serjeants told these words unto the magistrates: and they feared, when they heard that they were Romans. And they came and besought them, and brought them out, and desired them to depart out of the city' (Acts 16:36-39).

Prayers to receive victory in court are for prisoners who still have pending court cases. As you pray these prayers, all your accusers will start fighting themselves. Every negative voice against you will be silenced and God's voice will prevail over every evil plans against your life. The voice of the blood of Jesus will influence the judges to pass true judgment to your favor. When you believe and entirely trust God, you can receive a miracle. All things are possible before God. Your case file can receive a miraculous attention motivated by the Holy Ghost, which will end every case to your favor. It is possible.

More so, it possible that all counsels of your conspirators can be turned into foolishness. These prayers will reverse arrows of your enemies to fall into the pit they have dug for you.

> *'Behold, they shall surely gather together, but not by me: whosoever shall gather together against thee shall fall for thy sake. Behold, I have created the smith that bloweth the coals in the fire, and that bringeth forth an instrument for his work; and I have created the waster to destroy. No weapon that is formed against thee shall prosper; and every tongue that shall rise against thee in judgment thou shalt condemn. This is the heritage of the servants of the Lord, and their righteousness is of me, saith the Lord'* (Isaiah 54:15-17).

Note that the Word of the Lord came to Jeremiah while he was still in prison. Likewise, take this message as God's Word, which has come to you prison, and God will give you all-round victory. Rise up now in faith, believe God and pray these prayers with all your heart and watch God fight for you.

PRAYERS TO RECEIVE VICTORY IN COURT

1. Father Lord, arise and vindicate me in the court, in the name of Jesus.
2. Any human judge assigned against me, be frustrated and work for my favor, in the name of Jesus.
3. Let any evil brain that is thinking evil against me in this case scatter, in the name of Jesus.
4. Fire of God, burn to ashes every evil document prepared against me, in the name of Jesus.
5. Blood of Jesus, speak for me in the court till my case is settled, in the name of Jesus.
6. Father Lord, visit the court for my sake and give me victory, in the name of Jesus.
7. Let all evil witnesses raised against me witness to my favor, in the name of Jesus.
8. O Lord, confuse my opponents and disgrace their lawyers, in the name of Jesus.
9. I command confusion that will give me victory to appear in the court, in the name of Jesus.
10. Let the truth of my matter manifest to my favor, in the name of Jesus.
11. Father Lord, command my false accusers to be arrested by Your Spirit, in the name of Jesus.
12. O Lord, give me victory and release me by Your power, in the name of Jesus.

13. Every arrow of confusion fired against me, backfire, in the name of Jesus.

14. Every work of native doctors and herbalists against me, be wasted, in the name of Jesus.

15. O Lord, cause my opponents to testify to my favor, in the name of Jesus.

16. I pull down every stumbling block mounted up against me, in the name of Jesus.

17. Every conspiracy going on against me, crash and disintegrate in the court, in the name of Jesus.

18. Let charms of my enemies fail to work against me in court, in the name of Jesus.

19. Every enemy of my destiny in the court, receive double shame, in the name of Jesus.

20. Any evil verdict and demonic judgment written against me, be reversed, in the name of Jesus.

TO BREAK INHERITED EVIL COVENANTS

'And Jabez was more honorable than his brethren: and his mother called his name Jabez, saying, Because I bare him with sorrow. And Jabez called on the God of Israel, saying, Oh that thou wouldest bless me indeed, and enlarge my coast, and that thine hand might be with me, and that thou wouldest keep me from evil, that it may not grieve me! And God granted him that which he requested' (1 Chronicles 4:9-10).

'Then there was a famine in the days of David three years, year after year; and David inquired of the Lord. And the Lord answered, It is for Saul, and for his bloody house, because he slew the Gibeonites. And the king called the Gibeonites, and said unto them; (now the Gibeonites were not of the children of Israel, but of the remnant of the Amorites; and the children of Israel had sworn unto them: and Saul sought to slay them in his zeal to the children of Israel and Judah.) Wherefore David said unto the Gibeonites, What shall I do for you? And wherewith shall I make

the atonement that ye may bless the inheritance of the Lord? And the Gibeonites said unto him, We will have no silver nor gold of Saul, nor of his house; neither for us shalt thou kill any man in Israel. And he said, What ye shall say, that will I do for you. And they answered the king, The man that consumed us, and that devised against us that we should be destroyed from remaining in any of the coasts of Israel, Let seven men of his sons be delivered unto us, and we will hang them up unto the Lord in Gibeah of Saul, whom the Lord did choose. And the king said, I will give them. But the king spared Mephibosheth, the son of Jonathan the son of Saul, because of the Lord's oath that was between them, between David and Jonathan the son of Saul. But the king took the two sons of Rizpah the daughter of Aiah, whom she bare unto Saul, Armoni and Mephibosheth; and the five sons of Michal the daughter of Saul, whom she brought up for Adriel the son of Barzillai the Meholathite: And he delivered them into the hands of the Gibeonites, and they hanged them in the hill before the Lord: and they fell all seven together, and were put to death in the days of harvest, in the first days, in the beginning of barley harvest' (2 Samuel 21:1-9).

A Covenant is a legal agreement made by two or more parties. Covenants are often designed for three major purposes:

1. *To establish friendship (See 1 Samuel 18:3).*
2. *For mutual protection (See Genesis 26:28-29).*
3. *To secure assistance in wars (See 1 Kings 15:18).*

As soon as any covenant is sealed, it becomes unalterable and difficult to break (See Galatians 3:15). For this reason, many evil covenants have lingered from one generation to another, affecting principle persons who entered it, extending to their families, born and unborn generations until it is broken. It is an irrevocable commitment and must be taken serious.

However, benefactors of holy covenants enjoy lots of benefits. They are made great even before birth. Their seeds multiply and prosper as dust of the earth everywhere they go. Whosoever blesses them is blessed and whosoever curses them is cursed (*See* Genesis 12:1-6, 13:14-17, 15:1-27, 17:1-14, 22:15-18).

In evil covenants, the reverse is always the case for benefactors of evil covenants are cursed even before they are born.

> *'Our fathers have sinned, and are not; and we have borne their iniquities'* (Lamentations 5:7).

> *'Now there cried a certain woman of the wives of the sons of the prophets unto Elisha, saying, Thy servant my husband is dead; and thou knowest that thy servant did fear the Lord: and the creditor is come to take unto him my two sons to be bondmen'* (2 Kings 4:1).

But you can break such covenants and remain free forever.

> *'And afterward when David heard it, he said, I and my kingdom are guiltless before the Lord for ever from the blood of Abner the son of Ner: Let it rest on the head of Joab, and on all his father's house; and let there not fail from the house of Joab one that hath an issue, or that is a leper, or that leaneth on a staff, or that falleth on the sword, or that lacketh bread'* (2 Samuel 3:28-29).

> *'Shall the prey be taken from the mighty, or the lawful captive delivered? But thus saith the Lord, Even the captives of the mighty shall be taken away, and the prey of the terrible shall be delivered: for I will contend with him that contendeth with thee, and I will save thy children. And I will feed them that oppress thee with their own flesh; and they shall be drunken with their own blood, as with sweet wine: and all flesh shall know that I the Lord am thy Savior and thy Redeemer, the mighty One of Jacob'* (Isaiah 49:24-26).

These prayers will help you break all manner of evil covenants, as you remain free of their consequences, in the name of Jesus.

PRAYERS TO BREAK INHERITED EVIL COVENANTS

1. Every inherited covenant designed to waste my life, break now, in the name of Jesus.

2. Fire of God, burn to ashes every evil covenant working against me, in the name of Jesus.

3. Let the covenant of my ancestors with evil spirits lose their hold over my life, in the name of Jesus.

4. You demons behind inherited covenants in my life, I cast you out by force, in the name of Jesus.

5. Any evil covenant of my parents with the grave, break now, in the name of Jesus.

6. I withdraw my entire life from consequences of evil covenants, in the name of Jesus.

7. I release myself from inherited marine covenants, in the name of Jesus.

8. I refuse to be harvested by demons over evil covenants in my life, in the name of Jesus.

9. All my possession in the hand of any evil spirit, I recover you now, in the name of Jesus.

10. Every satanic storehouse of my place of birth, release my blessings now, in the name of Jesus.

11. Any power assigned to waste my life, be wasted, in the name of Jesus.

12. You spirits behind evil covenants in my life, I cast you out, in the name of Jesus.

13. Blood of Jesus, speak death unto every inherited covenant in my life, in the name of Jesus.

14. Fire of God, burn to ashes every property of inherited evil covenant in my life, in the name of Jesus.

15. Every good thing enemies have stolen from my life because of evil covenant, I recover you now, in the name of Jesus.

16. Father Lord, break every inherited covenant in my life, in the name of Jesus.

17. I break and loose myself from the bondage of inherited evil covenants, in the name of Jesus.

18. I fire back every ancestral evil arrow, in the name of Jesus.

19. Blood of Jesus, recover all I have lost to my family's evil spirits, in the name of Jesus.

20. I walk out from captivities of evil inherited covenants, in the name of Jesus.

TO BREAK PERSONAL EVIL COVENANTS

> *'And ye have done worse than your fathers; for, behold, ye walk every one after the imagination of his evil heart, that they may not hearken unto me: Therefore will I cast you out of this land into a land that ye know not, neither ye nor your fathers; and there shall ye serve other gods day and night; where I will not shew you favor'* (Jeremiah 16:12-13).

> *'Reuben, thou art my firstborn, my might, and the beginning of my strength, the excellency of dignity, and the excellency of power: Unstable as water, thou shalt not excel; because thou wentest up to thy father's bed; then defiledst thou it: he went up to my couch'* (Genesis 49:3-4).

To break personal evil covenants, inherited evil covenants must be broken first.

> *'The word of the Lord came also unto me, saying, Thou shalt not take thee a wife, neither shalt thou have sons or daughters in this place. For thus saith the Lord concerning the sons and*

> *concerning the daughters that are born in this place, and concerning their mothers that bare them, and concerning their fathers that begat them in this land; They shall die of grievous deaths; they shall not be lamented; neither shall they be buried; but they shall be as dung upon the face of the earth: and they shall be consumed by the sword, and by famine; and their carcasses shall be meat for the fowls of heaven, and for the beasts of the earth'* (Jeremiah 16:1-4).

A personal evil covenant is a covenant you entered into personally, or an agreement you entered into without God's support. This kind of covenant can take someone out of God's plan, purpose and promises. It can impose visible and invincible barriers in the sight of any success or victory. The trials that come to victims of personal evil covenants are usually strange and frequent. This evil covenant attracts evil forces of backwardness, induces disappearances of good things and entrenches failures. Personal evil covenants are broken through –

(a) True repentance,
(b) Restitution and
(c) Forsaking of such sins.

> *'If I shut up heaven that there be no rain, or if I command the locusts to devour the land, or if I send pestilence among my people; If my people, which are called by my name, shall humble themselves, and pray, and seek my face, and turn*

> *from their wicked ways; then will I hear from heaven, and will forgive their sin, and will heal their land'* (2 Chronicles 7:13-14).

You need humility, obedience to God's Word and aggressive prayers to break personal evil covenants. When you handle these prayers with all diligence, you will be dissociated from spirits behind such evil covenants and new things will start happening in your life. Start praying today and witness your life delivered from these wicked spirits.

PRAYERS TO BREAK PERSONAL EVIL COVENANTS

1. Any evil covenant I entered into that is now tormenting my life, break, in the name of Jesus.

2. I recover every ground I handed over to Satan through personal evil covenant, in the name of Jesus.

3. Every demon militating against my life because of personal evil covenant, die, in the name of Jesus.

4. I break and loose myself from bondage of any personal evil covenant, in the name of Jesus.

5. Blood of Jesus, speak death against all personal evil covenants in my life, in the name of Jesus.

6. Every rod of the wicked in my life because of any personal evil covenant, become impotent, in the name of Jesus.

7. I release my destiny from grips of evil covenants, in the name of Jesus.

8. I disassociate myself from collective captivity of evil covenants, in the name of Jesus.

9. I break the yoke of witchcraft emanating from any personal evil covenant in my life, in the name of Jesus.

10. I cancel every manifestation of evil in my life because evil personal covenants, in the name of Jesus.

11. Every aggressive demon attacking my life because of any evil covenant, die, in the name of Jesus.

12. Every stubborn altar attacking my life, scatter by fire, in the name of Jesus.

13. I withdraw my entire life from spiritual and physical prisons, in the name of Jesus.

14. Every local altar troubling my life, catch fire and burn to ashes, in the name of Jesus.

15. Any problem in my life coming from personal evil covenants, die by force, in the name of Jesus.

16. Let the hammer of the Lord smash every personal evil covenant working against me, in the name of Jesus.

17. Any evil priest ministering against my life, be frustrated now, in the name of Jesus.

18. Anything representing me in any evil altar, catch fire and burn to ashes, in the name of Jesus.

19. Let all my glory in any evil altar begin to come out by fire, in the name of Jesus.

20. Fire of God burn to ashes every evil in my life, in the name of Jesus.

FOR THE CONDEMNED

'And it came to pass, when his master heard the words of his wife, which she spake unto him, saying, After this manner did thy servant to me; that his wrath was kindled. And Joseph's master took him, and put him into the prison, a place where the king's prisoners were bound: and he was there in the prison' (Genesis 39:19-20).

'Now about that time Herod the king stretched forth his hands to vex certain of the church. And he killed James the brother of John with the sword. And because he saw it pleased the Jews, he proceeded further to take Peter also. (Then were the days of unleavened bread.) And when he had apprehended him, he put him in prison, and delivered him to four quaternions of soldiers to keep him; intending after Easter to bring him forth to the people. Peter therefore was kept in prison: but prayer was made without ceasing of the church unto God for him. And when Herod would have brought him forth, the same night Peter was sleeping between two soldiers, bound with two chains: and the keepers before the door kept the prison' (Acts 12:1-6).

Joseph went to jail liken outright-condemned criminal who never received any appropriate trial. His imprisonment was ordered by his own master without a fair trial. Previously, he was hated by his own brothers, and was later tempted by Potiphar's wife, but he overcame by fleeing, and indeed, he overcame all and God honored him in the end.

> *'Dearly beloved, I beseech you as strangers and pilgrims, abstain from fleshly lusts, which war against the soul; Having your conversation honest among the Gentiles: that, whereas they speak against you as evildoers, they may by your good works, which they shall behold, glorify God in the day of visitation'* (1 Peter 2:11-12).

> *'Flee fornication. Every sin that a man doeth is without the body; but he that committeth fornication sinneth against his own body'* (1 Corinthians 6:18).

Therefore, being judged and condemned by human courts does not mean that your end has come. Even when you are guilty of what you are being accused of, the only thing you need to do is to repent of it and renounce it. A certain woman was once found guilty, judged and condemned to die. When she was about to be killed, she encountered Jesus and her death verdict was overturned miraculously, and all her accusers disappeared in shame.

Who says that such cannot be said of your case when you encounter Jesus? When you pray and trust God, even if you die, you will be with Christ in paradise.

> *'Jesus went unto the mount of Olives. And early in the morning he came again into the temple, and all the people came unto him; and he sat down, and taught them. And the scribes and Pharisees brought unto him a woman taken in adultery; and when they had set her in the midst, They say unto him, Master, this woman was taken in adultery, in the very act. Now Moses in the law commanded us, that such should be stoned: but what sayest thou? This they said, tempting him that they might have to accuse him. But Jesus stooped down, and with his finger wrote on the ground, as though he heard them not. So when they continued asking him, he lifted up himself, and said unto them, He that is without sin among you, let him first cast a stone at her. And again he stooped down, and wrote on the ground. And they which heard it, being convicted by their own conscience, went out one by one, beginning at the eldest, even unto the last: and Jesus was left alone, and the woman standing in the midst. When Jesus had lifted up himself, and saw none but the woman, he said unto her, Woman, where are those thine accusers? hath no man condemned thee? She said, No man, Lord. And Jesus said unto her, Neither do I condemn thee: go, and sin no more'* (John 8:1-11).

> *'And one of the malefactors which were hanged railed on him, saying, If thou be Christ, save thyself and us. But the other answering rebuked him, saying, Dost not thou fear God, seeing thou art in the same condemnation? And we indeed justly; for we receive the due reward of our deeds: but this man hath done nothing amiss. And he said unto Jesus, Lord, remember me when thou comest into thy kingdom. And Jesus said unto him, Verily I say unto thee, Today shalt thou be with me in paradise'* (Luke 23:39-43).

Despite how bad your story or history is, when you repent, confess and be ready to forsake your sins, your judgment can be reversed miraculously. There is a story of a boy, an only child of a widow, who was condemned and killed by devil. However, at the point when he was about to be buried, Jesus showed up, confronted devil, rebuked death and released this young boy to live again. There is nothing that Jesus cannot do.

> *'And it came to pass the day after, that he went into a city called Nain; and many of his disciples went with him, and much people. Now when he came nigh to the gate of the city, behold, there was a dead man carried out, the only son of his mother, and she was a widow: and much people of the city was with her. And when the Lord saw her, he had compassion on her, and said unto her, Weep not. And he came and touched the bier: and*

> *they that bare him stood still. And he said, Young man, I say unto thee, Arise. And he that was dead sat up, and began to speak. And he delivered him to his mother'* (Luke 7:11-15).

If you can handle these prayers with *enough-is-enough* spirit, every property of death in your life will be removed, and the verdict of death hanging over your life will be reversed and Jesus will give you abundant life.

> *'The thief cometh not, but for to steal, and to kill, and to destroy: I am come that they might have life, and that they might have it more abundantly'* (John 10:10).

PRAYERS FOR THE CONDEMNED

1. Any curse placed upon me, I reverse you by force, in the name of Jesus.

2. Father Lord, rearrange my destiny to suit Your purpose, in the name of Jesus.

3. Any evil utterance ever said against me, be reversed, in the name of Jesus.

4. You judgment of death delivered upon me, be reversed by the heavens, in the name of Jesus.

5. Any power that has hijacked my life, released it by force, in the name of Jesus.

6. Destiny killers in my life, I cast you out by fire, in the name of Jesus.

7. Let my life escape every verdict of death passed against it, in the name of Jesus.

8. I wipe out any damage done to my life by devil, in the name of Jesus.

9. I command every agent of destruction inside me to come out now, in the name of Jesus.

10. Blood of Jesus, destroy the raging fire of death inside of me, in the name of Jesus.

11. Every property of death inside me, come out and die, in the name of Jesus.

12. Abundant life of Christ, appear and possess me, in the name of Jesus.

13. Father Lord, arise in Your power and deliver me from hell, in the name of Jesus.

14. Death and hell, lose your hold over my life now, in the name of Jesus.

15. Powers of righteousness, divine fellowship, rest and anointing for eternity posses me, in the name of Jesus.

16. Let the joy of my salvation empower me to make heaven, in the name of Jesus.

17. Blood of Jesus, wash me by Your cleansing power, in the name of Jesus.

18. Blood of Jesus, speak righteousness unto my foundation, in the name of Jesus.

19. I receive victory over death and hell, in the name of Jesus.

20. Any power blocking my heaven, give way by force, in the name of Jesus.

21. Let the angels of God appear for my sake and take me to heaven, in the name of Jesus.

22. Any evil personality assigned to exclude me from making heaven, be arrested by fire, in the name of Jesus.

O LORD, VINDICATE ME

'Then spake the chief butler unto Pharaoh, saying, I do remember my faults this day… Then Pharaoh sent and called Joseph, and they brought him hastily out of the dungeon: and he shaved himself, and changed his raiment, and came in unto Pharaoh… And Pharaoh said unto Joseph, See, I have set thee over all the land of Egypt. And Pharaoh took off his ring from his hand, and put it upon Joseph's hand, and arrayed him in vestures of fine linen, and put a gold chain about his neck; And he made him to ride in the second chariot which he had; and they cried before him, Bow the knee: and he made him ruler over all the land of Egypt. And Pharaoh said unto Joseph, I am Pharaoh, and without thee shall no man lift up his hand or foot in all the land of Egypt. And Pharaoh called Joseph's name Zaphnath-paaneah; and he gave him to wife Asenath the daughter of Poti-pherah priest of On. And Joseph went out over all the land of Egypt' (Genesis 41:9, 14, 41-45).

These are prayers for people who are either in police detention or under police or house arrest, and also for those whose cases are in court. Even as a guilty person, you can still benefit from these prayers by first repenting and confessing your sins. Commit your case to Christ and stick to truth. You may have been judged and condemned, but Christ will vindicate you in a mysterious way.

> *'And ye shall know the truth, and the truth shall make you free. They answered him, We be Abraham's seed, and were never in bondage to any man: how sayest thou, Ye shall be made free?'* (John 8:32-33).

Accept that you have sinned and you need help. Cry unto God for mercy. Even when you are viewed as the worst criminal, Jesus can take up your case and deliver you in deed. Pray these prayers and all your enemies will be exposed and disgraced. With Christ, you can overcome all determined spiritual and physical enemies.

> *'And when it was day, certain of the Jews banded together, and bound themselves under a curse, saying that they would neither eat nor drink till they had killed Paul. And they were more than forty which had made this conspiracy. And they came to the chief priests and elders, and said, We have bound ourselves under a great curse, that we will eat nothing until we have slain Paul. Now therefore ye with the council signify to the chief captain that he bring him down unto you tomorrow, as though ye would inquire something*

> *more perfectly concerning him: and we, or ever he come near, are ready to kill him. And when Paul's sister's son heard of their lying in wait, he went and entered into the castle, and told Paul'* (Acts 23:12-16).

Wherever your down fall is being plotted, God is there to fight for you. You will surely be delivered, and your enemies will die in your place. As you engage in these prayers, evil men conspiring against you in secrets and openly will be frustrated. Your time for vindication has come. Believe God and take authority over every enemy of your freedom and you will be vindicated.

PRAYERS FOR GOD TO VINDICATE YOU

1. Father Lord, perfect my salvation now, in the name of Jesus.
2. Holy Ghost fire, burn to ashes every sin in my life, in the name of Jesus.
3. O Lord, arise and vindicate me by fire, in the name of Jesus.
4. Father Lord, deliver me from the hands of all determined enemies, in the name of Jesus.
5. Every false allegation raised up against me, be cancelled now, in the name of Jesus.
6. Any man or woman hired to convict me falsely, be disgraced, in the name of Jesus.
7. Let all conspiracies against me be exposed and destroyed, in the name of Jesus.
8. Any evil write-up against me, disappear mysteriously, in the name of Jesus.
9. O Lord, remove my enemies from all their positions, in the name of Jesus.
10. Any evil plan to eliminate me, be exposed by force, in the name of Jesus.
11. Spirit of bribery and corruption designed to rope me to destruction, die, in the name of Jesus.
12. Father Lord, raise men and women that will oppose my enemies, in the name of Jesus.

13. I reject every evil influence working against my freedom, in the name of Jesus.

14. Let any power that is working hard to destroy me in this case fail woefully, in the name of Jesus.

15. Every occult manipulation going on against my life, fail, in the name of Jesus.

16. Let charms prepared against me work to my favor, in the name of Jesus.

17. Every instrument of death fashioned against me in this case, backfire, in the name of Jesus.

18. Every chain of darkness assigned to keep me in bondage, break, in the name of Jesus.

19. Any evil agreement working against me, scatter, in the name of Jesus.

20. Blood of Jesus, speak death unto every enemy of my deliverance, in the name of Jesus.

21. O Lord, raise bold witnesses that will favor me in this case, in the name of Jesus.

22. Any evil power keeping me away from my blessings, die, in the name of Jesus.

23. Angels of the living God, appear for my sake and silence my enemies, in the name of Jesus.

TO DESTROY EVIL CHARACTERS

'For we know that the law is spiritual: but I am carnal, sold under sin. For that which I do I allow not: for what I would, that do I not; but what I hate, that do I. If then I do that which I would not, I consent unto the law that it is good. Now then it is no more I that do it, but sin that dwelleth in me. For I know that in me (that is, in my flesh,) dwelleth no good thing: for to will is present with me; but how to perform that which is good I find not. For the good that I would I do not: but the evil which I would not, that I do. Now if I do that I would not, it is no more I that do it, but sin that dwelleth in me. I find then a law, that, when I would do good, evil is present with me. For I delight in the law of God after the inward man: But I see another law in my members, warring against the law of my mind, and bringing me into captivity to the law of sin which is in my members. O wretched man that I am! Who shall deliver me from the body of this death? I thank God through Jesus Christ our Lord. So then with

the mind I myself serve the law of God; but with the flesh the law of sin' (Romans 7:14-25).

The divine nature of God in man, which was the original nature of God at creation, was destroyed by devil in the Garden of Eden. This has long since darkened man's understanding (*See* Ephesians 4:18), deceived man's heart and made it wicked (*See* Jeremiah 17:9). Through deception, Satan enslaved man's heart and began controlling man's behaviors (*See* Romans 7:18). Sin became a dominating tyrant; an inward enemy and an invader of the divine nature of God in man.

Sin begets evil characters. Many evil characters are punishable with prison sentences. It is these characters that I termed prison-bound characters. Prison-bound characters are evil characters that can either put you in prison or earn you a prison sentence. It is devil that installs these evil characters in men and women. The purpose of this book is to help all prisoners worldwide understand their worst enemy, which is Satan, and sin.

In a figurative sense, sin is a terrorist that must be dealt with and hated with perfect hatred. Another important aspect to note about sin is that evil characters are first conceived in the heart and premeditated before they are finally committed (*See* Mark 7:21-23, Revelation 21:8, Romans 1:29-32, 1 Corinthians 6:9, 10, Colossians 3:5-6, Galatians 5:19-21).

To allow prison-bound characters flourish in your life is synonymous with failure in life. The worst thing that can happen to you is not being imprisoned, but to live and die with evil characters.

> *'There was a certain rich man, which was clothed in purple and fine linen, and fared sumptuously every day: And there was a certain beggar named Lazarus, which was laid at his gate, full of sores, And desiring to be fed with the crumbs which fell from the rich man's table: moreover the dogs came and licked his sores. And it came to pass, that the beggar died, and was carried by the angels into Abraham's bosom: the rich man also died, and was buried; And in hell he lift up his eyes, being in torments, and seeth Abraham afar off, and Lazarus in his bosom. And he cried and said, Father Abraham, have mercy on me, and send Lazarus, that he may dip the tip of his finger in water, and cool my tongue; for I am tormented in this flame'* (Luke 16:19-24).

However, it is possible for you to come out of prison and become a wealthy man. But if you fail to deal with prison-bound characters in your life, you are as good as having achieved nothing and have failed beyond explanation. More strategic than a church, prison is the best place in life to settle everything about sin. Do everything possible to deal with sin and every prison-bound character in your life now or you will live to regret it.

'And he said, A certain man had two sons: And the younger of them said to his father, Father, give me the portion of goods that falleth to me. And he divided unto them his living. And not many days after the younger son gathered all together, and took his journey into a far country, and there wasted his substance with riotous living. And when he had spent all, there arose a mighty famine in that land; and he began to be in want. And he went and joined himself to a citizen of that country; and he sent him into his fields to feed swine. And he would fain have filled his belly with the husks that the swine did eat: and no man gave unto him. And when he came to himself, he said, How many hired servants of my father's have bread enough and to spare, and I perish with hunger! I will arise and go to my father, and will say unto him, Father, I have sinned against heaven, and before thee, And am no more worthy to be called thy son: make me as one of thy hired servants. And he arose, and came to his father. But when he was yet a great way off, his father saw him, and had compassion, and ran, and fell on his neck, and kissed him. And the son said unto him, Father, I have sinned against heaven, and in thy sight, and am no more worthy to be called thy son' (Luke 15:11-21).

Think. Take time out to remember all your sins, repent of all of them one by one. Confess and forsake them. Go into prayers. I recommend one of my books '***Confront***

and Conquer'. In that book, I listed all evil and prison-bound characters. Take time to pray against prison-bound characters and all will be well with your future.

PRAYERS FOR DESTROYING EVIL CHARACTERS

1. Every imprisonment character inside me designed to waste my life, die, in the name of Jesus.

2. I command every invisible force working against my character to die, in the name of Jesus.

3. Any power assigned to return me to evil lifestyle, be frustrated, in the name of Jesus.

4. Every stubborn yoke of sin dragging me into errors, break, in the name of Jesus.

5. Any power that has vowed to keep me in prison forever, die, in the name of Jesus.

6. You that power that darken my understanding, I cast you out, in the name of Jesus.

7. Spirit of laziness assigned to waste my destiny, be wasted, in the name of Jesus.

8. Any power from the grave militating against my destiny, die, in the name of Jesus.

9. Every yoke of lasciviousness in my life, break, in the name of Jesus.

10. Any satanic training camp teaching me evil, catch fire, in the name of Jesus.

11. Spirit of lesbianism and gay raising ugly head inside me, be destroyed, in the name of Jesus.

12. You the serpent of licentiousness dragging my destiny down, die, in the name of Jesus.

13. Any evil force causing me to limit God, scatter in shame, in the name of Jesus.

14. Any part of my life being used by devil, receive your deliverance, in the name of Jesus.

15. Anything in me that loves money more than God, be delivered, in the name of Jesus.

16. You the garment of mammon spirit in my life, catch fire, in the name of Jesus.

17. Unclean spirits of demonic pleasures in my life, I cast you out, in the name of Jesus.

18. Let the yoke of lovers of self in my life break now, in the name of Jesus.

19. Any party spirit demon working against my destiny, I cast you out, in the name of Jesus.

20. Spirit of oppression living inside me, come out and die, in the name of Jesus.

21. Evil desires of oral/anal sex living inside of me, walk back and die, in the name of Jesus.

22. Any evil oath I have taken in the past, die, in the name of Jesus.

23. Every demon of murmuring eating me up, I cast you out, in the name of Jesus.

24. Spirit of murder working hard to terminate my life, die, in the name of Jesus.

25. Agents of mockery, pulling me into disgrace, die, in the name of Jesus.

26. You those powers of mischief harassing my life, I cut you off, in the name of Jesus.

27. Every arrow of masturbation fired against me, backfire, in the name of Jesus.

28. You the spirit of malignity living inside of me, receive shock and die, in the name of Jesus.

29. Every dragon of malice in the garden of my life, die, in the name of Jesus.

30. Spirit of lies and insincerity in my life, I cast you out, in the name of Jesus.

31. Demons in charge of luxury in my life, be disgraced, in the name of Jesus.

32. You demon of lust in my life, be dismantled, in the name of Jesus.

33. Every agent of lukewarm spirit in my life, be disgraced, in the name of Jesus.

34. Any power causing me to love the world, I cast you out, in the name of Jesus.

35. Let the fire of perversion in me be cast out forever, in the name of Jesus.

36. Reveling demon moving my life into destruction, die, in the name of Jesus.

37. You revengeful spirits attacking my life, be disgraced, in the name of Jesus.

38. Arrows of pollution fired against me, I fire you back, in the name of Jesus.

39. Spirit of polygamy or polyandry working against me, die, in the name of Jesus.

40. Every serpent of rebellion living inside of me, I cast you out, in the name of Jesus.

41. You the strongman of pride ruining my life, be wasted unto death, in the name of Jesus.

42. You railing serpent living inside me, come out and die, in the name of Jesus.

43. Every worm of quarrelling all the time living inside of me, receive utter destruction, in the name of Jesus.

44. Dragon of fighting and destruction in my life, come out by force, in the name of Jesus.

45. You that spirit of madness and provocation in my life, die, in the name of Jesus.

46. Spirit of prostitution assigned to disgrace me, be disgraced, in the name of Jesus.

47. Every yoke of profligacy upon my life, break, in the name of Jesus.

48. Every influence of promiscuity warring against me, die, in the name of Jesus.

49. Rioting spirit of my father's house, I cast you out, in the name of Jesus.

50. Every ruthless spirit dragging me up and down, receive destruction, in the name of Jesus.

51. Any chain of seduction moving me into destruction, break, in the name of Jesus.

52. Let every seductive demon inside me come out and die, in the name of Jesus.

53. You evil spell of stealing working against my life, expire, in the name of Jesus.

54. Serpent of sexual perversion in my body, I cut you to pieces, in the name of Jesus.

55. Spirit of self-destruction assigned to destroy me, be destroyed, in the name of Jesus.

56. Anything in me exalting itself above God, I cut you off, in the name of Jesus.

57. Any tongue of serpentine power speaking guile in me, die, in the name of Jesus.

58. Every demon of sorcery using me like an evil tool, die, in the name of Jesus.

59. Anything inside of me sinning against the Holy Spirit, die, in the name of Jesus.

60. Let the strongman that uses me to shed innocent blood be frustrated to death, in the name of Jesus.

61. I command the spirit of self-will to leave me alone, in the name of Jesus.

62. Fire of self-exaltation inside of me, quench forever, in the name of Jesus.

63. Every selfishness spirit inside of me, receive confusion unto death, in the name of Jesus.

64. Every yoke of self-management upon my life, break, in the name of Jesus.

65. Spirit of slavery limiting my life, be consumed by fire, in the name of Jesus.

66. O Lord, arise and take away slander from my life, in the name of Jesus.

67. Every spirit of whoredom living inside of me, I cast you out, in the name of Jesus.

68. Horrible tempest of God, destroy every trace of unruliness in my life, in the name of Jesus.

69. Every unrighteous spirit in my life, I cast you out, in the name of Jesus.

70. Let every wicked spirit using me to destroy others be destroyed, in the name of Jesus.

71. You subtle serpent manipulating my life, be manipulated to death, in the name of Jesus.

72. Any evil power pairing me with wrong people, receive death, in the name of Jesus.

73. You the spirit of usury inside of me, come out and die, in the name of Jesus.

74. Every unforgiving spirit inside of me, be cast out, in the name of Jesus.

75. Let the anger of God destroy traitorous spirits in me, in the name of Jesus.

76. Serpent of violence using me to destroy others, be destroyed, in the name of Jesus.

77. Every weapon of worldliness inside of me, come out and die, in the name of Jesus.

78. Spirit of worry and anxiety designed to destroy me, die, in the name of Jesus.

79. You serpentine spirit of anger, leave me alone and die, in the name of Jesus.

80. Powers of idolatry confusing my destiny, be destroyed, in the name of Jesus.

81. Any witchcraft seed planted inside of me, die, in the name of Jesus.

82. Any witchcraft material that I have swallowed, I vomit you now, in the name of Jesus.

83. I break and loose myself from my family's evil partners, in the name of Jesus.

84. You the spirit of wickedness living inside of me, be cast out, in the name of Jesus.

85. Any evil power that causes me to walk by sight, you must die, in the name of Jesus.

86. Fire of arrogance burning inside of me, quench now, in the name of Jesus.

87. You spirit of fornication and adultery, I cast you out now by force, in the name of Jesus.

88. Every root of bitterness inside of me, be uprooted, in the name of Jesus.

89. Powers of bribery and corruption, you are wicked, die, in the name of Jesus.

90. Any demon causing me to defraud others, receive destruction, in the name of Jesus.

91. Any corrupt demon corrupting my life, be cast out, in the name of Jesus.

92. Every arrow of conspiracy fired into my life, backfire, in the name of Jesus.

93. Anything in me devising iniquity, be cast out, in the name of Jesus.

94. Powers of darkness assigned to defile me, die, in the name of Jesus.

95. You spirit of confusion and cowardice in me, come out and die, in the name of Jesus.

96. Powers that promote covetousness in my life, be paralyzed, in the name of Jesus.

97. You spirit of divorce in my family lineage, I cast you out, in the name of Jesus.

98. Powers that create enmity between people and me, be cast out, in the name of Jesus.

99. Fire of God, burn to ashes every evil in my life, in the name of Jesus.

100. I command every weapon of foolishness to leave me alone, in the name of Jesus.

101. Every garment of jealousy upon my life, catch Holy Ghost fire, in the name of Jesus.

102. Any power that uses me to invent evil, be paralyzed, in the name of Jesus.

103. Every spell of incest cast upon me, I cast you out, in the name of Jesus.

104. Let every implacable demon inside of me be cast out, in the name of Jesus.

105. Spirit of immorality prospering in my family, be wasted now, in the name of Jesus.

106. Powers of inordinate affection designed to destroy me, die, in the name of Jesus.

107. Spirit of insult, using me to insult people, die, in the name of Jesus.

108. Powers of indignation using me at will, I cast you out, in the name of Jesus.

109. Every weapon of impatience in my life, catch fire, in the name of Jesus.

110. O Lord, arise and deliver me from hating God, in the name of Jesus.

TO PREPARE FOR LIFE AFTER PRISON

'And they went out of the prison, and entered into the house of Lydia and when they had seen the brethren, they comforted them, and departed... Now when they had passed through Amphipolis and Apollonian, they came to Thessalonica, where was a synagogue of the Jews: And Paul, as his manner was, went in unto them, and three Sabbath days reasoned with them out of the scriptures, Opening and alleging, that Christ must needs have suffered, and risen again from the dead; and that this Jesus, whom I preach unto you, is Christ. And some of them believed, and consorted with Paul and Silas; and of the devout Greeks a great multitude, and of the chief women not a few.... Now while Paul waited for them at Athens, his spirit was stirred in him, when he saw the city wholly given to idolatry. Therefore disputed he in the synagogue with the Jews, and with the devout persons, and in the market daily with them that met with him. Then certain philosophers of the Epicureans, and of the Stoicks,

> *encountered him. And some said, What will this babbler say? other some, He seemeth to be a setter forth of strange gods: because he preached unto them Jesus, and the resurrection. And they took him, and brought him unto Areopagus, saying, May we know what this new doctrine, whereof thou speakest, is?'* (Acts 16:40, 17:1-4, 16-19).

Every prisoner is expected to prepare himself to face the world before coming out of prison. Otherwise, he or she will be returned back to prison sooner or later, or live on earth with notorious prison-bound characters (*See* Romans 7:14-25).

Just as a foundation of a building is very essential to its survival, a foundation for a new life is fundamental for every prisoner coming back into the world. In order words, you cannot come out of prison and expect to continue life as usual. What if you lose every investment or businesses you labored for years to build, would you have to kill in other to feel relieved? What will you do in such a case? The best thing to do is to run back to God, identify with other true Christians and start all over again with God. Everything belongs to God, and He is able to restore all to you if you can trust Him.

> *'If the foundations be destroyed, what can the righteous do?'* (Psalms 11:3).

> *'For which of you, intending to build a tower, sitteth not down first, and counteth the cost,*

> *whether he has sufficient to finish it? Lest haply, after he hath laid the foundation, and is not able to finish it, all that behold it begin to mock him, Saying, This man began to build, and was not able to finish'* (Luke 14:28-30).

> *'Not forsaking the assembling of ourselves together, as the manner of some is; but exhorting one another: and so much the more, as ye see the day approaching'* (Hebrews 10:25).

Do not fight with anyone or join your bad old friends. Start all over again with God for with Him, you will bounce back and all things will be possible and much better than before. If you pray the prayers here before leaving the prison and remain with God after your release you will prosper more than ever before.

> *'And the Lord turned the captivity of Job, when he prayed for his friends: also the Lord gave Job twice as much as he had before. Then came there unto him all his brethren, and all his sisters, and all they that had been of his acquaintance before, and did eat bread with him in his house: and they bemoaned him, and comforted him over all the evil that the Lord had brought upon him: every man also gave him a piece of money, and everyone an earring of gold. So the Lord blessed the latter end of Job more than his beginning: for he had fourteen thousand sheep, and six thousand camels, and a thousand yoke of oxen, and a thousand she asses'* (Job 42:10-12).

> *'And when the king asked the woman, she told him. So the king appointed unto her a certain officer, saying, Restore all that was hers, and all the fruits of the field since the day that she left the land, even until now'* (2 Kings 8:6).

The prayers here will disconnect your life from the evil powers that brought you into prison and deal with the strongman of your place of birth. No evil covenant, curses, old lifestyle or sinful partner will be able to influence your life again if only you can prayerfully remain loyal to God after your prison terms (*See* John 15:1-8, Psalms 1:1-3, 92:13-14, Romans 7: 4, Colossians 1:5-8, Romans 1:13-17, John 15:16).

To abide in Christ means to continue to believe in Him; to continue to live in the grace and Word of Christ after prison. You have to bear Christ-like fruits that constantly bring glory to God alone.

PRAYERS TO PREPARE FOR LIFE AFTER PRISON

1. You any hidden enemy waiting to destroy me outside prison, die before my release, in the name of Jesus.
2. Every hidden giant assigned to disgrace me in the world, be disgraced, in the name of Jesus.
3. Powers that brought me into this prison, I bury you alive, in the name of Jesus.
4. I receive power from on high to overcome evil powers outside the prison, in the name of Jesus.
5. I command evil powers waiting to destroy me after my release to die, in the name of Jesus.
6. I withdraw the control over my life from any family spirit, in the name of Jesus.
7. Any evil priest that is making sacrifices to return me to prison, fail woefully, in the name of Jesus.
8. Let every problem waiting to waste my life, be wasted, in the name of Jesus.
9. You the strongman of my place of birth assigned to destabilize me, be destabilized, in the name of Jesus.
10. Fire of God burn to ashes every evil yoke placed upon my life, in the name of Jesus.
11. Every destructive covenant wasting people in my family, break, in the name of Jesus.
12. Every curse placed upon my life to pull me back to bondage, expire, in the name of Jesus.

13. Let every evil action or mistake prepared against me be avoided, in the name of Jesus.

14. Every yoke of worldliness pulling me down, break, in the name of Jesus.

15. O Lord, anoint me to live my life for You forever, in the name of Jesus.

16. Holy Ghost fire, burn to ashes any evil thing that will return me to jail, in the name of Jesus.

17. I receive anointing to do God's work outside the prison, in the name of Jesus.

18. Fire of God, burn to ashes every marine deposit in my life, in the name of Jesus.

19. Every yoke of trouble upon my life, be broken by force, in the name of Jesus.

20. I receive power for personal evangelism, in the name of Jesus.

21. Father Lord, give me the grace to carry the good news to all the nations, in the name of Jesus.

22. O Lord, give me power to forgive all my offenders, in the name of Jesus.

23. Let the grace to remain a new creature outside the prison possess me, in the name of Jesus.

24. I receive divine conversion, conviction, commission and compassion for lost souls, in the name of Jesus.

25. Power to proclaim the gospel to nations of the world, possess me forever, in the name of Jesus.

26. Anointing to devote my time, talents, strength and money to preach, possess me, in the name of Jesus.

27. Father Lord, empower me for mass evangelism, in the name of Jesus.

28. Any power assigned to delay my determination to evangelize, I cut you off, in the name of Jesus.

29. Every yoke of ignorance, worldly cares, and falseness of riches in my life, break, in the name of Jesus.

30. I reject and refuse a wasteful and extravagant lifestyle, in the name of Jesus.

31. Spirit of prayerlessness, lack of compassion for lost souls, leave me alone and die, in the name of Jesus.

32. Divine power of sacrifice, self-denial and discipline possess me now, in the name of Jesus.

33. O Lord, saturate my life with deeply burning compassion to win souls for Christ, in the name of Jesus.

34. Anointing to share my personal experiences with Christ, fall upon me, in the name of Jesus.

35. I receive enough grace to follow up new converts, in the name of Jesus.

36. Power for daily study of God's Word and fellowship with other Christians, possess me, in the name of Jesus.

37. I receive divine wisdom to convince, convict and convert sinners, in the name of Jesus.

38. Anointing and grace to overcome Satan, possess me now, in the name of Jesus.

39. O Lord, endue me with wisdom from above to lead sinners unto Christ, in the name of Jesus.

40. You my brain, memorize all relevant Scriptures for soul winning, in the name of Jesus.

41. Father Lord, give me power to overcome every persecution and temptation, in the name of Jesus.

42. Power to reject every worldliness and worldly entertainment, fall upon me, in the name of Jesus.

43. I refuse to love the world more than God, in the name of Jesus.

44. You the pride things of this world, I reject you all, in the name of Jesus.

45. I separate and distinct from people whose affections and desire are worldly only, in the name of Jesus.

46. I refuse to attend any evil feast or evil gatherings, in the name of Jesus.

47. Anything that is not pleasing to God, or profitable for evangelism, I reject you, in the name of Jesus.

48. Powers to obey God's Word, possess me, in the name of Jesus.

49. Anointing for perfect obedience in all things, possess me, in the name of Jesus.

50. Evil forces assigned to frustrate me in the world, I destroy you all, in the name of Jesus.

51. Let all unprofitable relationships designed to waste my life and time to be destroyed, in the name of Jesus.

52. Little forces that spoil the vines in my life, catch fire and die, in the name of Jesus.

53. I reject every demonic conversation designed to trap my life, in the name of Jesus.

54. I refuse to put on worldly dressings and questionable ornaments to Christian living, in the name of Jesus.

55. Every daydreaming and worldly cares designed to destroy me, I reject you, in the name of Jesus.

56. Demonic motivated ambitions and evil pursuits, I reject you, in the name of Jesus.

57. Every garment of worldly enjoyment and pleasure without God in my life, catch fire, in the name of Jesus.

58. Demonic motivated parties and time consuming film shows, I reject you, in the name of Jesus.

59. Every yoke of evil habit in my life, break by force, in the name of Jesus.

60. You demons demonic entertainments, smoking and drugs, die, in the name of Jesus.

61. Let evil spirit of alcoholic drinks in me come out and die, in the name of Jesus.

62. Christ-centered affections and ambitions, manifest in my life, in the name of Jesus.

63. Power to be quickened with Christ, possess me, in the name of Jesus.

64. Power to die to sin, to the world and to things of this world, possess me, in the name of Jesus.

65. You my emotions, die to all the works of devil forever, in the name of Jesus.

66. I set my affection on things above from now onward, in the name of Jesus.

67. You my life and destiny, get rid of evil and inordinate affections for people, place and things, in the name of Jesus.

68. Every ambition that will take me away from Christ, I sacrifice you to death, in the name of Jesus.

69. I destroy every deceit in my heart and I cast away every demon of wickedness, in the name of Jesus.

70. O Lord, bring Your light and understanding into my life, in the name of Jesus.

71. Let every defiling thing in my mind and conscience be purged, in the name of Jesus.

72. You my life, you will serve and worship God forever, in the name of Jesus.

73. Every root of sin, sickness and works of devil in my life, be uprooted, in the name of Jesus.

74. Let the root of sin, all filthiness and carnality in my life die, in the name of Jesus.

75. Every work of the flesh in me, come out and die, in the name of Jesus.

76. Every evil inheritance, corruption of my moral nature, die, in the name of Jesus.

77. Father Lord, sanctify me and give me abundant life, in the name of Jesus.

78. Blood of Jesus cleanse me, perfect my love for God and cast out evil fears, in the name of Jesus.

79. O hand of God, plant in me the joy of God and cause me to inherit Your nature, in the name of Jesus.

80. Lord Jesus, prepare me to enter the world and empower me for heaven, in the name of Jesus.

81. Lord Jesus, cause the nine fruits of the Spirit to begin to manifest in my life, in the name of Jesus.

82. Father Lord, make me a renewed and matured man with divine wisdom, in the name of Jesus.

83. Fire of God, make me zealous, cloth me with humility and compassion, in the name of Jesus.

84. You my faith, be strong in the Lord and keep your first love, in the name of Jesus.

85. I consecrate my life fully to God and His service forever, in the name of Jesus.

86. Let a live coal from off the altar of God touch my lips, purge me and renew me, in the name of Jesus.

87. Holy Spirit, sanctify me, anoint me and empower me to pray always, in the name of Jesus.

88. Power of praise, purity, preaching and sound principle, possess me, in the name of Jesus.

89. Every yoke of laziness, selfishness, carelessness, indifference and worldliness, break in my life, in the name of Jesus.

90. O Lord, make me a man of secret prayers, supernatural power and saintly purpose, in the name of Jesus.

91. Power for letter writing evangelism and telephone witnessing, possess me, in the name of Jesus.

92. Anointing to distribute Christian materials, to visit and invite people to Christ, fall upon me, in the name of Jesus.

93. I receive the grace to testily about Christ to my generation, in the name of Jesus.

94. O Lord, lead me into Spirit-filled evangelism, in the name of Jesus.

95. Blood of Jesus, empower me to live a dynamic life, in the name of Jesus.

96. Holy Spirit of God, help me to preach with eternity in view, in the name of Jesus.

97. Any yoke of sin, sickness and hell upon my life, break, in the name of Jesus.

98. Father Lord, make me to be conscious of Your presence at all times, in the name of Jesus.

99. I receive power to partake in the first resurrection and rapture, in the name of Jesus.

100. Any power assigned to take away heaven from me, die now, in the name of Jesus.

101. O Lord, empower me to find favor everywhere I go, in the name of Jesus.

102. Let my life attract divine motivated helpers, in the name of Jesus.

103. Lord Jesus, give me a Job that will give me the time to serve You, in the name of Jesus.

104. Father Lord, show me where to cast my nets, in the name of Jesus.

105. The divine motivated substitution that will rightly place me where I belong, appears, in the name of Jesus.

106. Let all my adversaries waiting to destroy me be disgraced, in the name of Jesus.

107. Every evil plan of my household enemies, be exposed and be disgraced, in the name of Jesus.

108. Every evil record waiting somewhere to destroy me, catch fire, in the name of Jesus.

109. Lord Jesus, dispatch Your angels to make things easy for me, in the name of Jesus.

110. I receive anointing to excel above my masters in the world without sin, in the name of Jesus.

111. Blood of Jesus, flow in and out of my life, and prepare me for release, in the name of Jesus.

112. Let all evil arrows fired at my star begin to leave, in the name of Jesus.

113. Father Lord, open every good door the enemy has closed against me, in the name of Jesus.

114. Every enemy of my advancement, I trample upon you, in the name of Jesus.

115. As I leave this place, let every good thing I have lost begin to come back, in the name of Jesus.

116. O Lord, arise and enlarge my coast by fire, in the name of Jesus.

117. I command my destiny to escape every demonic confinement, in the name of Jesus.

118. You my angel of blessings, wherever you are now appear and lead me, in the name of Jesus.

119. Any evil mouth opened against me out there, close in shame, in the name of Jesus.

120. Any problem waiting for me to be released, you are wicked, die, in the name of Jesus.

121. O Lord, prepare a table for me in the midst of my enemies, in the name of Jesus.

122. Every good thing I lost all these years, I recover you double, in the name of Jesus.

123. O Lord, give me Your prosperity and peace, in the name of Jesus.

124. Every established enemy assigned to destroy me, arise and help me, in the name of Jesus.

125. Any evil power challenging my freedom, be disgraced, in the name of Jesus.

INTERCESSION FOR PRISONERS

'Peter therefore was kept in prison: but prayer was made without ceasing of the church unto God for him. And when Herod would have brought him forth, the same night Peter was sleeping between two soldiers, bound with two chains: and the keepers before the door kept the prison. And, behold, the angel of the Lord came upon him, and a light shined in the prison: and he smote Peter on the side, and raised him up, saying, Arise up quickly. And his chains fell off from his hands. And the angel said unto him, Gird thyself, and bind on thy sandals. And so he did. And he saith unto him, Cast thy garment about thee, and follow me. And he went out, and followed him; and wist not that it was true which was done by the angel; but thought he saw a vision. When they were past the first and the second ward, they came unto the iron gate that leadeth unto the city; which opened to them of his own accord: and they went out, and passed on through one street; and forthwith the angel departed from him. And when Peter was come to himself, he said, Now I know of a surety, that the Lord hath sent his angel, and

hath delivered me out of the hand of Herod, and from all the expectation of the people of the Jews. And when he had considered the thing, he came to the house of Mary the mother of John, whose surname was Mark; where many were gathered together praying. And as Peter knocked at the door of the gate, a damsel came to hearken, named Rhoda' (Acts 12:5-13).

The ministry of intercession is the ministry of praying for others. It is a ministry that helps us to pray for others instead of criticizing them, or opposing them, finding faults and causing divisions.

'Paul, an apostle of Jesus Christ by the will of God, to the saints which are at Ephesus, and to the faithful in Christ Jesus: Grace be to you, and peace, from God our Father, and from the Lord Jesus Christ. Blessed be the God and Father of our Lord Jesus Christ, who hath blessed us with all spiritual blessings in heavenly places in Christ: According as he hath chosen us in him before the foundation of the world, that we should be holy and without blame before him in love: Having predestinated us unto the adoption of children by Jesus Christ to himself, according to the good pleasure of his will, To the praise of the glory of his grace, wherein he hath made us accepted in the beloved. In whom we have redemption through his blood, the forgiveness of sins, according to the riches of his grace; Wherein he hath abounded

toward us in all wisdom and prudence; Having made known unto us the mystery of his will, according to his good pleasure which he hath purposed in himself: That in the dispensation of the fullness of times he might gather together in one all things in Christ, both which are in heaven, and which are on earth; even in him: In whom also we have obtained an inheritance, being predestinated according to the purpose of him who worketh all things after the counsel of his own will: That we should be to the praise of his glory, who first trusted in Christ. In whom ye also trusted, after that ye heard the word of truth, the gospel of your salvation: in whom also after that ye believed, ye were sealed with that holy Spirit of promise, Which is the earnest of our inheritance until the redemption of the purchased possession, unto the praise of his glory. Wherefore I also, after I heard of your faith in the Lord Jesus, and love unto all the saints, Cease not to give thanks for you, making mention of you in my prayers' (Ephesians 1:1-16).

'First, I thank my God through Jesus Christ for you all, that your faith is spoken of throughout the whole world. For God is my witness, whom I serve with my spirit in the gospel of his Son, that without ceasing I make mention of you always in my prayers' (Romans 1:8-9).

> *'I thank my God upon every remembrance of you, Always in every prayer of mine for you all making request with joy'* (Philippians 1:3-4).

> *'We give thanks to God always for you all, making mention of you in our prayers'* (1 Thessalonians 1:2).

As a prisoner of hope, when you pray for other prisoners, you are also praying for yourself. It is so unfortunate that many people are born to be presidents of their countries and great leaders of many nations wallow in prison. While others have long died in prisons or have come out to become useless. The major cause of this is lack of faith. If prisoners can pray in faith and love, many will make it in life. Intercession is a heart concern for others in which one stands between them and God making request on their behalf (*See* Isaiah 53:12, Hebrews 7:25, John 17:15, 20-21, Romans 8:34, Genesis 18:20-33, Exodus 32:9-14, 1 Samuel 7:8-10, 12:18-23, Romans 8:26-28).

Prison ministry can bring peace to many nations if faithful and dedicated believers can be interceding for prisoners before the Lord daily.

> *'And he saw that there was no man, and wondered that there was no intercessor: therefore his arm brought salvation unto him; and his righteousness, it sustained him. For he put on righteousness as a breastplate, and an helmet of salvation upon his head; and he put on the*

garments of vengeance for clothing, and was clad with zeal as a cloke. According to their deeds, accordingly he will repay, fury to his adversaries, recompense to his enemies; to the islands he will repay recompense. So shall they fear the name of the Lord from the west, and his glory from the rising of the sun. When the enemy shall come in like a flood, the Spirit of the Lord shall lift up a standard against him' (Isaiah 59:16-19).

'At what instant I shall speak concerning a nation, and concerning a kingdom, to pluck up, and to pull down, and to destroy it; If that nation, against whom I have pronounced, turn from their evil, I will repent of the evil that I thought to do unto them' (Jeremiah 18:7-8).

'And I sought for a man among them that should make up the hedge, and stand in the gap before me for the land, that I should not destroy it: but I found none' (Ezekiel 22:30).

History has proven that when men pray to God for prisoners, great leaders emanate from prison to save their people. Prison yards can provide best human assets.

'And Pharaoh said unto his servants, Can we find such a one as this is, a man in whom the Spirit of God is? And Pharaoh said unto Joseph, Forasmuch as God hath shewed thee all this, there is none so discreet and wise as thou art: Thou

> *shalt be over my house, and according unto thy word shall all my people be ruled: only in the throne will I be greater than thou. And Pharaoh said unto Joseph, See, I have set thee over all the land of Egypt. And Pharaoh took off his ring from his hand, and put it upon Joseph's hand, and arrayed him in vestures of fine linen, and put a gold chain about his neck; And he made him to ride in the second chariot which he had; and they cried before him, Bow the knee: and he made him ruler over all the land of Egypt. And Pharaoh said unto Joseph, I am Pharaoh, and without thee shall no man lift up his hand or foot in all the land of Egypt'* (Genesis 41:38-44).

Lacking intercessors to beat back the tide of iniquity is a great tragedy in our generation. The neglect of intercessory ministry is affecting every nation.

> *'I exhort therefore, that, first of all, supplications, prayers, intercessions, and giving of thanks, be made for all men; For kings, and for all that are in authority; that we may lead a quiet and peaceable life in all godliness and honesty. For this is good and acceptable in the sight of God our Savior; Who will have all men to be saved, and to come unto the knowledge of the truth'* (1 Timothy 2:1-4).

> *'After this manner therefore pray ye: Our Father which art in heaven, Hallowed be thy name. Thy kingdom come. Thy will be done in earth, as it is*

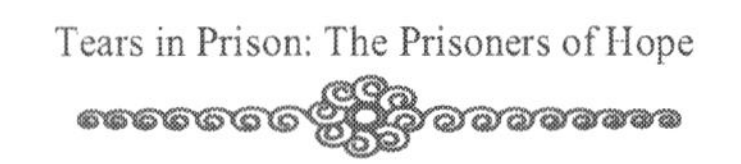

> *in heaven. Give us this day our daily bread. And forgive us our debts, as we forgive our debtors. And lead us not into temptation, but deliver us from evil: For thine is the kingdom, and the power, and the glory, forever. Amen'* (Matthew 6:9-13).

You can begin today to intercede for prisoners and people in authority. There are blessings attached to all obedience to God's Word. Let us pray and intercede for one another, for the people in authority and sinners in the world to repent.

PRAYERS OF INTERCESSION FOR PRISONERS

1. Blessed Holy Trinity, visit every prisoner in the world today, in the name of Jesus.

2. Lord Jesus, appear and convert every prisoner worldwide, in the name of Jesus.

3. Blood of Jesus, flow into the foundation of every prison, in the name of Jesus.

4. Let every evil character in every prisoner be roasted by fire, in the name of Jesus.

5. Blessed Holy Spirit, bring revival to every prison in my nation, in the name of Jesus.

6. Spirit of the living God, raise prison evangelists to evangelize prisons in my country, in the name of Jesus.

7. Any satanic roadblock in every prison, be dismantled, in the name of Jesus.

8. Miracle of salvation, manifest in the life of every prisoner in this world, in the name of Jesus.

9. Let every prisoner begin to have understanding about Christ, in the name of Jesus.

10. Any darkness in the heart of any prisoner, receive divine light, in the name of Jesus.

11. Fire of God, burn to ashes every deceit and wickedness in prisoners' hearts, in the name of Jesus.

12. Blood of Jesus, destroy defiled thoughts in all prisoners' consciences, in the name of Jesus.

13. Let the enslaved wills of all hardened prisoners be delivered, in the name of Jesus.

14. Let the hammer of the Word of God break the power of sin in prisoners' lives, in the name of Jesus.

15. Father Lord, kill the old man, which is the body of sin in every prisoner's, in the name of Jesus.

16. Carnal mindedness in any of prisoner, die forever, in the name of Jesus.

17. Let every fleshly motivated prisoner receive salvation today, in the name of Jesus.

18. I command filthiness to depart from the life of every prisoner, in the name of Jesus.

19. Any evil character dominating and tormenting prisoners, die now, in the name of Jesus.

20. I command every sinful inheritance militating against prisoners to cease, in the name of Jesus.

21. Every spiritual enemy living inside any prisoner, be overthrown, in the name of Jesus.

22. Any corruption in the moral nature of every prisoner, die, in the name of Jesus.

23. Father Lord, Let Your presence appear in every prison, in the name of Jesus.

24. Let every common problem in prisons worldwide receive solution today, in the name of Jesus.

25. Let those evil spirits wasting lives of prisoners be destroyed now, in the name of Jesus.

26. Let all manner of immoral tendencies in every prison cease by force, in the name of Jesus.

27. O Lord, establish prayer groups in every prison of the world, in the name of Jesus.

28. Every evil covenant and curse existing in any prison, expire, in the name of Jesus.

29. Father Lord, make every prisoner suitable for rapture, in the name of Jesus.

30. Heaven, what are you waiting for? Come down in every prison, in the name of Jesus.

31. I command general and individual peace to come down in every prison, in the name of Jesus.

32. Let divine joy, holiness, glory, comfort, justice and knowledge of God appear to all prisoners, in the name of Jesus.

33. Father Lord, bring healing, health, economic prosperity and love of God to every prison, in the name of Jesus.

34. I command every prisoner to develop a life of fellowship with God, in the name of Jesus.

35. I command rest, divine abundance and life of abundance in every prison, in the name of Jesus.

INTERCESSION FOR PEOPLE IN AUTHORITY

'I exhort therefore, that, first of all, supplications, prayers, intercessions, and giving of thanks, be made for all men; For kings, and for all that are in authority; that we may lead a quiet and peaceable life in all godliness and honesty. For this is good and acceptable in the sight of God our Savior; Who will have all men to be saved, and to come unto the knowledge of the truth' (1 Timothy 2:1-4).

'And the children of Israel said to Samuel, Cease not to cry unto the Lord our God for us, that he will save us out of the hand of the Philistines... And all the people said unto Samuel, Pray for thy servants unto the Lord thy God that we die not: for we have added unto all our sins this evil, to ask us a king. And Samuel said unto the people, Fear not: ye have done all this wickedness: yet turn not aside from following the Lord, but serve the Lord with all your heart; And turn ye not aside: for then should ye go after vain things, which cannot profit nor deliver; for they are vain. For the Lord will not forsake his people for his

great name's sake: because it hath pleased the Lord to make you his people. Moreover as for me, God forbid that I should sin against the Lord in ceasing to pray for you: but I will teach you the good and the right way: Only fear the Lord, and serve him in truth with all your heart: for consider how great things he hath done for you. But if ye shall still do wickedly, ye shall be consumed, both ye and your king.' (1 Samuel 7:8, 12:19-25)

The Latin word for intercession is *'interceddo'*, meaning *'to go (or pass) between'*. It is a heart concern for others in which one stands between them and God, making requests on their behalf. No matter how bad or good a government is, Christ urged us to pray for those who despitefully hate us.

'But I say unto you, Love your enemies, bless them that curse you, do good to them that hate you, and pray for them which despitefully use you, and persecute you' (Matthew 5:44).

When you refuse to pray for the government, devil will use them to bring policies that will hinder your freedom. Some of the laws that brought people to prison are contrary to Biblical stipulated principles. Some laws in many nations have thrown out the Bible and replaced it with brutal police. The Bible is the best police on earth. Without the influence of the Bible, value clarification will rule. When in 1962, prayer in public schools was declared unconstitutional in

America (Engel v. Vitale)and the Ten Commandments thrown into the gutters (Stone V. Gramm), rape, armed robbery, murder, cheating and gang warfare took over. Not only in America. So many other nations have in their national lifestyles and values done worse than America. They despised the written Word of God and adopted evolution, disrespect and rebellion against God. There are many outcries against our leaders, but the core problem is demons behind their actions. When you refuse to pray, you will find out that the world will be continuously ruled by evil leaders. We must all pray to bring God back to our cities.

> *'But I say unto you, Love your enemies, bless them that curse you, do good to them that hate you, and pray for them which despitefully use you, and persecute you'* (Psalms 60:9).

Let us pray for leaders who will bring back traditional values to root out the culture of making families without being married. History has been thrown out and revisionism has taken over. Social engineering has killed true learning and condom and abortion has over thrown abstinence. Let us all pray for our leaders to respect God.

PRAYERS OF INTERCESSION FOR PEOPLE IN AUTHORITY

1. Any evil personality, sitting upon the throne of the world, be dethroned, in the name of Jesus.

2. Blood of Jesus, flow into every throne and destroy demonized leaders, in the name of Jesus.

3. Fire of God, burn to ashes every evil throne on earth, in the name of Jesus.

4. Let all invisible personalities in every throne be dethroned, in the name of Jesus.

5. Eternal rock of ages, establish Your kingdom upon every throne, in the name of Jesus.

6. Every throne of darkness, confusing the nations, scatter, in the name of Jesus.

7. Any evil throne fighting against Christ's kingdom, be disintegrated, in the name of Jesus.

8. Any satanic motivated policy on earth, expire now, in the name of Jesus.

9. Father Lord, raise good people to occupy every throne on earth, in the name of Jesus.

10. Let the government in-charge of every prison embrace Christ, in the name of Jesus.

11. Lord Jesus, bring a better change to every government on earth, in the name of Jesus.

12. Any problem that will bring end time revival and mass repentance, appear, in the name of Jesus.

13. Let the whole world begin to embrace Christ without difficulties, in the name of Jesus.

14. Father Lord, raise intercessors in my nation by fire, in the name of Jesus.

15. Let the body of Christ take its rightful position worldwide, in the name of Jesus.

16. Any demonic motivated war in every nation, be aborted, in the name of Jesus.

17. Father Lord, intervene in every election in the world, in the name of Jesus.

18. I command every believer in the whole world to represent Christ actively, in the name of Jesus.

19. Any wicked lawyer sitting in the throne, be disgraced, in the name of Jesus.

20. Any wicked judge working for devil, repent or perish, in the name of Jesus.

21. Let worldwide courts deliver judgment in righteousness, in the name of Jesus.

22. Any evil verdict prepared by any evil court, be reversed, in the name of Jesus.

23. Any judge or magistrate working for devil, be disgraced, in the name of Jesus.

24. Father Lord, raise God-fearing men and women in the courts, in the name of Jesus.

25. Any evil personality that has clearly manipulated himself in the throne, be disgraced, in the name of Jesus.

26. Let all decision makers in every nation take sides with God, in the name of Jesus.

27. I command all lawmakers and other leaders to honor God's Word, in the name of Jesus.

28. I Command deliverance to take place in lives of all demon possessed leaders, in the name of Jesus.

29. Let every evil group in the world scatter in shame, in the name of Jesus.

30. Fire of God, burn to ashes every evil document against God's people, in the name of Jesus.

31. Father Lord, re-organize the court, police and all military groups, in the name of Jesus.

32. Let every policy that is opposed to God be discarded worldwide, in the name of Jesus.

33. O Lord, arise and deliver every nation from doom, in the name of Jesus.

34. Blood of Jesus. speak destruction to every anti-gospel agent, in the name of Jesus.

35. Any blockage to the gospel in any nation, be dismantled, in the name of Jesus.

36. Father Lord, raise missionaries to enter into every nation and make impact, in the name of Jesus.

TO PULL DOWN PRISON STRONGHOLDS

'Then Pharaoh sent and called Joseph, and they brought him hastily out of the dungeon: and he shaved himself, and changed his raiment, and came in unto Pharaoh' (Genesis 41:14).

'Peter therefore was kept in prison: but prayer was made without ceasing of the church unto God for him. And when Herod would have brought him forth, the same night Peter was sleeping between two soldiers, bound with two chains: and the keepers before the door kept the prison. And, behold, the angel of the Lord came upon him, and a light shined in the prison: and he smote Peter on the side, and raised him up, saying, Arise up quickly. And his chains fell off from his hands… And at midnight Paul and Silas prayed, and sang praises unto God: and the prisoners heard them. And suddenly there was a great earthquake, so that the foundations of the prison were shaken: and immediately all the doors were opened, and every one's bands were loosed' (Acts 12:5-7, 16:25-26).

The purpose of this prayer section is to command the powers in prisons to release people who have met God's demand and conditions. Because of scarcity of these kinds of prayers over the years, many prisoners have overstayed in prisons. Some have been killed or died in pains without justice. Do not keep quiet when you know you should be out of prison. Do not plan to break out or disobey authorities. Start praying the prayers in this book. Peter and Joseph never kept quiet in prison. They prayed until they were released. This is your time and you need to force your prison doors open, not physically but with spiritual weapons.

> *'For though we walk in the flesh, we do not war after the flesh: (For the weapons of our warfare are not carnal, but mighty through God to the pulling down of strong holds) Casting down imaginations, and every high thing that exalteth itself against the knowledge of God, and bringing into captivity every thought to the obedience of Christ'* (2 Corinthians 10:3-5).

Prison strongholds can only be pulled down with spiritual weapons. The greatest struggle that lies before every prisoner is the plan of Satan to keep him or her beyond the divine stipulated time of release. To pull down your personal prison stronghold, you have to put off the carnal man, and put on you divine armor which is as follows:

1. *The belt of truth (See Ephesians 6:14, Luke 12:35, 1 Peter 1:13).*

2. *The breastplate of righteousness (See Ephesians 6:14, 1 Peter 1:14-16).*
3. *The shoes of the gospel of peace (See Ephesians 6:15, Romans 1:16-17).*
4. *The shield of faith (See Ephesians 6:16, Hebrews 11:32-34, 1 Peter 5:9, 1 John 5:4).*
5. *The helmet of salvation (See Ephesians 6:17, 1 Thessalonians 5:8).*
6. *The sword of the Spirit (See Ephesians 6:17, Matthew 4:1-11, Psalms 119:11, Hebrews 4:12, 1 Peter 3:15).*

Many strong and great Christians have failed in the days of battle simply because they do not pray against satanic strongholds, which is the backbone behind their problems. Do not let your name be enlisted among those that have failed. Rise up now and start praying for your life.

PRAYERS FOR PULLING DOWN PRISON STRONGHOLDS

1. Every environmental power controlling this prison, be arrested and cast out, in the name of Jesus.

2. You the strongman of this prison, I cut off your head, in the name of Jesus.

3. Every resident evil power assigned to waste my life, be wasted, in the name of Jesus.

4. Every dark room in this prison yard, catch fire, in the name of Jesus.

5. Any evil personality inside anyone to torment my life, be disgraced, in the name of Jesus.

6. Blood of Jesus, flow into the foundation of this prison for my sake, in the name of Jesus.

7. Lord Jesus, deliver me from common problems in this prison, in the name of Jesus.

8. Any established evil covenant in this prison, break by force, in the name of Jesus.

9. Let any collective evil yoke in this prison break and release me, in the name of Jesus.

10. Every arrow of hatred fired against my life, I fire you back, in the name of Jesus.

11. Any power following me about in this prison to waste my life, be wasted, in the name of Jesus.

12. Fire of God, burn to ashes every problem that entered into my life in this prison, in the name of Jesus.

13. Every evil material in the root of this prison, catch fire, in the name of Jesus.

14. You the dragon of this prison, I cut of your head, die, in the name of Jesus.

15. Any power that wants me to overstay in this prison, die, in the name of Jesus.

16. Every chain of darkness holding me in bondage, break to pieces, in the name of Jesus.

17. Every good thing enemies are wasting in my life, receive life, in the name of Jesus.

18. Any environmental spirit that has entered into my life, come out and die, in the name of Jesus.

19. Blood of Jesus, deliver me from all evil power in this prison, in the name of Jesus.

20. Every evil gateman in this prison, blocking my helpers, fall down and die, in the name of Jesus.

21. Every Herodic instruction against me in this prison, be rejected and abandoned, in the name of Jesus.

22. Let all invisible satanic soldiers monitoring me in this prison be knocked down, in the name of Jesus.

23. Let the angel of God bring light from heaven for my sake in this prison, in the name of Jesus.

24. Every invisible chain holding me down in this prison, break to pieces, in the name of Jesus.

25. You my life, what are you waiting for? Walk out of this bondage, in the name of Jesus.

26. Every garment of imprisonment upon my life, catch fire, in the name of Jesus.

27. Every good dream about my freedom manifest by force, in the name of Jesus.

28. Any evil padlock keeping me behind bars, break by force, in the name of Jesus.

29. Every evil foundation in this prison constructed against me, collapse, in the name of Jesus.

30. Every evil expectation of my enemies in this prison, fail woefully, in the name of Jesus.

31. Blood of Jesus, flow into every strong room in this prison and deliver me, in the name of Jesus.

32. Fire of God, burn to ashes every curse placed upon me in this prison, in the name of Jesus.

33. Every evil plan to waste me in this prison, be frustrated in shame, in the name of Jesus.

34. Every demonic arrow that has entered into my life in this prison, come out now, in the name of Jesus.

35. Every enemy of my joy in this prison, die and die forever, in the name of Jesus.

36. Any evil sacrifice going on against me in this prison, expire, in the name of Jesus.

37. Holy Ghost fire, burn to ashes every problem planted against me in this prison, in the name of Jesus.

38. Let every yoke of bondage placed upon me in this prison catch fire, in the name of Jesus.

39. Any evil womb swallowing my blessing in this prison, burst open, in the name of Jesus.

40. I command every demonic distraction working against me in this prison to die, in the name of Jesus.

41. O Lord, arise and engage me profitably in this prison to Your own glory, in the name of Jesus.

42. Any evil chain holding me down in this prison, break by force, in the name of Jesus.

43. Let the angels of God on assignment appear and set me free, in the name of Jesus.

44. Any power working against my freedom, die, in the name of Jesus.

45. I command every official in this government responsible for my release to respond now, in the name of Jesus.

46. You that strongman in this prison keeping me behind bars, collapse, in the name of Jesus.

47. Let powers that took away Joseph from prison appear for my sake, in the name of Jesus.

48. Any visible and invisible gate locking me up, open by force, in the name of Jesus.

49. You that personality that has vowed to keep me here in prison, repent or die, in the name of Jesus.

50. O Lord, take me back to my true inheritance and place in life, in the name of Jesus.

FOR PRISON SPONSORSHIP & MINISTRIES

'When the Son of man shall come in his glory, and all the holy angels with him, then shall he sit upon the throne of his glory: And before him shall be gathered all nations: and he shall separate them one from another, as a shepherd divideth his sheep from the goats: And he shall set the sheep on his right hand, but the goats on the left. Then shall the King say unto them on his right hand, Come, ye blessed of my Father, inherit the kingdom prepared for you from the foundation of the world: For I was an hungred, and ye gave me meat: I was thirsty, and ye gave me drink: I was a stranger, and ye took me in: Naked, and ye clothed me: I was sick, and ye visited me: I was in prison, and ye came unto me… Then shall he say also unto them on the left hand, Depart from me, ye cursed, into everlasting fire, prepared for the devil and his angels: For I was an hungred, and ye gave me no meat: I was thirsty, and ye gave me no drink: I was a stranger, and ye took me not in: naked, and ye clothed me not: sick, and in prison, and ye visited me not. Then shall they also answer him, saying, Lord, when saw we thee an hungred, or athirst, or a stranger, or naked, or sick, or in prison, and did not minister unto

thee? Then shall he answer them, saying, Verily I say unto you, Inasmuch as ye did it not to one of the least of these, ye did it not to me. And these shall go away into everlasting punishment: but the righteous into life eternal' (Matthew 25:31-36, 41-46).

There are millions of hungry prisoners all over the world looking for what to eat. In Africa, many prisoners are dehumanized and treated like animals. Many go naked and over time turn ferocious as result of brutal and cruel treatments meted out to them in prisons. They live in crowded prisons without ventilations, no access to good water or care from anyone. Others become sick, and die while cursing God, their governments and their enemies. Curses coming from the lips of many suffering prisoners can trigger bitter spiritual wars and spiritual barricade for the nations in question. Other prisoners are either abandoned by their parents, friends and former loved ones. Christ expects every Christian on earth to visit prisoners at least occasionally.

'After this there was a feast of the Jews; and Jesus went up to Jerusalem. Now there is at Jerusalem by the sheep market a pool, which is called in the Hebrew tongue Bethesda, having five porches. In these lay a great multitude of impotent folk, of blind, halt, withered, waiting for the moving of the water. For an angel went down at a certain season into the pool, and troubled the water: whosoever then first after the troubling of the water stepped in was made whole of whatsoever disease he had. And a certain man was there, which had an infirmity thirty and eight years. When Jesus saw him lie, and knew that he had been now a long time in that case, he saith unto him, Wilt

> *thou be made whole? The impotent man answered him, Sir, I have no man, when the water is troubled, to put me into the pool: but while I am coming, another steppeth down before me. Jesus saith unto him, Rise, take up thy bed, and walk. And immediately the man was made whole, and took up his bed, and walked: and on the same day was the Sabbath'* (John 5:1-9).

Abandoning the needy and the helpless like prisoners attracts curses. When you survey the wondrous cross on which the Prince of life and glory died, no price will seem too high to be paid. No sacrifice is too great to make, and no problem will be too big not to be surmounted for the sake of salvation of the lost souls. Prison evangelism is not charity but a debt which you must pay. As a Christian prisoner, you owe other prisoners the gospel of salvation and peace, and ensuring they become born again.

> *'I am debtor both to the Greeks, and to the Barbarians; both to the wise, and to the unwise'* (Romans 1:14).

The prayers below are meant for people who sponsor prison evangelism, send Bibles, Christian materials, food, clothes and other needs of prisoners. Also as a prisoner, pray for the author of this book and all other people who care for prisoners. You can also minister to people who watch over you, including the warders, prison keepers, etc.

> *'And the keeper of the prison awaking out of his sleep, and seeing the prison doors open, he drew out his sword, and would have killed himself, supposing that the prisoners had been fled. But Paul cried with a loud voice, saying, Do thyself no harm: for we are all here. Then he called for a light, and sprang in, and came trembling, and fell down before Paul and Silas, And*

> *brought them out, and said, Sirs, what must I do to be saved? And they said, Believe on the Lord Jesus Christ, and thou shalt be saved, and thy house. And they spake unto him the word of the Lord, and to all that were in his house. And he took them the same hour of the night, and washed their stripes; and was baptized, he and all his, straightway. And when he had brought them into his house, he set meat before them, and rejoiced, believing in God with all his house'* (Acts 16:27-34).

Pray that God helps the author of this book to receive favor, and for this book to attract sponsors who can sponsor this book to all the prisons worldwide, in order to minister to every prisoner on earth. Pray that prisons worldwide be converted to places of worship.

PRAYERS FOR PRISON SPONSORSHIPS &MINISTRIES

1. O Lord, bless men and women that sponsor the spread of this book to prisoners, in the name of Jesus.

2. Every enemy of the spread of this book in every prison of the world, be frustrated, in the name of Jesus.

3. Let God protect every sponsor of prison ministries, in the name of Jesus.

4. I command all powers of darkness to disappear from the life of sponsors of this book, in the name of Jesus.

5. Blood of Jesus, chase away every problem in the families of prison ministers, in the name of Jesus.

6. Satan, I remove you from the finances of the sponsors of prison ministries, in the name of Jesus.

7. O Lord, restore every good thing sponsors of prison ministries has ever lost, in the name of Jesus.

8. You the polluters of the mind of sponsors of prison ministries, I paralyze you now, in the name of Jesus.

9. O Lord, anoint the writer of this book with the power of the Holy Ghost, in the name of Jesus.

10. Let every enemy of sponsors of prison ministries be exposed and disgraced, in the name of Jesus.

11. Let sponsors of prison ministries prosper beyond measures in their businesses, in the name of Jesus.

12. Any strange finance in the businesses of prison ministries sponsors, disappear, in the name of Jesus.

13. Let sponsors of prison ministries arise and prosper beyond their equals, in the name of Jesus.

14. Spirit of death, disappear from the lives of sponsors of this book, in the name of Jesus.

15. Father Lord, use this book to attract other materials needed in prisons worldwide, in the name of Jesus.

16. Powers of darkness diverting the progress of sponsors of this book, die, in the name of Jesus.

17. Lord Jesus, visit everything sponsors of this book do with blessings, in the name of Jesus.

18. Let divine whirlwind fight for the sponsors of this book, in the name of Jesus.

19. I blind every evil eye observing the progress of the sponsors of this book, in the name of Jesus.

20. Any stubborn curse in the lives of the writer and sponsors of this book, expire, in the name of Jesus.

21. Every handwriting of the enemy in the destiny of the sponsors of prison ministries, die, in the name of Jesus.

22. Heavenly Father, walk into the lives of the sponsors of this book today, in the name of Jesus.

23. Let the anger of the Lord destroy problems in the life of writer of this book and the editor, in the name of Jesus.

24. Let the raging fire of God burn to ashes problems of the sponsors of this book, in the name of Jesus.

25. O Lord, use the sponsors of this book to provide other urgent needs in prisons worldwide, in the name of Jesus.

26. Father Lord, raise more sponsors all over the world to provide for prisoners, in the name of Jesus.

27. Lord Jesus, put a copy of this book in the hand of every prisoner on earth, in the name of Jesus.

28. Father Lord, use this book to convert every prisoner on earth, in the name of Jesus.

29. Blood of Jesus, flow into this book and use it to convert every prisoner, in the name of Jesus.

30. Holy Ghost fire, burn every problem in the life of the writer of this book and replace it with the nine gifts of the Holy Ghost, in the name of Jesus.

31. Let this book carry anointing that will solve every problem on earth, especially in prisons, in the name of Jesus.

AN OPEN LETTER TO PARTNER IN PRISON MINISTRY

God is looking for partners all over the world that will activate His works in prisons (*See* Psalms 60:9, Matthew 25:31-46). All prisoners are bound with two kinds of chains – the first is the physical chain or gate, and the second is spiritual chain of sin and condemnation.

Therefore, God has purposed that every prisoner be given a chance to hear the gospel of Jesus in order to believe the living Word of God. In other words, it is God's plan to deliver every prisoner out of these two bondages so prisoners can also reign in Christ Jesus (*See* Ecclesiastes 4:14a).

The distribution of this book - ***Tears in Prison***, to all prisoners is an effective way of bringing hope and solace to prisoners who have lost all hope. The whole church in Jerusalem felt very bad when they learnt that Peter was imprisoned. They gathered and prayed day and night for Peter. You can do a lot for prisoners and God honors you.

Many Non-governmental Organizations are rendering great services all over the world to see that incarcerated people receive some form of love. On Thursday, 5 August 2010, I picked a daily mail newspaper at Heathrow Airport, United Kingdom, and on the seventh page, I read a story titled, '***Billionaires give half their Fortunes to Charity***'. Among those was Bill Gates.

Bill and Melinda Gates Foundation is one of the largest charity organizations in the world. It has donated more than £17 Billion to charitable trusts. Another person mentioned was Barron Hilton, who once announced he wanted to leave 79% of his wealth to charitable trusts. Ted Turner who is the founder of CNN supports UN causes.

Warren Buffet rose to rank among the richest in the world as he gave away money. Michael Bloomberg, 68,once said, *'I have always said that the best financial planning ends with bouncing the cheque to the undertaker'*. And Rockefeller gave $100 Million to Harvard.

These are leaders who are leading by examples. It is a challenge to the body of Christ and other millionaires in the world to join forces to help the poor. Critical neglect of the poor causes economic problems all over the world. This has contributed adversely to increasing wars, terrorism and global bloodshed. I want to use this medium to appeal to pastors, Christians, churches and millionaires all over the world to collaborate in distributing copies of this book to prisoners all over the world.

This book should be read by all prisoners, making it necessary to translate this book into all major languages of the world, so that every prisoner of every tribe can read this book and be helped. Translators, who can translate this book into various local languages, are needed to partner in the spreading of this book to foreign prisons. Likewise, sponsorships for translations are needed. You can buy a copy, ten, a hundred, a thousand, or millions to donate to prisoners or churches who engage in prison ministries.

Robert Arthington of Leeds, England, a Cambridge graduate, lived in a single room and cooked his own meals. He gave all his earnings to foreign missions. He said, '*Gladly would I make floor my bed, a box my chair, and another box my table, rather than men should perish for lack of the knowledge of Christ*'.

Would you remain silent then, or keep back your money and ignore the cries of millions of prisoners dying and rushing to the endless pit of hell without being given any privilege of meeting God here on earth while you possess huge estates and businesses? (*See* Matthew 9:36-37; John 4:35-38).

When you survey the wondrous cross on which the Prince of Glory died, no price will be too high to pay, and no sacrifice will be too great to make, and no problems will be too big to be encountered for the sake of the salvation of imprisoned sinners. If you can purchase a million copies of this book, do not hesitate to do it today. This is one of the greatest charities on earth.

With a gift of this book, reach out to one of the most neglected and abandoned class of people on earth today and you will be richly blessed by God (*See* Matthew 25:31-46, John 5:1-9).

This book can be purchase locally from the author or directly from Amazon.

Thank You So Much!

Beloved, I hope you enjoyed this Book as much as I believe God has touched your heart today. I cannot thank you enough for your continued support for this prayer ministry.

I appreciate you so much for taking out of time to read this wonderful prayer book, and if you have an extra second, I would love to hear what you think about this book.

Please, do share your testimonies with me by sending an email to me at pastor@prayermadueke.com, also in Facebook at www.facebook.com/prayer.madueke. I personally invite you to my website at www.prayermadueke.com to view many other books I have written on various issues of life, especially on marriage, family, sexual problems and money.

I will be delighted to collaborate with you in organized Crusades, Ceremonies, Marriages and Marriage seminars, Special Events, Church Ministration and Fellowship for the advancement of God's Kingdom here on earth.

Thank you again, and I wish you nothing less than success in life.

God bless you.

Prayer M. Madueke

OTHER BOOKS BY PRAYER M. MADUEKE

- *21/40 Nights Of Decrees And Your Enemies Will Surrender*
- *Confront And Conquer*
- *35 Special Dangerous Decrees*
- *Tears in Prison*
- *The Reality of Spirit Marriage*
- *Queen of Heaven*
- *Leviathan the Beast*
- *100 Days Prayer To Wake Up Your Lazarus*
- *Dangerous Decrees To Destroy Your Destroyers*
- *The spirit of Christmas*
- *More Kingdoms To Conquer*
- *Your Dream Directory*
- *The Sword Of New Testament Deliverance*
- *Alphabetic Battle For Unmerited Favors*
- *Alphabetic Character Deliverance*
- *Holiness*
- *The Witchcraft Of The Woman That Sits Upon Many Waters*
- *The Operations Of The Woman That Sits Upon Many Waters*
- *Powers To Pray Once And Receive Answers*
- *Prayer Riots To Overthrow Divorce*
- *Prayers To Get Married Happily*
- *Prayers To Keep Your Marriage Out of Troubles*
- *Prayers For Conception And Power To Retain*
- *Prayer Retreat – Prayers to Possess Your Year*
- *Prayers for Nation Building (Vol. 1,2 & 3)*
- *Organized student in a disorganized school*
- *Welcome to Campus*
- *Alone with God (10 series)*

CONTACTS

AFRICA

#1 Babatunde close,
Off Olaitan Street, Surulere
Lagos, Nigeria
+234 803 353 0599
pastor@prayermadueke.com,

#28B Ubiaja Crescent
Garki II Abuja,
FCT - Nigeria
+234 807 065 4159

IRELAND

Ps Emmanuel Oko
#84 Thornfield Square
Cloudalkin D22
Ireland
Tel: +353 872 820 909, +353 872 977 422
aghaoko2003@yahoo.com

EUROPE/SCHENGEN

Collins Kwame
#46 Felton Road
Barking
Essex IG11 7XZ GB
Tel: +44 208 507 8083, +44 787 703 2386, +44 780 703 6916
aghaoko2003@yahoo.com

Printed by Amazon Italia Logistica S.r.l.
Torrazza Piemonte (TO), Italy